The United Nations and Business

The United Nations and Business

A Partnership Recovered

Sandrine Tesner
with the Collaboration of
Georg Kell

St. Martin's Press
New York

THE UNITED NATIONS AND BUSINESS
Copyright © Sandrine Tesner, 2000. All rights reserved. Printed in the United States of America. No part of this book may be used or reproduced in any manner whatsoever without written permission except in the case of brief quotations embodied in critical articles or reviews. For information, address St. Martin's Press, New York, N.Y. 10010.

ISBN 0-312-23071-0

Library of Congress Cataloging-in-Publication Data
to be found at the Library of Congress

Design by Letra Libre, Inc.

First edition: August, 2000
10 9 8 7 6 5 4 3 2 1

To Mitch Werner

Contents

The UNITED NATIONS system

PRINCIPAL ORGANS OF THE UNITED NATIONS

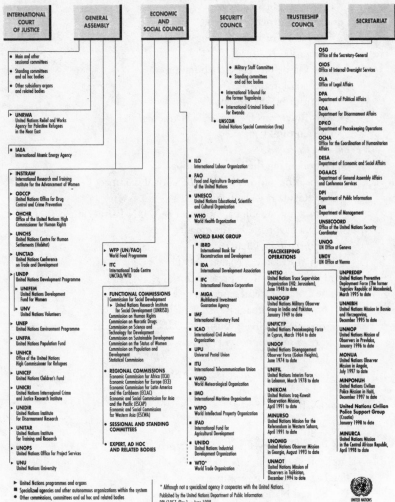

INTERNATIONAL COURT OF JUSTICE

GENERAL ASSEMBLY

ECONOMIC AND SOCIAL COUNCIL

SECURITY COUNCIL

TRUSTEESHIP COUNCIL

SECRETARIAT

- Main and other sessional committees
- Standing committees and ad hoc bodies
- Other subsidiary organs and related bodies

► UNRWA
United Nations Relief and Works Agency for Palestine Refugees in the Near East

■ IAEA
International Atomic Energy Agency

► INSTRAW
International Research and Training Institute for the Advancement of Women

► ODCCP
United Nations Office for Drug Control and Crime Prevention

► OHCHR
Office of the United Nations High Commissioner for Human Rights

► UNCHS
United Nations Centre for Human Settlements (Habitat)

► UNCTAD
United Nations Conference on Trade and Development

► UNDP
United Nations Development Programme
- ► UNIFEM
  United Nations Development Fund for Women
- ► UNV
  United Nations Volunteers

► UNEP
United Nations Environment Programme

► UNFPA
United Nations Population Fund

► UNHCR
Office of the United Nations High Commissioner for Refugees

► UNICEF
United Nations Children's Fund

► UNICRI
United Nations Interregional Crime and Justice Research Institute

► UNIDIR
United Nations Institute for Disarmament Research

► UNITAR
United Nations Institute for Training and Research

► UNOPS
United Nations Office for Project Services

► UNU
United Nations University

► WFP (UN/FAO)
World Food Programme

► ITC
International Trade Centre UNCTAD/WTO

● FUNCTIONAL COMMISSIONS
Commission for Social Development
  ► United Nations Research Institute for Social Development (UNRISD)
Commission on Human Rights
Commission on Narcotic Drugs
Commission on Science and Technology for Development
Commission on Sustainable Development
Commission on the Status of Women
Commission on Population and Development
Statistical Commission

● REGIONAL COMMISSIONS
Economic Commission for Africa (ECA)
Economic Commission for Europe (ECE)
Economic Commission for Latin America and the Caribbean (ECLAC)
Economic and Social Commission for Asia and the Pacific (ESCAP)
Economic and Social Commission for Western Asia (ESCWA)

● SESSIONAL AND STANDING COMMITTEES

● EXPERT, AD HOC AND RELATED BODIES

- Military Staff Committee
- Standing committees and ad hoc bodies
- International Tribunal for the former Yugoslavia
- International Criminal Tribunal for Rwanda

● UNSCOM
United Nations Special Commission (Iraq)

■ ILO
International Labour Organization

■ FAO
Food and Agriculture Organization of the United Nations

■ UNESCO
United Nations Educational, Scientific and Cultural Organization

■ WHO
World Health Organization

WORLD BANK GROUP
■ IBRD
International Bank for Reconstruction and Development
■ IDA
International Development Association
■ IFC
International Finance Corporation
■ MIGA
Multilateral Investment Guarantee Agency

■ IMF
International Monetary Fund

■ ICAO
International Civil Aviation Organization

■ UPU
Universal Postal Union

■ ITU
International Telecommunication Union

■ WMO
World Meteorological Organization

■ IMO
International Maritime Organization

■ WIPO
World Intellectual Property Organization

■ IFAD
International Fund for Agricultural Development

■ UNIDO
United Nations Industrial Development Organization

■ WTO*
World Trade Organization

PEACEKEEPING OPERATIONS

UNTSO
United Nations Truce Supervision Organization (HQ: Jerusalem), June 1948 to date

UNMOGIP
United Nations Military Observer Group in India and Pakistan, January 1949 to date

UNFICYP
United Nations Peacekeeping Force in Cyprus, March 1964 to date

UNDOF
United Nations Disengagement Observer Force (Golan Heights), June 1974 to date

UNIFIL
United Nations Interim Force in Lebanon, March 1978 to date

UNIKOM
United Nations Iraq-Kuwait Observation Mission, April 1991 to date

MINURSO
United Nations Mission for the Referendum in Western Sahara, April 1991 to date

UNOMIG
United Nations Observer Mission in Georgia, August 1993 to date

UNMOT
United Nations Mission of Observers in Tajikistan, December 1994 to date

OSG
Office of the Secretary-General

OIOS
Office of Internal Oversight Services

OLA
Office of Legal Affairs

DPA
Department of Political Affairs

DDA
Department for Disarmament Affairs

DPKO
Department of Peacekeeping Operations

OCHA
Office for the Coordination of Humanitarian Affairs

DESA
Department of Economic and Social Affairs

DGAACS
Department of General Assembly Affairs and Conference Services

DPI
Department of Public Information

DM
Department of Management

UNSECOORD
Office of the United Nations Security Coordinator

UNOG
UN Office at Geneva

UNOV
UN Office at Vienna

UNPREDEP
United Nations Preventive Deployment Force (The former Yugoslav Republic of Macedonia), March 1995 to date

UNMIBH
United Nations Mission in Bosnia and Herzegovina, December 1995 to date

UNMOP
United Nations Mission of Observers in Prevlaka, January 1996 to date

MONUA
United Nations Observer Mission in Angola, July 1997 to date

MINPONUH
United Nations Civilian Police Mission in Haiti, December 1997 to date

United Nations Civilian Police Support Group (Croatia) January 1998 to date

MINURCA
United Nations Mission in the Central African Republic, April 1998 to date

► United Nations programmes and organs
■ Specialized agencies and other autonomous organizations within the system
● Other commissions, committees and ad hoc and related bodies

* Although not a specialized agency it cooperates with the United Nations.

Published by the United Nations Department of Public Information
DPI/1857/Rev.1—June 1998

UNITED NATIONS

List of Acronyms and Websites

United Nations System

UN website: www.un.org
UN business website: www.un.org/partners/business
Global Compact website: www.unglobalcompact.org

ACC	Administrative Committee on Coordination (www.acc.unsystem.org)
ACABQ	Advisory Committee on Administrative and Budgetary Questions
CCPOQ	Consultative Committee on Program and Operational Questions
DPA	Department of Political Affairs (www.un.org/depts/dpa)
DPI	Department of Public Information (www.un.org/depts/dpi)
DPKO	Department of Peacekeeping Operations (www.un.org/depts/dpko)
ECA	Economic Commission for Africa (www.un.org/depts/eca)
ECE	Economic Commission for Europe (www.unece.org)
ECLAC	Economic Commission for Latin America and the Caribbean (www.eclac.cl/index1.html)
ECOSOC	Economic and Social Council (www.un.org/esa/coordination/ecosoc)
ESCAP	Economic and Social Commission for Asia and the Pacific (www.un.org/depts/escap)
ESCWA	Economic and Social Commission for Western Asia (www.escwa.org)
FAO	Food and Agriculture Organization of the United Nations (www.fao.org)
IAEA	International Atomic Energy Agency (www.iaea.org)

IBRD	International Bank for Reconstruction and Development, also known as the World Bank (www.worldbank.org)
ICAO	International Civil Aviation Organization (www.icao.org)
ICJ	International Court of Justice (www.icj-cij.org)
IFAD	International Fund for Agricultural Development (www.ifad.org)
IFC	International Finance Corporation (www.ifc.org)
ILO	International Labor Organization (www.ilo.org)
ILO/ITC	International Training Center of the ILO (www.itcilo.it)
IMF	International Monetary Fund (www.imf.org)
IMO	International Maritime Organization (www.imo.org)
INSTRAW	International Research and Training Institute for the Advancement of Women
ITC	International Trade Center (www.intracen.org)
ITU	International Telecommunications Union (www.itu.org)
JIU	Joint Inspection Unit
OCHA	Office for the Coordination of Humanitarian Affairs (www.reliefweb.int/ocha_ol/index.html)
OLA	Office of Legal Affairs
UNAIDS	Joint United Nations Program on HIV/AIDS (www.unaids.org)
UNCHS	United Nations Center for Human Settlements or Habitat (www.unchs.org)
UNCSD	United Nations Commission on Sustainable Development (www.uncsd.org)
UNCTAD	United Nations Conference on Trade and Development (www.unctad.org)
UNDCP	United Nations International Drug Control Program (www.undcp.org)
UNDP	United Nations Development Program (www.undp.org)
UNEP	United Nations Environment Program (www.unep.org)
UNESCO	United Nations Educational, Scientific and Cultural Organization (www.unesco.org)
UNFIP	United Nations Fund for International Partnerships (www.unfip.org)
UNFPA	United Nations Population Fund (www.unfpa.org)
UNHCHR	United Nations High Commissioner for Human Rights (www.unhchr.ch)
UNHCR	United Nations High Commissioner for Refugees (www.unhcr.ch)
UNICEF	United Nations Children's Fund (www.unicef.org)

UNCITRAL	United Nations Commission on International Trade Law (www.uncitral.org)
UNIDO	United Nations Industrial Development Organization (www.unido.org)
UNIFEM	United Nations Development Fund for Women (www.unifem.org)
UNITAR	United Nations Institute for Training and Research (www.unitar.org)
UNOPS	United Nations Office for Project Services (www.unops.org and www.unops.org/partnerships)
UNRWA	United Nations Relief and Works Agency for Palestine Refugees inthe Near East (www.unrwa.org)
UNSC	United Nations Staff College (www.itcilo.it/unscp)
UNU	United Nations University (www.unu.org)
UNV	United Nations Volunteers (www.unv.org)
UPU	Universal Postal Union (www.upu.org)
WFP	World Food Program (www.wfp.org)
WHO	World Health Organization (www.who.org)
WIPO	World Intellectual Property Organization (www.wipo.org)
WMO	World Meteorological Organization (www.wmo.org)
WTO	World Tourism Organization (www.world-tourism.org)

Other International Organizations and Acronyms

AFDB	African Development Bank (www.afdb.org)
ASDB	Asian Development Bank (www.adb.org)
EBRD	European Bank for Reconstruction and Development (www.ebrd.org)
EU	European Union (www.eu.org)
GATT	General Agreement on Tariffs and Trade (www.wto.org/wto/legal/ursum_wp.htm)
IADB	Inter-American Development Bank (www.iadb.org)
MIGA	Multilateral Investment Guarantee Agency (www.miga.org)
NGO	Non-Governmental Organization
OECD	Organization for Economic Cooperation and Development (www.oecd.org)
OSCE	Organization for Security and Cooperation in Europe (www.osce.org)
USAID	United States Agency for International Development (www.usaid.org)

WTO	World Trade Organization (www.wto.org) **Business Associations, Think Tanks, and Other Relevant Sites**
BCIU	Business Council for International Understanding (www.bciu.org)
BCUN	Business Council for the United Nations (www.unausa.org)
BSR	Business for Social Responsibility (www.bsr.org)
CEPAA	Center for Economic Priorities Accreditation Agency (www.cepaa.org)
CFR	Council on Foreign Relations (www.cfr.org)
Copenhagen Center	www.copenhagencentre.org
Global Public Policy	www.globalpublicpolicy.net
GRI	Global Reporting Initiative (www.globalreporting.org)
ICC	International Chamber of Commerce (www.iccwbo.org)
IOE	International Organization of Employers (www.ioe-emp.org)
Netaid	www.netaid.com
Sullivan Principles	www.sullivanprinciples.org
The Conference Board	www.conference-board.org
UNF	UN Foundation(www.unfoundation.org)
UN Business Wire	www.unfoundation.org/unwirebw
UN Wire	www.unfoundation.org/unwire
USCIB	U.S. Council for International Business (www.uscib.org)
WBCSD	World Business Council for Sustainable Development (www.wbcsd.org)
WEF	World Economic Forum (www.wef.org)

Acknowledgements

This book is dedicated to Mitch Werner, a dear friend and former colleague whose untimely passing in December 1999 shocked all those who knew him. I had the privilege of meeting Mitch while still a student at Columbia. As my advisor under the school's alumni program, he helped me to sort out my new career options, which included the United Nations. A few years later, I worked with him on UN programs for corporate executives at the United Nations Association of the U.S.A. Unfortunately for me, our collaboration was interrupted when Secretary-General Kofi Annan, seeking people of talent and great achievements, invited Mitch to join his cabinet shortly after taking office. Mitch remained a mentor and a friend, however, and when I joined the UN in 1999 we were able to collaborate again, albeit remotely. Mitch was a pioneer in the effort to reconnect the UN and the business community, and he understood the need for a strong relationship between them earlier than anyone I know. The ideas contained herein are in part his, and I know that he would have supported the overall argument of this book. He certainly encouraged me to write it and he should have been around to help implement its vision. His counsel, genuine concern, and equal respect for all those who worked with him were unique, and they are sorely missed.

This book owes much to the work of John Ruggie, who as former dean of Columbia's School of International and Public Affairs has influenced my thinking since my school days. Now senior advisor to UN Secretary-General Kofi Annan, John Ruggie is along with Georg Kell the author of the UN's policy of rapprochement with the business community. The Global Compact owes a large debt to his earlier writings, as I do. He supported this project since I first mentioned it to him in March 1999, and I only hope that the student has not irremediably misrepresented the ideas of the master. Whatever conclusions I have drawn from the policy he has designed are my own, and I take full responsibility for them.

At UNOPS, I want to thank Michael Dudley for his timely advice and support. Now back in his native Belgium, my friend and predecessor at UNOPS, Dominique Michel, made himself available by E-mail and telephone and provided guidance and generous encouragement. My associate, Elise Colomer, was an able research assistant and an authority on websites. Our executive director, Reinhart Helmke, was the first reader and editor of this book. His comments enabled me to correct a number of historical and other errors. With over 30 years of professional experience in the service of developing countries, six languages, ten international moves around the world, and a scholar's knowledge of fifteenth-century public-private partnerships in the Duchy of Burgundy, Reinhart Helmke is the quintessential global citizen. His knowledge, wisdom, and unbounded kindness are a gift to his entire staff. I am deeply grateful for his support and his understanding, as I rushed to meet my publisher's deadline.

Working as UNOPS interns during the fall of 1999 in addition to carrying a full load of courses, two Columbia students, Gina Dario and David Zehner, read several books and carried out excellent research on a number of economic issues that bear on the argument of this book. Their collaboration in the less rewarding tasks of proofreading and bibliographical compilation is equally appreciated. I wish them well in the pursuit of their degrees and have no doubt that they will thrive as professionals of international affairs.

I am grateful to Maria Cattaui, secretary-general of the ICC, and Richard McCormick, former CEO of US West and ICC president-elect—two globetrotting business leaders who continue to play paramount roles in redefining UN-business relations—for taking the time to reply to my survey of business attitudes toward the UN. I thank also my friends, Stephen Halloway, a former UN official, and Lew Cramer, adviser to Richard McCormick, for expressing their interest in this project and always extending a hand when I needed it. At the U.S. Council for International Business (USCIB), William Stibravy supplied numerous and precious pieces of evidence on the early phase of the UN-business relationship. Bill's oral history of the ICC and its role in supporting multilateralism from the start is unmatchable, and I am grateful for his openness to sharing his knowledge and materials. Equally committed to the cause of UN-business relations, USCIB Senior Vice President Ronnie Goldberg facilitated access to sources and executives.

At St. Martin's Press, my editor, Karen Wolny, deserves full credit and admiration for believing in a "UN book" after multilateralism has been under consistent attack in the United States for a decade. Her trust honors me and I hope that the debate generated by this book will vindicate her early conviction.

Last but not least, I owe my deepest gratitude to my parents, Michèle and Michel, also known as M&M. The gift of freedom is the greatest of all, and on that account alone their generosity can never be matched. But it is their love and involvement in my daily life that, despite the thousands of miles separating us, enable me to succeed in all my undertakings. As I prepare to usher in a new millennium, I only wish they lived closer by.

Sandrine Tesner
December 31, 1999

Introduction

In 1945, 51 nations and hundreds of civil society organizations from around the world gathered in San Francisco to witness the birth of the first universal multilateral organization in human history. The State Department had worked assiduously during the war years to contribute to the text of the United Nations Charter. Having borrowed its heading from the American constitution, the Charter's liberal value framework placed on "We the Peoples" the responsibility of crafting a peaceful future.[1] Fulfilling President Roosevelt's savvy political plans, the American delegation to the San Francisco conference included numerous religious, civic, labor, and business groups. Representatives of the U.S. Chamber of Commerce, still today America's largest business organization, joined a delegation of the Paris-based International Chamber of Commerce, of which the American Chamber was a member. In July 1945, as the Senate Foreign Relations Committee pondered whether to ratify the UN Charter, Philip D. Reed, then chairman of General Electric and one of America's senior business leaders, sent a telegram to the committee's chairman expressing the "earnest and enthusiastic support" of the U.S. Chamber to the Charter and urging unanimous ratification by the Senate. Yet in the 55 years since the UN's creation, business and UN leaders have exhibited at best a mutual disdain toward each other—when they did not engage in a virulent war of words. This book seeks to explain what kept the United Nations and the private sector apart for five decades, why they have renewed their ties since 1997, and why the future of multilateral institutions hinges on the latter's ability to integrate the private sector in the entire spectrum of activities.

The international business community has long been favorable to the concept of multilateralism. The history of the International Chamber of Commerce (ICC), whose establishment was decided at a meeting held in Atlantic City in 1919, demonstrates that cosmopolitan business leaders understood the need for multilateral solutions to international problems well before governments. Had their support for the League of Nations been heeded during the 1930s, the protectionism and autarkism that fueled the already disastrous effects of the Great Depression might have been avoided, thereby stalling the ineluctable march toward a global war. It is not surprising therefore that both the ICC and its powerful American cousin, the U.S. Chamber, wary of the isolationist sentiments that might derail once again the creation of a multilateral body, made their views known to their national leaders by urging ratification of the UN Charter. What is more interesting yet is that the UN Charter presupposed a governmental role in regulating the economy, favoring employment, and providing safety nets to the hardest-hit social groups during recessions. Based on the work of British economist J. M. Keynes, this "compromise of embedded liberalism"[2] had been formulated in response to the Great Depression. The idea that a degree of intervention was necessary to maintain openness, while protecting the most disfavored from utter poverty and its inherent destabilizing effects, was not seen as "anti-business." Indeed, the creation of the UN system on the one hand, and the World Bank and International Monetary Fund—the so-called Bretton Woods institutions—on the other, was premised on macroeconomic management. In 1945 international business was not only pro-UN; it was also pro-regulation.

The relationship between the UN and the private sector began to unravel during the 1950s as the former colonies of Asia and Africa gained independence and joined the ranks of the UN General Assembly as equal members with equal rights. The ensuing debates over the objectives and methods of development policy consumed the rupture. The choice of infant-industry policies, accompanied by attempts to regulate the prices of commodities for the benefit of the newly formed "South," seemed to undermine the compromise of 1945, predicated as it was upon the maintenance of open trade. The estrangement reached its nadir with the call for a New International Economic Order in 1974, and the contemporaneous attempt by the Organization of Oil Exporting Countries (OPEC) to accrue wealth and power through a commodity threat backed by high oil prices. The hardened political context of the Cold War fueled poor policy choices: it is only because they served ideological purposes in the war-by-other-means imposed by nuclear weapons that such bad economics prevailed for almost four decades.

During the 1970s, the successes of export-led growth in Asia, the return to a level of interdependence that had eroded ever since 1913, and the liberal reaction that began with the elections of Margaret Thatcher and Ronald Reagan signaled the beginning of the end of the UN-business chasm. When the Berlin Wall came tumbling down, discrediting irremediably the techniques of central command economies, the UN faced the challenge of fashioning for itself a relevant role in the transition of socialist countries to market economies. The end of the Cold War also meant that governments would no longer look at development policies as instruments of their political positioning in the East-West rivalry, but rather as ends in themselves in the expansion of world markets. As some spoke of the "end of history," a rapprochement between the UN and the business community could not be far away.[3]

The process of globalization that began when bipolarity ended has dramatically altered the premise of the "compromise of embedded liberalism." Not only have the failures of central command economies undermined support for government intervention in the economy, but were a consensus in favor of such a role to emerge anew, the conditions of globalization would prevent governments from exercising their traditional regulatory functions. While nation-states retain authority over their territory, population, and an array of symbolic and real capacities, they have lost control over a large portion of economic activities now taking place in a metanational space above borders, nations, and cultures.[4] Because it limits the state's capacity to tax the product of economic activity, this loss of control undermines the provision of safety nets and national public goods. The international community has therefore entered a transitory phase where large-scale openness and free circulation of goods, money, and ideas coincide with a limitation of governmental power not seen since the fifteenth century.

Two factors make this state of affairs necessarily temporary. Firstly, this regulatory gap is fraught with dangers. The uncontrolled penetration of goods and ideas that accompanies and characterizes globalization has resulted in increased inequality and social dislocations, on the one hand, and the perception of threats to national and ethnic identities, on the other. Poverty and cultural insecurity, added to the spread of such metanational problems as environmental degradation and the AIDS pandemic, constitute potent ingredients for social explosions and a general backlash against globalization. These conditions require solutions, lest the promise of openness turns into a nightmare of exclusion and national introversion, whose consequences in the context of a global world would far surpass the closure of the 1930s. Secondly, and more optimistically, man being a cultural creature whose survival depends on the construction of ideas and values, and the institutions in which to embed them, the international community is bound to fashion and build the institutional mechanisms that will ensure its survival and well-being in the twenty-first century.[5] As unexpected as it may seem, the ongoing rapprochement between the United Nations and the business community is crucial to the construction of this new world order.

Understanding the meaning of these systemic changes, shortly after his appointment on January 1, 1997, UN Secretary-General Kofi Annan announced that strengthening relations between the United Nations and the private sector would constitute a priority of his mandate. His commitment rang loud and clear when, addressing the World Economic Forum in Davos four weeks after taking office, Kofi Annan stated that: "Today, market capitalism has no rival. . . . In today's world, the private sector is the dominant engine of growth; the principal creator of value and wealth. . . . This is why I call today for a new partnership among governments, the private sector, and the international community."[6] The Davos speech signaled the beginning of a consistent outreach to business leaders of goodwill. Since 1997 the secretary-general has issued unprecedented policy statements with the ICC and other business organizations, calling for a partnership between the United Nations and business in constructing the rules that will sustain globalization by cushioning its blows on some of its victims—real or perceived. His vision came full circle in 1999 when, speaking again at Davos, he challenged the international private sector to adopt a "Global Compact of shared values and principles" focusing on three negative externalities of globalization: attacks on human rights, labor rights, and the environment.[7]

The rationale for this recovered partnership is simple, yet strong and visionary. Three global actors have emerged as key participants and shapers of the new global reality. Multinational corporations, multinational civil society groups, and the United Nations all share a metanational dimension in that their allegiance is not tied to any state or nation but reaches above them. Of the three, business and civil society are clearly the most global, having established networks above borders and deriving their legitimacy from their shareholders and members, respectively. The United Nations, of course, is an intergovernmental organization in which member states wield ultimate power. But the UN Charter already acknowledged the role of civil society in international affairs by providing under Article 71 an accreditation mechanism for NGOs, business, and labor groups. The ICC obtained accreditation to the UN in 1946, and over 1,500 NGOs currently enjoy consultative status to the world body. In the context of globalization, the United Nations will fight the battle of its relevance on its capacity to integrate nonstate actors in its work.

Globalization is not solely an economic phenomenon. Its cultural, political, and social dimensions may play as influential a role in reshaping the world order as economic exchanges. But the former are more elusive and harder to quantify than the latter. Furthermore, globalization was first visible in the economic sphere and it remains to this day a business-led process. This fact alone argues in favor of a UN-business alliance in the construction of global rules. More importantly, corporations are in a unique position to act on behalf of the three negative externalities outlined by the Global Compact. As employers, they can decide to eliminate child labor and other human rights abuses. As investors, they can pressure their partners to respect fundamental values. As manufacturers, they can exercise responsibility toward the global commons of air, sea, and land. In the creation of a normative framework to accompany globalization, the private sector is the necessary and privileged partner of the United Nations.

Having set the stage in chapters 1 and 2 for a recovered partnership between the UN and the business community, this book provides the first comprehensive account of the objectives, modalities, accomplishments, and challenges of these partnerships to date. Chapter 3 describes the formats of partnerships in the four main areas of policy, fund-raising, advocacy and awareness, and operations. The cases presented below demonstrate that corporations and UN agencies work together more often than is generally assumed, in a myriad of ways, and with diverse objectives. Successful partnerships are predicated on so-called win-win situations based on mutual benefits and common objectives. No UN body has failed to increase its outreach to the private sector in recent years and, contrary to commonly held clichés, filling the UN's coffers with corporate funds does not constitute the primary motivation for partnering. The UN looks to business to provide technical expertise, expert staff, policy guidance, management skills, goods and services, and general support for the UN's mandates. Crucial to the sustainability of globalization is a corporate commitment to investing in and extending the benefits of open trade to the poorest nations, many of which are in Africa. Poverty and war have never formed the basis of wealth and business expansion, giving the UN and the private sector a common interest in their elimination.

Chapter 4 takes stock of the short history of renewed cooperation and looks to the future. Many obstacles remain in the path of sustained partnership. Firstly, the new approach to UN-business relations is too recent to have become embedded in UN and corporate structures. It is therefore fragile and easily damageable. If corporations have developed a stake in this renewed relationship, as I believe they have, they will have to defend it and use their influence to prevent a reversal of the course. At the UN too, those officials and staff members who believe in the approach will have to make a constant case for it and counter critics of all stripes—internal and external, governmental and nongovernmental, domestic and international. The battle of ideas over the UN's future is far from over. Operational and legal challenges also stand in the way of increasing the opportunities for and the formulation of UN-business partnerships. These hurdles, however, are manageable, and assuming that the political will remains intact, there is good hope that modernized guidelines for private sector collaboration can be put in place in 2000.

One last and sizeable question mark deserves mention in this introduction. As has been stated, the UN Charter already envisaged the participation of nonstate actors in its deliberations. If the UN cannot hope to accomplish its work in the twenty-first century without the contribution and support of civil society and business, these nonstate actors can be expected to request an official representative status within UN debates and forums. The private sector has remained discreet on the matter, but civil society organizations have been clamoring for a more influential and official role in UN international conferences, and by extension, in those UN bodies charged with implementing their recommendations. Were the support of business for a renewed and relevant United Nations to increase and broaden internationally, business associations may follow the lead of NGOs in asking for stepped-up representation. Such a development ought not to be surprising, nor should it be dismissed as politically infeasible. If the international system of the past four centuries relied on the capacities of the nation-state, the global order of the next hundred years will have to depend on those of non-state actors. What format their representation might take within the United Nations is open for debate, but it is doubtful that the only universal multilateral body available to the global community can achieve its ends in the future without reinterpreting the foundations of its legitimacy, and therefore of its membership. Were the United Nations to fail in enacting this transformation, a novel multipartite governance mechanism would likely arise to take its place.

CHAPTER 1

Overcoming the Past

The end of the Cold War, the globalization of the economy, and the announced "end of history" were all factors in the UN's decision to renew its ties with the private sector. Although nothing precluded such collaboration from the time of the UN's creation in 1945, the conditions required to strike that partnership did not prevail until the 1990s. Private-public partnerships are not a new concept, however. They existed in the fifteenth century in the form of associations between the rising traders of Spain, Italy, and the Netherlands, and political leaders all over Europe. Taking place at the crossroads between the economic and the political realms, the fairs of the Hanseatic League can be seen as the forerunners to such contemporary summits as the World Economic Forum's annual meeting in Davos, Switzerland. But once the nation-state made its entrance on the world stage in the seventeenth century, it became the responsibility of political bureaucracies to regulate the content and format of economic relations. Governmental control over the economy remained in place until increasing exchanges and the rise of an international business class in the second half of the nineteenth century challenged the nationalist model of mercantilism. The new state of affairs had its credo, liberalism, whose laissez-faire version ruled economic discourse until 1945. The drafters of the United Nations Charter did not question the key assumptions of free trade and free capital flows, but the Great Depression imposed some compromises on nineteenth-century laissez-faire. The UN's economic organs would rest on the principles of multilateralism and nondiscrimination, but their stated goals would include economic growth and full employment.

This central compromise was not questioned until the onset of decolonization in the early 1960s. The ensuing dramatic shift in UN membership heralded a neo-Marxist analysis of the international economic system and a new emphasis on redistribution. The concerns of the newly independent nations, which soon acquired a collective identity under such labels as the

"South" and the "Third World," were addressed by the creation of a slew of UN agencies mandated to develop their economies through the transfer of capital and skills. For a while it looked as if the new generation of UN member states would question the original compromise of the UN Charter. But the failure of their policies only made the return of liberalism in the 1980s more assertive and uncompromising. By the end of the 1980s, the world had passed from the ideologues to the managers in both the North and the South.

Enter the end of the Cold War and globalization. By discrediting all forms of central planning, the end of the Cold War meant that the UN no longer needed to remain neutral as to the effectiveness of markets. In 1992, Francis Fukuyama gave this apparent victory of economic liberalism the infamous label of "end of history."[1] The end of the Cold War also meant that governments would no longer look at development policies as instruments of their political positioning in the East-West rivalry, but rather as ends in themselves in the expansion of world markets. Globalization had two main implications. Firstly, maintaining an open global economy and turning developing countries into emerging markets became the primary objectives of most developed nations—a concern that was reflected in UN debates and forced a reformulation of UN development policies. Secondly, and more importantly, because the activities of multinationals increasingly escape national regulatory frameworks, globalization implies that governments no longer boast the capacities to fully regulate economic relations. In this context, bridging the gap between international business and international organizations has become critical to maintaining an open and expanding economy in the twenty-first century. How the UN came to realize the centrality of this new fact is in large part due to the appointment of Kofi Annan as secretary-general in 1996 and the policies he began to shape in 1997.

Back to the Future?

What is known as "public-private partnership" has become a cliché of daily political discourse; yet it is not an invention of the late twentieth century. Similar alliances between political rulers and business leaders were quite common in the Italy of Machiavelli and the Spain of Philip II. The artistic patronage of the Renaissance, without which that period would never have known its treasures, is a fifteenth-century form of corporate responsibility. The reign and role of Venice in fifteenth-century commerce remind one of the vitality and centrality of New York today, and its "Cinque Savii alla Mercanzia"—a council of five experts on commerce—calls to mind our Council of Economic Advisers. Attempts to control trade and limit competition already existed in the form of the "Fondaco dei Tedeschi," an organization that constrained the activities of German merchants seeking to foster commercial relations with the Levant—modern Turkey. In an effort to consolidate Venice's commercial preeminence, the Venetian Republic built large ships, the "galere da mercato," which it put at the disposal of the merchants.[2] Before the invention of national armies, even wars followed an economic rationale as princes hired mercenaries, the so-called "condottieri," to fight on their behalf.[3]

Looking at human history over the long haul, the next millennium may have more in common with the fifteenth century than meets the eye. The international system of the late Middle Ages and Renaissance presented a diversity in the sources and distribution of power that is closer to our own age than it is to eighteenth-century inter-national politics. In a system where statehood did not yet exist, power was distributed among various polities ("civitates"), principalities, fiefdoms, and local republics. "To these must be added" according to Ruggie, "cities, associations of trades, commercial leagues, and even universities, not to mention papacy and empire—all of which, for certain purposes, were considered to be legitimate 'international' political actors."[4] Religious power merits particular attention, as it was the main competitor to political power until religion was submitted to the state in the seventeenth century.

What are today's parallels to the diverse power units of the fifteenth century? In his book *The Lexus and the Olive Tree,* Thomas Friedman uses storytelling to illustrate the many sources of identity for the global citizen at the end of the twentieth century. In addition to belonging to a nation-state to which she still pays taxes and may still defend in war, the citizen of the year 2000 may belong to the community of the Internet, a religious community of her choice (which may have little to do with the one she was born into), a corporation or any other employer, her university's alumni society, various neighborhood organizations, a sports club—and the list is far from exhaustive. These diverse communities are symbolized by McDonalds's Golden Arches, CNN.com, thousands of civil society organizations—domestic and global—and the flags of the European Union and the United Nations flying alongside each other in Kosovo. As military men and women, today's citizens may indeed serve in multilateral peacekeeping operations that bear little resemblance to the national armies that won World War II.

In some ways, therefore, today's global life shows signs of bringing us back to the future—the future of the Renaissance and the Middle Ages. But this historical return is taking place after a long period of centralization of power from the seventeenth to the late nineteenth century.

Signed in 1648 at the end of the Thirty Years' War, the Treaty of Westphalia is commonly seen as the act of creation of the sovereign state. The modern state became a centralizing force, separate and standing above religious power, which it was created to contain. The state also became solely responsible for the safety of its citizens, and uniquely capable of mobilizing economic resources for the national benefit. The modern age that began in the mid-seventeenth century was therefore characterized by the primacy of the political over the economic. Its economic system, mercantilism, had nationalistic connotations. To become rich, nations had to accumulate gold and silver, whose prices were fixed. To do so, they had to export more than they imported, which necessarily came at the expense of other nations' efforts to enrich themselves. The prevalence of zero-sum gains was the central assumption of international politics, therefore making international peace contingent on maintaining a precarious balance of power. The latter assigned leaders and diplomats a central role in international policymaking, as the stability of the system rested on their skills and craftiness in preventing the formation of overwhelming alliances that constituted the main threats to the system. Metternich, Talleyrand, and Bismarck are some of the men who epitomized the genius of classical diplomacy.[5] Until the early nineteenth century, international life was therefore characterized by well-defined and centralized units—so many atoms moving independently in a controlled pattern and cautiously avoiding any hint of fusion. Its style was classical and civilized, reminiscent of the Louis XVI aesthetics copied throughout Europe. Its language was French, whose Cartesian grammar and rhetoric fit admirably the inescapable logic of national sovereignty.

The nineteenth century introduced ominous changes in this dignified arrangement. For one, what François Furet called the revolution in the singular—1770–1880—produced the three ideologies that were to divide the world in the twentieth century: liberalism first, followed by nationalism and socialism. Second, central government found a rival in the rise of what became known as "society." This creation of the revolution, which does not fully overlap with our concept of "civil society," refers not only to the right but, even more so, the inclination of members of a same community to organize themselves in ways that do not fully overlap with the state. Civil society would become the subject of Tocqueville's admiration in his analysis of the American political system, but it was a newcomer to European politics in the nineteenth century. Thirdly, by spurring the rise of new industries and transforming the entire globe into an open market, the Industrial Revolution spelled the bankruptcy of mercantilism. In the process it created a class of international business leaders and gave rise to a future world power, although no one could tell until after World War I. Finally, a mushrooming number of press organizations meant the end of secret diplomacy.[6] By the time President Wilson called for open international negotiations in 1918, the media—and the public opinion it created—had irremediably transformed the career of diplomat, one of the world's oldest.

A new international system began to emerge at the Paris Conference in 1919. Based on the principle of self-determination for the world's peoples, President Wilson's Fourteen Points introduced concepts that were at odds with the unitary dimension of classical diplomacy. National self-determination, a concern for public opinion, and the submission of foreign policy to moral values were among many ideas that brought a fluidity to international politics uncharacteristic of the previous era. Under Wilson's influence and despite the resistance of the European powers, the 1919 Paris Conference turned on its head what the Congress of Vienna had adamantly sought to construct in 1815. The principle of collective security, which was to be enshrined in Wilson's proposed League of Nations, epitomized the new thinking. Collective security could only be upheld if all states in the international system were equal. Equality was the prerequisite to reciprocity, and reciprocity called for the intervention of all against the aggression of one. Wilson's principle of collective security based on equality was revolutionary: no claim would have sounded more preposterous to a Metternich or a Bismarck than stating that all states are equal in the international system. In inventing multilateralism, Wilson was both a pioneer and a visionary, but few at the time could follow him down the multilateral path. As a unilateralist vision of America's international role prevailed in the U.S. Congress, America's entry into the League was defeated, thereby dooming the organization from its inception.[7]

Yet, some principles of multilateralism won the day, as evidenced by the creation in 1919 of the International Labor Organization (ILO), a UN agency since 1946. Part of the Versailles Treaty that formally ended World War I, the ILO has a tripartite structure that is unique among UN bodies. In addition to member states, its members include representatives of labor and employers' groups, the latter two enjoying equal policymaking and management responsibilities with governments.[8] The International Labor Conference, for example, sets international labor standards and adopts the ILO's budget. In this sense, the ILO was the UN's first private-public partnership, a position that puts it at the center of current discussions on UN-business collaboration.

By 1945, the liberal credo according to which political stability is contingent on economic exchange had gained many adepts. Concretely, it meant that postwar reconstruction could not proceed without significant participation from private sector firms. Retrospectively, it seemed that the failure to maintain an open trading system during the interwar period accounted for many of the societal ills that had led to the outbreak of World War II. In his classic study of the period, Kindleberger ascribed to a benevolent hegemon—at that time the United States—the responsibility of providing the public goods of free trade and financial stability.[9] The job could also be performed by institutions embodying similar values, and the latter formula was not incompatible with the former. Indeed, the Roosevelt administration would play a leading role in shaping these new institutions.

At the UN's Creation

Initial discussions on a future international institution began before America's entry into the war in 1941. Subsequently, work on drafting the UN Charter took place mostly in the State Department under the leadership of Secretary of State Cordell Hull. When the Dumbarton Oaks conference convened in August 1944, its delegates focused on the "U.S. Tentative Proposals for a General International Organization," to be comprised of a small "executive council" concerned with the maintenance of peace and security, a General Assembly, an International Court of Justice, and autonomous specialized agencies.[10] The UN Charter was signed in San Francisco in June 1945, after a two-month conference gathering 51 states. As a result of President Roosevelt's conscious strategy of building public support for the Charter, ratification by the United States Congress was close to unanimous. Moreover, President Roosevelt's decision to send to the San Francisco conference 42 American organizations in such fields as business, law, education, and labor, set a significant precedent for future UN partnerships with civil society and the private sector.[11]

To understand the concepts that would guide the new organization's work in the economic and social areas, it is useful to contrast them with the principles set by the UN Charter in peace and security matters. Although the principle of collective security introduced by the defunct League of Nations still informed the UN Charter, it was substantially modified to guarantee, it was argued, the UN's success where the League had failed. The principle of multilateralism, according to which rules apply equally to all members, was generally enshrined in the Charter. However, in the security realm, some members would be more equal than others. This reality struck home when five nations—the United States, the United Kingdom, France, the Soviet Union, and later China—obtained permanent seats and a right of veto on the Security Council. The existence of two categories of membership in the Security Council meant that military intervention by the UN would not proceed on the basis of collective security, which spells out joint response to an attack on any single member of an organization.[12] Rather, any of the five permanent members could veto an intervention with which it disagreed, thereby condemning the organization to paralysis, as it did during most of the Cold War. Moreover, a Military Staff Committee consisting of the Chiefs of Staff of the five permanent members of the council would be "responsible for the strategic direction of any armed forces placed at the disposal of the Security Council." This was a seriously amended concept of collective security—Roosevelt called it collective security "with teeth"—but it was the only one the president could sell the U.S. Congress.

In the economic realm, however, no similar dual membership would apply. Work to chart the UN's structure and mandate in the economic and social area can be traced back to 1939 when the Bruce Committee, named after the Australian representative to the League of Nations, issued a report arguing for the creation of a Central Committee for Economic and Social Questions.[13] There again, American drafters gave the final plan its key concepts and values. Papers that emerged from the State Department were based on four principles: the end of autarky and other nationalist economic systems, nondiscrimination in international trade, equal access to raw materials, and the creation of a financial system to sustain an open and growing economy. Proposals for a "Joint Economic and Social Council" or a "Bureau of Technical Services" concerned with economic and social issues were made during 1942–43. By 1944, the U.S. Tentative Proposals for a General International Organization included provisions for a Social and Economic Council under the authority of the UN General Assembly. Its rationale, centered on the liberal credo of peace through trade, was stated as follows: "With a view to the creation of stability and well-being which are necessary for peaceful and friendly relations among nations, the general international organization should facilitate and promote solutions of economic and social problems, including educational and cultural problems."[14]

At the Dumbarton Oaks conference in August 1944, these proposals fell prey to the diverging interests of various delegations. The Soviet view was that an international organization's "primary and indeed only task" was to maintain peace and security. Soviet Foreign Minister Gromyko asserted that the League of Nations had lost enough time with "secondary" economic and social matters.[15] The British delegation, for its part, was concerned about the implications of an open recognition of human rights for the longevity of its empire. It also favored restricting the membership of the UN's economic council to 18, with a view to making it more effective. Indeed, arguing that economic well-being and international peace were intimately linked, the United Kingdom initially proposed to give the Security Council mandate over economic and social issues.[16]

While it was discussing the mandates of the UN's economic organs, the United States was concurrently laying the groundwork for the Bretton Woods conference that, in July 1944, created the International Monetary Fund (IMF) and the World Bank (officially called International Bank for Reconstruction and Development, IBRD). In 1945, President Roosevelt stressed the functional division of labor between the Bretton Woods institutions and the UN. Addressing Congress, he stated: "the cornerstone for international political cooperation is the Dumbarton Oaks proposal for a

permanent United Nations. . . . The cornerstone for international economic cooperation is the Bretton Woods proposal for an International
Monetary Fund and an International Bank for Reconstruction and Development."[17] Therefore, while the United States was not indifferent to the ultimate values and goals of the UN's future economic bodies, it relied mostly
on the Bretton Woods institutions to manage the major task of ensuring an
open and stable financial and trading system.

While they stayed away from the discussions taking place at Dumbarton
Oaks on the creation of the future UN, the involvement of business representatives in the Bretton Woods negotiations provides added evidence of the
role the latter institutions were expected to play in rebuilding and sustaining
the world economy. American business leaders were consulted by the Department of the Treasury and invited to Capitol Hill for Senate hearings on
the creation of the IMF and the World Bank. Several business associations
and union groups braved the State Department's indifference and made a
case in favor of attending the San Francisco conference in June 1945.[18] Yet,
only one business organization, the International Chamber of Commerce
(ICC), asked for and received immediate accreditation to the UN under Article 71 of the Charter.

The ICC's history is enlightening regarding the role of the private sector
in creating and supporting multilateral institutions in the early part of the
century, and it deserves a short digression. The decision to establish "a permanent world business organization" was made in October 1919 in Atlantic
City, New Jersey, by a group of internationalist and highbrow business leaders from Europe who had come to New Jersey at the invitation of the U.S.
Chamber of Commerce. The ICC was finally established the following year
in Paris—its seat to this day—and was immediately accredited to the League
of Nations. The ICC's first president, and one of its main conceivers, was Etienne Clémentel, a former French minister of commerce who harbored firmly
liberal views on economic interdependence and the link between peace and
prosperity. During the 1920s and 1930s, the ICC took part in most economic conferences convened by the League. Enjoying equal membership status with governments, three ICC representatives joined a "special committee"
on trade at the 1927 World Economic Conference, allowing the ICC to play
a policy role that would be inconceivable in the context of current UN forums.[19] The ICC also helped to address one of the major political challenges
of the day, the level and pace of German reparations, and contributed to the
creation of the Dawes Commission. As the world came ever closer to the
brink of war, ICC presidents worked tirelessly on behalf of peace, as testified
by *Merchants of Peace,* a book published by the organization in 1938. Then
President of the ICC Thomas J. Watson, founder of IBM, traveled to 21 European countries in 1938–39 in an effort to prevent the outbreak of war.[20]

In 1945, arguing in favor of obtaining consultative status to the UN, the ICC could point to its long history of collaboration with the League of Nations. Consultative status was obtained in 1946 at the highest level authorized by the Charter (Level A). The notion that the UN was an anti-business organization was not present at the creation. It developed with the emergence of the Cold War and became cast in stone with the accession of the former colonies of Asia and Africa to independence in the 1950s. A telegram sent by Philip D. Reed, then chairman and CEO of General Electric, to the U.S. Senate Foreign Relations Committee in July 1945 demonstrates strong American business support for the Charter. As the Senate prepared to take up the ratification debate, Reed wrote: "We believe that no finer nor more fruitful gesture could be made toward its successful implementation than for the Foreign Relations Committee and subsequently the Senate itself to ratify the Charter unanimously."[21] In 1946, therefore, the ICC became the UN's leading counterpart in the private sector, although labor unions later obtained NGO status before the world body.

Despite corporate participation in the San Francisco conference, the developing countries gave the future UN's economic council its final shape on that occasion. Under their pressure, and with the support of smaller developed nations such as Canada and Australia, the UN Economic and Social Council (ECOSOC) became one of the principal organs of the world organization and received larger powers. Rallying under the motto of "justice for all," developing countries followed the leadership of India to remind the developed world that "it is economic injustice, and even more so, social injustice, that has bred for all time in the past the great causes of war." Antiliberal proposals were put forth by France to allow the future ECOSOC to "insure access, on equal terms, to trade, raw materials, and to capital goods." But the whiff of antiliberalism that would prevail at the UN in the 1960s and 1970s was defeated at this early stage, as "the urgency of creating a new international organization took precedence over a prior elucidation and resolution of the ambiguities of the political consensus which underpinned it."[22] All ECOSOC was finally granted was greater autonomy in issuing reports, convening conferences, and submitting information on economic matters to the General Assembly on its own initiative.

Still, the UN Charter placed economic and social progress at the center of its search for peace. Article 1 of the Charter cites the achievement of "international cooperation in solving international problems of an economic, social, cultural, or humanitarian character" as the third purpose of the UN.[23] Article 55 stipulates the principles and values that were to guide the work of the United Nations in the area of international economic and social cooperation. These included the promotion of "higher standards of living, full employment, and conditions of economic and social progress and development;" solutions to problems related to health and education; and a "universal respect for, and observance of, human rights and fundamental freedom."[24]

These principles reflect what John Ruggie has termed the "compromise of embedded liberalism."[25] Embedded liberalism as it applied to the UN and the Bretton Woods institutions meant nothing else than an international translation of the domestic parameters of the New Deal. In a departure from nineteenth-century laissez-faire, the New Deal, it will be recalled, had legitimized government intervention in the economy—a necessity that British economist John Maynard Keynes had demonstrated in his *General Theory of Employment, Interest, and Money,* published in 1936. Similarly, the international institutions created after World War II would acknowledge the legitimacy of full employment policies, as underlined in the UN Charter itself, as well as the need for stabilization policies in the financial system—a public good the IMF was mandated to provide.

Where, then, was the compromise? It lay in two principles of critical importance to the American architects of the UN. The first principle was the maintenance of an open trading and financial system. As has been stated above, the UN's economic organs were primarily envisioned to help developing countries help themselves. The engine of growth and development, however, would remain free and nondiscriminatory exchange, in negation of some of the autarkic policies that had been attempted during the interwar period. Nondiscrimination meant the acceptance of multilateralism—the second principle of the American drafters—by and for all members of the new organization. In the sense in which it is used here, "multilateralism" does not refer to action by several states, as "unilateral" means action by one state or "bilateral" refers to action by two states. Rather, multilateralism is based on the equality of all states and the denial of any form of discrimination among them.[26] The result of multilateral relations between states is reciprocity: if A is equal to B, which is equal to C, then A and C are also equal (transitivity) and all are entitled to expect the same treatment from each other (reciprocity). This is the basis of most-favored-nation status in trade: whatever advantages a nation grants another apply equally to a third party. Trade is multilateral when similar trading conditions apply equally to all members of the system. In the name of the "compromise of embedded liberalism," the drafters of the UN Charter therefore inscribed full employment, financial stabilization, and later on economic development policies among its stated objectives in exchange for the recognition of the principle of multilateralism in international financial and trade relations.

Although ECOSOC was mandated to carry out and monitor the UN economic and social functions, the UN Charter did not grant it clear-cut authority. According to Article 62 of the Charter, ECOSOC was to be a policymaking body charged with publishing reports and studies on economic and social issues, calling for conferences on these matters, and making recommendations to the General Assembly in its mandate area. It was also envisaged that ECOSOC would coordinate the functions of the UN specialized agencies. However, the prescription that such coordinating functions would be undertaken "through recommendations to the General Assembly" represented a substantial restriction on ECOSOC's autonomy.[27] The General Assembly could also assign tasks to ECOSOC as it saw fit.[28] Moreover, the Charter allowed for overlapping functions between ECOSOC and the General Assembly, since the latter was also entitled to submit reports on economic issues.[29] In the end, the assembly retained legislative power and ECOSOC received neither legislative nor executive authority. ECOSOC's power deficit would prove heavy in consequences during the peacekeeping missions of the 1990s, as well as in UN-business partnerships in the current period. Regarding ECOSOC's partners in its field of activity, Article 71 specified that ECOSOC could "make suitable arrangements for consultation with non-governmental organizations," but it said nothing about ECOSOC's interaction with the private sector specifically.[30] Finally, ECOSOC was given oversight on several regional economic commissions, created as early as 1947–48 to focus on economic problems and cooperation in specific regions.[31]

The establishment of several specialized agencies prior to ECOSOC's creation further complicated ECOSOC's mission from its inception. As stated above, the ILO had been created in 1919. The International Telecommunication Union (ITU) became a UN body in 1947, but dated back to 1865, when it was founded as the International Telegraph Union. Another technical agency, the Universal Postal Union (UPU), had been established in 1874 and became a UN agency in 1948. Although established in October 1945, the UN Food and Agriculture Organization (FAO, headquartered in Rome) was the product of talks initiated by the U.S. Department of Agriculture in 1943 to address short-term emergency food needs and longer-term issues of nutrition and food distribution in the wake of the war. Another meeting held under U.S. auspices in Chicago in 1944 led to the creation that year of the International Civil Aviation Organization (ICAO, headquartered in Montreal), which regulates civil aviation. This apparently haphazard institution-building was not entirely unplanned. In a reinterpretation of "divide and conquer," the United States believed that separate and autonomous agencies would be easier to control and would not fall prey to the political debates that were meant to become the hallmark of an intergovernmental organization such as the UN. The specialized agencies were to be just that: expert bodies minding their technical business away from the political wrangling of UN member states.

As most plans, this scheme suffered from unintended consequences. The ILO, for example, should have played a major role in promoting full employment, labor standards, and labor rights, a stated purpose of UN economic bodies. In fact, the ILO fell victim to the ideological warfare of the 1960s and 1970s, a plight that marginalized its role until recently.[32] UNESCO became infamous for turning its specialized mandate in the areas of education and science into an antiliberal crusade during the same period. A similar trend affected most UN specialized agencies, including the most technical among them, such as the ITU and the UPU.[33] The agencies ECOSOC was expected to coordinate therefore followed their own paths during most of the UN's history, limiting ECOSOC's potential role and dooming the intent that had led to their establishment separate from ECOSOC. Ironically, that original plan has come back to haunt its very authors as they seek to reform the UN's economic organs today. Attempting to coordinate, let alone integrate, UN economic and social activities has proven particularly challenging, as each agency has self-righteously claimed its legal autonomy to resist falling under the authority of a single UN economic organ.

Before closing the immediate post–World War II period, a word must be said about trade issues. Plans to establish an International Trade Organization (ITO) were debated during the postwar period. It proved impossible to reconcile the divergent agendas of its potential members, however, and the ITO's proposed mandate contained too many contradictory provisions to allow its creation at the time. The British insistence on maintaining its imperial preferences in trade represented an unacceptable blow to the sacrosanct principles of nondiscrimination and multilateralism. In the end, the U.S. Congress defeated the ITO proposal, and no business lobby could rescue a trade organization at a time when too few American corporations depended on international trade to survive.[34] Trade was entrusted to a regime rather than an institution. The General Agreement on Tariffs and Trade (GATT), instituted in 1947, sequentially negotiated and widened free trade agreements until the creation of the World Trade Organization (WTO) in 1995, which remains officially outside the UN system.

From Partnership to Cold War

The attention of the world community was soon diverted from economic recovery and reconstruction to the resumption of war—a cold war—on a global scale. In the early 1950s, the Korean War monopolized the attention of policymakers and constrained the UN's role in the economic and social realm. The UN had little to do with the reconstruction of Europe, entrusted to the American-designed Marshall Plan. The general movement toward decolonization that began in the early part of the 1950s and accelerated in the 1960s would transform "development policy" into the UN's leading concern for three decades.

While the discussion of this policy may seem unrelated to our topic, it has in fact a direct bearing on the history of the UN's relations with the private sector. The policy frameworks chosen by developing countries during that period, often with UN support, contributed to a long estrangement between the United Nations and business leaders and built a legacy of misperceptions and mistrust. It is not possible to understand why the UN and business failed for decades to deliver on the partnership they had struck in 1945 without reviewing the ebb and flow of development policy since 1950.

Although many of the delegations attending the 1945 San Francisco conference belonged to what would later be called "the developing world," the power and prestige of the victors of World War II covered their voices at that time. But membership from developing countries grew steadily between 1945 and 1960. Sixteen new states were added to the UN rostrum in 1955, among them Jordan, Laos, Libya, Sri Lanka, and Nepal. All records were beaten in 1960, when 17 new states joined the ranks of the organization, 16 of which originated in Africa.[35] The evolution of UN debates on economic development faithfully mirrored these transformations.

In the 1950s, UN work in the economic and social arena focused on identifying and defining the scope of the "problem" of underdevelopment and initiating some discussion on how to tackle it. Technical assistance came into being in 1948, with an endowment of $350,000 to a UN Technical Assistance Program that would distribute aid at the request of governments irrespective of political considerations. The only developing countries having gained full independence by 1950, India and Pakistan were the initial focus of discussions on the best uses of technical assistance and budding development policies.

In 1950, President Truman proposed an ambitious program aimed at transferring large-scale technical assistance to all developing countries through such channels as the UN specialized agencies. Truman insisted on the linkage between social and economic development—a position that would be the hallmark of Western technical cooperation until the mid-1960s. The initial philosophy of technical cooperation focused on nurturing the human conditions of development through the transfer of experts, volunteers, and other personnel charged with developing the skills of the yet unformed workforce of the "South." It emphasized education, vocational training, public health, as well as the development of communication and transportation—all seen as prerequisites to future economic growth. This UN Expanded Program of Technical Assistance (EPTA) received voluntary pledges from governments. From $20 million in 1950, these contributions grew to $54 million in 1965. In 1958, signaling an early concern with creating the institutional conditions of development, ECOSOC initiated an experimental program named Operational Administrative and Executive Personnel, under which senior administrators and civil servants from developed nations were dispatched to strengthen the administrations of developing countries.

As newly independent nations accrued to the UN's membership, signs of an impending rift over the objectives and methods of development assistance began to surface. The initial bone of contention focused on the financing of development policies. In 1952, a proposal emerged for the creation of a Special UN Fund for Economic Development (SUNFED), which would provide grants and long-term, low-interest loans to finance infrastructure in the developing world. However, the developing countries' insistence on giving the General Assembly, where they held the majority of votes, control over the fund doomed SUNFED from the start. A compromise solution emerged in the form of a UN Special Fund created in 1959. The 18 members of its governing council, elected by ECOSOC, were distributed evenly between developed and developing nations, and the requirement of two-third majority votes guaranteed the developed nations' control over the Special Fund. Under the direction of the American Paul Hoffman, former chief administrator of the Marshall Plan, the Special Fund refined the techniques of EPTA and financed multiyear regional and national programs aimed at promoting investment and raising productivity in developing nations.

Kennedy's election in 1960 was undoubtedly accompanied by the expectation of a new understanding for the special circumstances of the developing world. "The emergence of a sizable number of independent states in Africa," Kennedy told Congress in 1960 "has introduced an additional element of urgency to the process of accelerating the economic development of the less developed countries."[36] He added that developing countries expected the United Nations to play an operational role, "particularly in connection with the financing of economic development," and to place a "new emphasis on international economic policy."[37] To demonstrate his goodwill, he proposed to declare the 1960s the "Decade of Development." The UN General Assembly applauded the idea, although it soon transpired that the majority of its members did not share Kennedy's views as to what such a "decade" should accomplish.

American policy continued to stress "human development," a term that made its first appearance at an Asian population conference convened in 1963. According to U.S. policymakers, the development decade meant to provide a "symbolic framework in which concerted efforts based on soundly conceived country plans would lead to the improvement of economic and social conditions around the world."[38] Family planning was now seen as a "new, distinct, and challenging frontier for public health workers."[39] The proponents of this view argued that no nation in human history had managed to increase its wealth without controlling the rate of growth of its population. In addition to straining food supplies, uncontrolled population growth also taxed a country's infrastructure beyond capacity. Very high birth rates also often coincided with high illiteracy rates, and education was seen as the hinge on which successful development policies would rotate.[40] In a similar vein, the United States supported the creation in 1963 of the UN Institute on Research and Training (UNITAR).

But a cursory reading of the UN General Assembly's resolution that launched the Development Decade in 1961 would have uncovered the philosophical gap that blew into the open in the mid-1960s. The resolution invited member countries to do the following: First, "enable the less developing countries . . . to sell more of their products at stable and remunerative prices in expanding markets;" second, "ensure to the developing countries an equitable share of earnings from the extraction and marketing of their natural resources by foreign capital;" third, "increase the flow of development resources, public and private, to developing countries on mutually acceptable terms;" and fourth, "stimulate the flow of private investment capital for the economic development of developing countries." This was a call for "hard development," as opposed to the "soft development" approach favored by the West. As it turned out, the final break would occur on the double pitfall of trade and direct capital transfers.

As seen above, trade policy had been the province of GATT since 1948. In 1961, the UN General Assembly suggested the creation of a Development Insurance Fund aimed at protecting the developing countries from the "adverse effects of instability in commodity trade" and the resulting setbacks in their economic development.[41] Approving of the general proposal, the developing countries wanted trade issues to be revisited at an international conference that would examine "all vital questions relating to international trade, primary commodity trade, and economic relations between developing and developed countries."[42] After almost three years of preparatory work, the UN Conference on Trade and Development (UNCTAD) convened in Geneva in 1964 with two thousand delegates present. Interestingly enough, the opening of UNCTAD coincided with the creation of the Group of 77 (G-77), a coalition of developing countries mostly identified with the so-called Non-Aligned Movement that proposed to adopt unified positions in favor of their common interests.[43]

UNCTAD would profoundly influence the development policy debate in the ensuing decade. But before turning to its impact, a word must be said about the role of the private sector during the early period of the UN's economic work. Firstly, one must keep in mind that the developing world did not represent a significant potential of earnings for private enterprise until the mid-1960s, at the earliest. Secondly, most commercial firms interested in the prospects of trade had their eyes set on a reconstructed Europe, and the benefits to be derived from years of delayed consumption in those countries. Participation in the Marshall Plan was therefore more enticing in the early 1950s than the far-off promises of African and Asian development. Finally, whatever private sector involvement existed in technical cooperation programs took place on a bilateral basis between donors and recipients. Once they had partially recovered, European countries established, usually within their foreign ministries, technical cooperation agencies to distribute aid and manage the development projects of their former colonies. Past colonial ties provided the structure within which private enterprise took root in the developing economies of the newly independent nations. French firms did business in Francophone Africa while British, Dutch, and Belgian companies had natural advantages in their former colonies.

Tracing their origin to the Monroe Doctrine—issued in 1823 and for some an American version of indirect colonialism—America's economic ties to the developing world were focused on Latin America and the Caribbean. Only in 1961 did the United States establish its own technical cooperation agency, USAID, as well as the Peace Corps—another Kennedy contribution to the cause of development. American and British firms were of course very active in the oil industry in the Middle East, which provides added evidence that private sector involvement in international economic development during the 1950s and 1960s took place at the bilateral level through the mediation of national governments. There was no direct participation of private enterprise in UN development policies, and the era that opened up with the creation of UNCTAD in 1964 would rule out such partnership for another two decades.

The Age of Revolutions, All over Again

Raul Prebisch, the man who became UNCTAD's first secretary-general in 1964, had elaborated his views on trade and development while heading the UN Economic Commission for Latin America and the Caribbean in the 1950s. A structuralist, Prebisch argued that the world was structured around a core of industrialized nations and a larger periphery of underdeveloped nations. The fundamental gap between North and South was reinforced by such structural factors as overpopulation, the predominance of agriculture in these nations' economies, weak political institutions, dependence on exports of raw materials, conservative social structures, and the long experience of marginalization.[44] According to structuralism, the terms of trade of developing countries constantly deteriorate because the latter spend an ever larger share of their national income importing expensive manufactured goods while their export earnings are constantly threatened by volatile commodity prices.

According to Prebisch, two solutions could alleviate the structural imbalance against the developing world. The first consisted of import-substitution strategies whereby developing countries closed their doors to foreign manufactured goods and made every effort to develop national substitutes. The second solution, which would become a priority of UNCTAD's agenda for almost two decades, was to institute commodity stabilization plans to protect the export earnings of developing countries. The ensuing North-South divide stemmed from the rejection of the compromise of the UN Charter implied in these schemes. Commodity price controls and other trade preferences, meant to protect the export earnings of the developing world, questioned the principles of multilateralism and reciprocity on which the UN's economic and social mandate had been based since 1945. The liberal economies could not go along with such revisionism, especially if they were expected to finance it.

The stir caused by the utterance of these ideas at the first UNCTAD conference is readily understood if one compares Prebisch's thinking to some of his predecessors' writings. Structuralist analysis has its roots in both Marxism and economic nationalism. Marx's theory of the class struggle was a domestic equivalent of the international structural struggle between poor and rich nations. Long before Prebisch, Lenin had argued that developed nations (in Lenin's era, the European colonial powers) needed to secure access to cheap raw materials and find markets on which to dump their manufactured goods. He called this imperial state "the last stage of capitalism."[45] Although Prebisch and his disciples did not openly claim Lenin's paternity, there are inescapable parallels between their approaches. Colonialism had been legally defeated by the mid-1960s, they argued, but the economic structure inherited from the colonial past had not been affected by nominal political independence. As for import-substitution, it was only the latest avatar of the nationalist economic policies advocated by the German School, among others, and attempted under Hitler's autarkic model. The common denominator of these analyses was their interpretation of trade as reinforcing structural inequalities rather than constituting the engine of growth, as seen by liberal economics.

The structuralist agenda initially struck some minimal victories. In addition to obtaining the establishment of UNCTAD as a UN agency—a victory in and of itself—import-substitution policies generated changes in the liberal trade regime. Import-substitution and its corollary, the protection of infant-industry, require the imposition of tariff barriers to discourage imports as well as quantitative controls, multiple exchange rates, and incentives to local consumption. In 1965, UNCTAD forced GATT to adopt a new section on trade and development, which provided for exceptions to free-trade rules for the less-developed countries.[46] In 1968, agreement was reached on establishing some forms of preferential schemes for the developing countries of varying duration. In addition, two new UN agencies, the UN Development Program (UNDP) and the UN Industrial Development Organization (UNIDO), came into being in 1965 and 1966, respectively.

UNDP was the result of the merger of the UN Special Fund and EPTA. But contrary to the latter, UNDP's governing body, although selected by ECOSOC, no longer maintained a balance between developed and developing countries. Although developed nations contributed 87 percent of UNDP's budget, the developing countries had the upper hand in UNDP's governing board, and UNDP's agenda reflected their influence.[47] Based on a consensus resolution adopted by the UN General Assembly in 1970, UNDP instituted five-year country programs, which gave developing nations greater control over UNDP expenditures. A decentralization reform inaugurated the system of the "resident representative," responsible for representing UNDP to local authorities and, much later, for coordinating UN economic programs on the ground. UNDP thus developed an operational structure all over the developing world, which its predecessors never enjoyed.[48] UNDP's first administrator, former head of the UN Special Fund Paul Hoffman, maintained the classical view that developing countries were responsible for breaking the bottlenecks of underdevelopment with the technical assistance of the developed world. Subsequent administrators showed greater sympathy for the structuralist analysis of the plight of the developing world.[49] Finally, created in 1966 despite American opposition, UNIDO was to develop policies and implement projects in the specific area of industrial development.[50] As a separate body with an independent governing board, it would report to the General Assembly, where it would enjoy the support of the developing countries.

On January 1, 1971, as it launched the Second Development Decade, the UN General Assembly issued a declaration that soon became embroiled in the promotion of a new economic doctrine still further removed from the compromise of the UN Charter than the UNCTAD agenda. Deriving confidence from the recent formation of the Organization of Oil Exporting Countries (OPEC) and the possibility of a commodity threat to be levied against the industrial world, the developing countries issued a declaration calling for a New International Economic Order (NIEO) at a special session of the General Assembly in May 1974.[51] Asserting that the developing world had become a "powerful factor," the declaration called for the "active, full and equal participation of the developing countries in the formulation and application of all decisions that concern the international community."[52]

Specifically, the program demanded a reduction in the tariff barriers of the developed countries on a nonreciprocal basis, improvements in the preference schemes already obtained from GATT, international commodity agreements, and various assistance programs to ease the cost of the developing countries' imports. UNCTAD in turn became a leading forum for the articulation of the NIEO. The most significant measure was the establishment within UNCTAD of an Integrated Program on Commodities, aimed at negotiating international commodity agreements between producers and consumers of raw materials. These agreements relied on a variety of schemes such as buffer-stocks, export quotas, and multilateral buying agreements, all aimed at guaranteeing or managing the prices of selected commodities.

Additional NIEO demands included the right of developing countries to form producer cartels, the right to nationalize transnational corporations and gain control over their natural resources, and the formulation of rules to regulate the operations of transnational corporations. In December 1974, the UN General Assembly adopted most of these principles under the Charter of Economic Rights and Duties of States.[53] As part of the agenda to control the behavior of transnational corporations in their countries of operations, the advocates of the NIEO managed to establish within the United Nations a Center on Transnational Corporations. Based on the premise of a necessary conflict between the interests of transnationals and those of host countries, the NIEO began negotiations on a Code of Conduct, which would regulate the operations of transnationals. At the initial stage of these negotiations, the demands of developing countries included the right to nationalize the assets of transnationals on their territories, and to decide whether and by how much to compensate shareholders for their losses.[54] But a new reality that soon received the name of "interdependence" was slowly rewriting the NIEO narrative.

Interdependence was already at the center of the only initiative that pointed the way to a future rapprochement between the UN and the private sector during the tumultuous decade of the 70s. Under the leadership of UN Secretary-General U Thant, a Consultative Committee was established in 1969 between the ICC, the UN, and GATT "to fill what is an urgent need on both sides—an established and permanent dialogue between business and intergovernmental organizations, with special reference to economic development."[55] Aimed at discussing such topics as "international production, development policies in the 1970s, transfer of technology, investment guarantees, . . . and the role and condition of foreign private investment in developing countries," the committee was expected to meet annually with the heads of UN economic and social agencies.[56] Members of the ICC attributed the committee's creation to a "reassessment within the United Nations of the role of private enterprise" and "a realization by the private sector that it has a vital role to play in the formulation and implementation of decisions of intergovernmental organizations on matters affecting business and economic affairs."[57] This was the spirit of 1945 back at work; yet a reenactment of that vision was premature. In time, attendance by the UN dwindled to the point of making the committee obsolete and irrelevant. Although the committee was never officially disbanded, business leaders gave up on the initiative for lack of UN interest.

Interdependence and the Return of Liberalism

While the mood reigning at the UN did not encourage private sector cooperation, business was forging ahead in more welcoming places—especially in Asia where the choice of export-led policies created conditions favorable to FDI. South Korea showed the way early on by devaluating its currency to encourage exports, replacing quotas with tariffs, and assisting those industries likely to produce exportable goods.[58] In the cases of Korea, Singapore, and Taiwan, strong government institutions enabled these countries to resist domestic protectionist pressures. By the mid-1970s, what became known as the newly-industrialized countries, or NICs, were enjoying growth rates far superior to those of countries that had maintained import-substitution policies.[59] During the first half of the 1970s, Korea enjoyed an average annual growth rate of 10.3 percent vs. 2.9 percent for the poorest developing countries.[60] Only the OPEC countries enjoyed similar growth levels during the 1970s by hiking up the price of oil.[61] The tactic, however, would prove short-lived, and the NIEO's reliance on the commodity threat would defeat its agenda by 1980–81.

The NICs received additional bonanza for their pro-trade policies and resistance to protectionism in the form of foreign direct investment (FDI) by transnational corporations. The flow of investments to the developing world grew from an annual average of $2.6 billion in the 1967–69 period to $10 billion in 1976–78 and $13 billion in 1979–81.[62] The NICs, however, were larger beneficiaries from this trend than the poorer LDCs, as multinationals favored propitious business environments with open trade policies, reliable and strong government institutions, and relatively good infrastructure. As a result of FDI, the NICs were able to create jobs; they also benefited from transfers of skills and technology that further fueled their export-led growth.

Increasing patterns of FDI produced what became known in the late 1970s as "interdependence," a phenomenon that may historically be seen as the precursor to globalization yet is fundamentally different, as is explained below. American political scientists Robert Keohane and Joseph Nye defined the new phenomenon and analyzed its implications for international politics in *Power and Interdependence*.[63] Interdependence, as they saw it, was characterized by several patterns of exchange among nations. For one, nations were connected through multiple channels, including but not limited to governmental ties. Economies were tied through transnational firms and increasingly interconnected financial and trade links. Citizens had direct, although informal, ties with nongovernmental organizations abroad. An international civil society was slowly developing. Moreover, the management of international economic relations was fast becoming a high priority of national foreign policies. The so-called "low politics" of trade and finance was replacing the "high politics" of security and arms control. Finally, domestic and international issues were becoming blurred as fewer areas of government action now escaped internationalization. In such a context, international institutions such as the IMF and GATT became the unavoidable forums for the management of an increasing array of international issues. In time, the United Nations would also have a role to play, but the policies of the 1970s would need to be defeated first and the economic principles of the Charter reaffirmed.

By the beginning of the 1980s, several developments had ruined the assumptions of the NIEO. Firstly, the international commodity agreements put in place to protect the commodity exports of developing nations foundered on the traditional pitfalls of quantity and price controls. Typically, producers and consumers cannot agree on such mechanisms, as the former have an interest in raising prices while the latter seek to lower them. This fundamental disagreement leads producers to cheat on price, quantity, or quality—or all of them at once. Control mechanisms are also expensive, as their management requires the skills of technical experts, not to mention the economic loss that is passed on to consumers in the form of higher prices. Secondly, import-substitution failed and left defects in the economic fabric of the developing countries, which the latter are still trying to mend. National markets were too small to transform goods produced locally into sources of wealth; by stifling competition, protectionism led to poor-quality products; and the need to import capital goods to manufacture domestic products inflated the debts of developing countries. Finally, the presumed alliance between OPEC and the LDCs, sealed at the creation of the G-77 in 1964, turned against the latter in two ways. Firstly, the OPEC nations never put their newly found wealth at the service of development.[64] Secondly, and more tragically, the second oil shock of 1979–81 nearly bankrupted a number of developing countries and plunged most of them into a debt crisis of catastrophic proportions. Between 1979 and 1981, the current account deficits of developing countries grew from $31.3 billion to $118.6 billion, while their interest payments went from $24.3 billion to $41.8 billion in the same period. In 1982, interest payments surpassed new lending by $3.5 billion.[65]

The NIEO was over, but its shadow lingers in two ways. Firstly, the loans approved by the IMF in the 1980s to bail the developing countries out of bankruptcy were tied to austerity programs that cut public expenditures to a trickle and had disastrous consequences on living standards. The dramatic increase in poverty that has ensued has set the developing world back by several decades and constitutes a plausible threat to global stability. Secondly, the ideology of the NIEO hurt the UN's credibility with the private sector so drastically that its legacy remains to this day an obstacle to enlisting business in UN activities.

Possibly because it followed two decades of neo-Marxist revival, the return of liberalism was not subdued. The elections of Margaret Thatcher and Ronald Reagan gave the reaffirmation of liberal values a missionary character that soon transpired at the United Nations. Appointed permanent representative to the United Nations by President Reagan in 1981, Ambassador Jeane Kirkpatrick set the tone by introducing a "diplomacy without apology."[66] Her policy had two initial objectives: it would combat antiliberal assumptions in the economic organs and debates of the United Nations; and it would seek to recover for the United States an influence commensurate with the level of American funding to the United Nations.

Points were struck on the first front in 1982–83 during the Law of the Sea Conference, a decade-long debate aimed at defining sovereignty over international waters and regulating the exploitation of deep-sea resources. The G-77 had called for the double establishment of an authority to regulate deep seabed exploitation and an enterprise charged with conducting mining operations, the profits of which would be shared internationally rather than accrue to mining corporations. Arguing that the UN Charter did not prescribe the redistribution of wealth from developed to developing nations, which he felt was implied in the G-77 scheme, President Reagan announced that the United States would not ratify the Law of the Sea Convention that was to emerge from the conference. In a move that signaled the beginning of a trend, he also refused to pay the American assessed contribution to the preparatory conference, since the latter's work contradicted the economic principles of the Charter.[67]

In public addresses at the UN and elsewhere, Ambassador Kirkpatrick reiterated the central tenets of liberalism: competition, free markets, innovation, and the incentives that only profit can create. She openly rejected the assumptions of the NIEO and faulted socialist and utopian policies for the "stagnation and decay" of the third world. To these policies she proposed to substitute such liberal ingredients as "innovation, investment, and entrepreneurship."[68] In 1984, the United States withdrew from the UN Educational, Scientific, and Cultural Organization (UNESCO) to protest Soviet-led efforts at regulating and controlling the free flow of information through governmental regulatory schemes. Nor was the United States alone in its decision. Singapore and the United Kingdom followed suit in 1985 and 1986, respectively.

By 1985, when Ambassador Vernon Walters replaced Kirkpatrick at the U.S. Mission, a more assertive United States adopted a new cause célèbre: reforming the United Nations. Interestingly, that agenda would lead to the first true UN-business partnerships in the 1990s. Development policy also began to bend under the new liberal wind. In 1986, the United States tabled a General Assembly resolution stressing the role of private property in "achieving economic and social development," and asked the secretary-general to undertake a study on the relationship between such fundamental human rights as the right to property and economic development. In the 1990s, such themes as the organization of free elections (what the UN calls governance programs), human development, measures favoring entrepreneurship in developing countries, and capacity-building became the new cornerstones of UN development policy.[69] Based on the premise that international organizations can only help create the conditions of economic and social progress rather than implement actual development policies, capacity-building in its variegated forms represented the triumph of the liberal viewpoint.[70] This approach received unquestioned acceptance once the Berlin Wall came tumbling down, giving the United Nations an entirely new mandate in assisting the transition of the former command economies of the Soviet Union and Eastern Europe to the free market.[71]

Another significant development in 1992 was the quiet burial of negotiations on the Code of Conduct on Transnational Corporations, an exercise that had begun under UNCTAD's auspices in 1974. Trying not to call undue attention to the failure of these discussions, the president of the 46th General Assembly reported that "delegations felt that the changed international economic environment and the importance attached to encouraging foreign investment required a fresh approach."[72] In fact, in the 1980s as negotiations had moved from the charged atmosphere of the NIEO, differences on the contents of the code had progressively been narrowed, to the point where a text acceptable to all parties was within reach.[73] The legacy of these discussions, however, and the suspicion they inspired because of their historical linkage to the NIEO, made it preferable to give up the entire enterprise. In the 1990s, the Center on Transnational Corporations gave up its hostile tune toward multinationals and began to praise their positive impact on job creation, technology transfers, and the facilitation of access to global markets by developing countries. In 1992, that body was transferred to UNCTAD's Division on Investment and Technology and UNCTAD's annual World Investment Report began to reflect the new thinking.

Major historical eras rarely begin with the first year of a century. If the twentieth century started in 1914, historians are likely to agree that the twenty-first started in 1991 when the Cold War completed its phased ending. Of course, the events that unfolded between President Gorbachev's watershed publication of *Perestroika* in 1987 and the final collapse of the Soviet system already transformed the picture of world politics.[74] In 1989, the UN fielded its first post–Cold War mission, the UN Transition Assistance Group (UNTAG), to guide Namibia from trusteeship to independence. In 1991, with the organization and monitoring of free national elections in Haiti, the United Nations went further, assisting for the first time the democratic transition of a sovereign nation. With the threat of a Soviet veto now removed, the UN Security Council was free to mandate increasingly large and complex peacekeeping operations. By demolishing the bipolar structure of post–World War II politics, 1991 formerly ushered in the new century. The new era became known as the age of globalization, a phrase that attempts to describe a single world no longer engaged in inter-national but rather in global relations. The nuance is substantial. The inter-national system that had prevailed since 1648 was managed by the diplomats of the world's most influential nation-states. In the world politics of the global era, states have lost their monopoly over policymaking. They now share it with civil society organizations, multilateral organizations, and corporations. And in the global economy, which at this stage constitutes most of the reality of globalization, corporations have become the unavoidable protagonists of global policymaking.

A Global World?

Before describing in detail the formidable changes that affected the UN system in the 1990s, it is essential to describe the fundamental differences that separate globalization from interdependence.[75] Interdependence is a phenomenon that took place within the context of national sovereignty and was therefore macroeconomic. In the 1970s, when firms traded and banks invested internationally, they did so within the regulatory frameworks of the host nations. Foreign Direct Investment (FDI) was motivated by low wages in the developing world as a stark contrast prevailed between conditions of production in those countries and those of industrialized nations. International exchanges left room for macroeconomic management between national governments. The G7 provided the forum for discussing and solving the debt crisis in the 1980s. Its leaders gathered to adjust exchange rates in the context of European monetary integration and slackening Japanese growth. National governments felt an obligation and some sense of kinship toward their corporate flagships: the U.S. government could not allow

Chrysler to sink into bankruptcy. Interdependence, while increasing the range and complexity of international economic relations, did not question the structure of political relations and the centrality of the state as regulator of last resort. Globalization attacks each of these assumptions.

Contrary to interdependence, globalization is a microeconomic phenomenon.[76] While international trade of the type that prevailed under interdependence remains a key component of exchanges across borders, intrafirm trade and investment is the new phenomenon of the global era. Because intrafirm transactions take place between the divisions of a single corporation wherever they are located, they are not aggregated under "international trade." Moreover, intrafirm trade is not based on differentials in labor costs. The costs of labor and other production factors have converged, as have consumption patterns. Firms now base relocation decisions on the competitiveness and excellence of R&D in a given area, a country's communication infrastructure, and the level of education of the local workforce. Under globalization, going for cheap does not pay. Additionally, all corporate functions are integrated into a global strategy. While the corporation of the 1970s had one division at headquarters mandated to strategize and manage the firm's international activities, the entire firm is now engaged in the global marketplace. Human resources, communication, production, marketing, and finance all elaborate their strategies at the global level—a change accompanied and made possible by the concurrent global integration of the financial markets, media, and communications.

Because it is a microeconomic phenomenon, globalization questions the efficacy of the macroeconomic regulatory tools of nation-states. To begin with, it is now difficult to compute the statistics of international trade. Intrafirm transactions of the types that take place between IBM Australia and IBM Brazil do not properly occur across borders. They involve two branches of IBM, but concern neither Australia, nor Brazil, nor the United States. The amount of these transactions eschews both computation and taxation. For all the increased economic activity it entails, globalization paradoxically affects both trade statistics and government coffers negatively. The share of trade in America's GNP was in 1990 only 1 percent higher than in 1913: 7 percent vs. 6.1 percent, respectively.[77] Similarly, "the net outflow of capital from Great Britain in the four decades before 1914 averaged 5 percent of gross domestic product, compared with 2 to 3 percent for Japan over the last decade."[78] Governments have therefore lost the capacity to regulate the activities of what was known in the 1970s as transnationals. The reason is simple: today's largest corporations are precisely no longer trans-nationals (the prefix "trans" meaning "across"). They may rather be called meta-nationals ("meta" meaning "above" as in metaphysics). In a global system where the nation-state no longer has a monopoly on the realm of politics, metanationals exist not across but above borders. They do not operate against the sovereign state, nor do they seek to deligitimize it. Rather they function in a space of their own, separate and above that of the nation-state—a metaspace. To the inter-national economic policy of the 1970s must be added a metanational policy that, while not questioning sovereignty, can palliate the impotence of the nation-state as it confronts the conundrums of the global economy. If the G-7 was the deus ex machina of international economics in the 1980s, the multilateral system can potentially become the mediator of the global crises of the new century and the guardian against a backlash toward globalization.

Globalization did not become a household name, however, until the late 1990s. Following the end of the Cold War, the UN faced in Eastern Europe and the former Soviet Union a new challenge and a new test to its relevance. The transition of these countries to market economies imposed a change in UN development policies that was reflected in both texts and programs. In addition to opening up offices throughout the region, UNDP created in 1990 a Division for Private Sector Development. The new policy focus was on investment promotion, governance, anticorruption programs, administrative reform, and the provision of advisory services, as opposed to the physical implementation of UN operational activities. The reason for the latter shift was that the scale and complexity of development problems had changed radically. While it was not overly costly or technologically ambitious to implement small rural development activities in African villages in the 1970s, the challenge of economic transition in such countries as Russia or Czechoslovakia was too large and complex for any UN agency to meet operationally. This realization of the UN's limitations played a significant role in pushing for a rapprochement between the UN and business. The UN was coming to accept that economic activity was better left to private sector firms, and that it could at best stir that activity in directions that would benefit the social and political development of nations as well as their economic growth. Liberalization and transition to markets therefore called for closer ties with the private sector, not only because the UN's newly adopted liberalism was now compatible with the values of business, but also because the private sector was finally recognized as the best vehicle of economic development.

This realization was at the center of international conferences organized by the UN in the 1990s, in which corporations were for the first time invited to participate. The first such conference convened in Rio de Janeiro (Brazil) in 1992 under the name of UN Conference for the Environment and Development (better known as the Rio Conference). Leading to the adoption of the famous Agenda 21 for climate change, it was attended by a record number of nongovernmental organizations and businesses. The former had been particularly active in defining the agenda of the conference and pushing for an ambitious platform of environmental controls and targets, and it is in part in reaction to their militancy that business groups organized and coalesced around Rio and Agenda 21. The brain-child of Swiss entrepreneur Stephan Schmiddheiny, the World Business Council on Sustainable Development (WBCSD) was formed in the run-up to the conference and quickly subscribed to the goals of environmentally sustainable growth.[79] Its 120 member firms, all international leaders in the fields of industrial ecology and energy technology, stand to gain from environmental awareness and standards and carry out studies and projects with various UN agencies.

Another megaconference that received wide publicity and nourished large expectations gathered in Istanbul (Turkey) in 1996 under the name of Habitat II. Convened by a UN agency devoted to human settlement and housing issues, it also called upon the private sector to attend and participate actively. Indeed, the conference was paired with an exhibition by nongovernmental organizations and corporations involved in the areas of construction, housing, and human settlement. However, like the Rio Conference before it, Habitat II disappointed those nonstate actors that had hoped to wield real influence on debates and define joint operational partnerships. Held in 1997 to review progress since the initial conference, the so-called Rio+5 meeting revealed the limitations of the UN machinery to construct a new framework and institutional setting for the participation of nonstate actors in UN debates. Corporations in particular continue to point to the lack of concreteness and operational viability of so-called partnerships, while nongovernmental organizations feel politically excluded.

Major Strides on the Terrain of UN Reform

Closer to UN Headquarters, however, the agenda of UN reform was offering new opportunities for successful UN-business partnerships. UN reform was not a new priority in the 1990s, but a number of developments added urgency to the theme. As a result of economic pressure and ideological changes, governments began reassessing the funding of a number of UN programs and agencies. While no other nation accumulated the debt that the United States now owes the UN, the reduction of official development assistance (ODA) gained new adepts in the 1990s, affecting the UN Development Program particularly strongly. The end of the Cold War was accompanied by a rising concern for economic efficiency that did not spare international organizations. The UN responded to this change of good fortune by cutting staff and budgets and slowly developing an approach to common services aimed at achieving savings through economies of scale. But these initially Malthusian methods soon proved insufficient and called for a more conceptual approach to reform for which the private sector provided some guidance.

The dramatic increase in the number and scale of peacekeeping operations in the early 1990s led to the first instance of private sector involvement in UN reform. As the UN Security Council voted ever larger and more complex mandates for UN peacekeeping operations in such places as Cambodia, Somalia, and later Bosnia, the UN Department of Peacekeeping Operations (DPKO) found itself unarmed to fulfill the logistics and communication requirements of these new missions. A term not even mentioned in the UN Charter, peacekeeping had evolved in a totally ad hoc manner since 1951, when the UN fielded its first enforcement operation in North Korea. That mission, however, had been led, financed, and mostly fought by the United States, as was its later equivalent, Desert Storm, in 1992. From Israel in 1948 to the Sinai in 1956 and Cyprus in 1964, UN peacekeepers had intervened to maintain the peace between signatories to a treaty in rarely violent or hostile environments. With Cambodia, Somalia, and Bosnia, the UN entered a "gray area"[80] of peacekeeping where member states expected it to separate parties to a civil war, feed the hungry, remove landmines, and monitor elections without necessarily giving the organization the military means and the command and control arrangements to succeed.[81]

Under the leadership of then Under-Secretary-General Kofi Annan, DPKO turned to the knowledge and practices of business to borrow what the UN could not develop internally. Already business had responded by supplying an increasing volume of goods and services through the UN's procurement system. While procurement for peacekeeping needs had barely reached a few hundred million in the 1980s, it approached $1.5 billion in 1993 and 1994 and surpassed $1 billion in 1995.[82] In the process of supplying the United Nations, business representatives began to understand what the UN did, where, and under what constraints. Suddenly, the sea of UN acronyms became familiar to export managers who now traveled to such places as Bailundo (Angola) or Mostar (Bosnia). These corporate executives also developed an appreciation for the courage and dedication of UN personnel operating in danger zones with no infrastructure and insecure budgets. The links forged through these commercial exchanges began to bridge the gap that had separated the UN from the business world for the better part of four decades.[83]

But DPKO pushed partnership beyond the contractual relationship of procurement. In 1992, an American consulting firm that had monitored the growing deployments of UN peacekeeping operations decided to contact DPKO, thinking that "the UN might need help to deal with changing mission requirements."[84] Under the leadership of Denis Beissel, then Director of the Field Operations Division (FOD, later renamed Field Administration and Logistics Division, FALD), the peacekeeping department acknowledged that it had neither the time nor the funds to develop internal solutions to its new problems. It then decided to hire the firm to transform the way DPKO approached mission planning and deployment. The method used for this partnership supplemented the transfer of technology and processes with the introduction of new working methods, whereby corporate and military personnel sat across the table of UN staff members for weeks in a row, watched them carry out their daily functions, and shared advice and ideas on how to improve working methods. According to Denis Beissel, "the interactions were informal and suggestions were made in a spirit of partnership aimed at transferring practices that had worked elsewhere and might work at the UN as well."[85] From the corporation's viewpoint, its involvement meant that the UN "did not have to reinvent the wheel but gained time in acquiring new technologies."[86] Among the tools the UN acquired through this transfer of know-how were mission templates outlining the basic requirements and operational assumptions of various missions; a standard Survey Mission Handbook, Mission Planning Manual, and Operational Support Manual; and a Standard Cost Manual providing specifications and costs for standard equipment and supplies used in peacekeeping operations. The firm also designed the communication system and procedures of the Situation Center, the first UN round-the-clock, global multimedia facility. But it is in the exchange of values, ideas, and working methods that this experiment qualifies as a true UN-business partnership.

During the same period, other initiatives also facilitated a direct dialogue between UN officials serving in peacekeeping operations and corporate leaders. Premised on the belief that the UN and business could be each other's best teachers, from 1992–96, the United Nations Association of the USA, an American nonprofit organization that researches and supports the UN, brought delegations of corporate leaders on visits to UN peacekeeping operations. As in the DPKO experiment described above, a rationale of exchange of values and ideas constituted the basis for these visits. Business leaders thought that budgetary pressure and increasingly complex mandates were forcing the UN to analyze its activities in terms of allocation of resources, cost and time efficiency, and value for money. They also realized that corporations had to become more sensitive to, and better aware of, international diversity and the complexity of some of the problems unleashed by globalization as they operated in an increasingly interdependent and multicultural business environment. The context of peacekeeping operations provided a forum for an exchange of views between business leaders and UN officials on the conditions of successful peace processes. In these exchanges, CEOs typically stressed the limited nature of governmental goodwill and resources, which they argued submitted the UN's political work to economic constraints. These constraints, in turn, could only be faced through such efficiency measures as improvements in procurement procedures and logistics, the submittal of operational mandates to a cost-benefit analysis, and the inclusion of economic rehabilitation programs in the early phase of peacekeeping mandates.[87] The infusion of such principles in the traditionally political sphere of diplomacy and military affairs was new to UN diplomats, to say the least, but it constituted a worthwhile exchange between two approaches to problem-solving that must necessarily move closer together if the UN is to succeed in its partnership with the private sector.

The creation of the UN Office for Project Services (UNOPS) as a separate UN body in 1995 was another UN reform that sought to adapt a business rationale to the UN system. The predecessor to UNOPS, OPS, had existed as a department of UNDP since 1973. In 1994, the governments that made up the UNDP Governing Council (now the UNDP Executive Board) decided that new operational demands arising from the complexity of UN activities since the end of the Cold War required the establishment of a separate entity solely devoted to project management and execution. As obvious as the decision may seem to a business executive, this development was significant within the UN context, as it was the first time that governments subscribed to an economic rationale of comparative advantage to justify the creation of a new UN organization.

A concern had arisen as to the potential conflict of interest that existed between UNDP's mandate to coordinate and rationalize UN activities in the area of development and its execution role as embodied by OPS. The former mandate implied the integration of UN development activities and the reduction of redundancies. The second mandate gave UNDP an interest in acquiring as many projects as possible in order to increase its income. The incompatibility of these roles led to the recommendation in 1993 to withdraw OPS from UNDP and fold the implementation of development activities into a single department under OPS's authority.[88] The new organization would remain guided by "the self-financing principle—the principle of an organization that expands or shrinks with its business."[89] Its personnel policies would be flexible enough to enable UNOPS to adjust to varying business levels—a very non-UN like recommendation.[90]

The principle of UNOPS's creation was accepted by the UNDP Executive Board in June 1994.[91] Endorsing the recommendation of ECOSOC, the UN General Assembly gave its imprimatur in September 1994.[92] UNOPS was to be "a demand-driven, client-oriented entity" providing project management services, project supervision, and loan administration, and other management services to UN and multilateral organizations.[93] Another document expounded on UNOPS's role as a provider of "high-quality, timely, and cost-effective development services" deriving its functions from "the constantly changing demands of its clients."[94] These statements constituted the first expression of a management culture at the UN and the first recognition of a linkage between economic efficiency and the UN's political mandates.

The creation and current operations of UNOPS therefore illustrate the UN's effort to put private sector methods at the service of the UN Charter. The growth and future status of UNOPS within the UN system will provide a key test of the UN's commitment to a rapprochement between the UN and the private sector in the name of UN reform, efficiency, and cost savings. At this stage, UNOPS embodies private sector values on the basis of three criteria. Firstly, as the only self-financing entity in the UN system, it receives no funding from governments and earns its budget from services rendered. Secondly, as the only UN body without a substantive mandate, its comparative advantage lies in management and technical expertise. In a system that has traditionally lacked a corporate culture, UNOPS strives (not without difficulty) to develop services in all areas of UN work based exclusively on the management of financial, legal, procurement, human resources, and other corporate functions. Finally, the creation of UNOPS promoted competitiveness in two ways. On the one hand, it eliminated execution monopolies within the UN system. On the other, because UN agencies are not required to choose UNOPS to execute their projects, UNOPS has no captive market and competes with the internal execution capacities of other UN bodies. Moreover, UNOPS does not enjoy the advantages of national technical cooperation agencies shielded from competitive pressure by exclusive working arrangements with their governments. While UNOPS faces the competitive pressures of a private corporation, it is constrained by two significant limitations. It is not listed publicly, has no access to capital, and is indeed legally precluded from raising its own project funds. As a public entity, it is also prohibited from deriving a profit from its activities other than a small overhead placed in reserve.

If the UN is to adhere to the conceptual framework of values and principles that has thus far defined and guided its approach to the private sector, it seems unavoidable and indeed desirable that the exchange of values should go both ways. While the symmetry of that exchange remains highly contentious in many circles, some UN experiments have already proved that it can be successful and work to the benefit of the UN's mandates in the respect of its Charter. The theme will be expanded at length in subsequent chapters.

1997: A Turning Point

Setting the Tone

The appointment of Kofi Annan as UN secretary-general in December 1996 was unarguably a turning point in the UN's approach to the private sector.[95] Educated in the United States where he obtained an MBA, and rich with the experience of several UN senior management positions, Kofi Annan brought with him an understanding of, and an appreciation for, the private sector that none of his predecessors had ever displayed. His business education constitutes, in and of itself, a radical departure from the traditional government and diplomatic background of every UN secretary-general before him. Rather than relying on bureaucratic responses to address the UN's various challenges, Kofi Annan soon sent the signal that his approach to problem-solving would rest on finding expertise where it lies and engaging the actors that are shaping today's world. Corporations would, of course, be chief among them.

The secretary-general wasted no time in outlining his vision and exposing his new thinking. On February 1, 1997, four weeks to the day after assuming office, he addressed the world's top business leaders at the World Economic Forum in Davos, Switzerland, and made the stunning statement that there now was a "new universal understanding that market forces are essential for sustainable development."[96] As obvious as the phrase may have sounded to an average American citizen, no UN secretary-general had ever dared to speak about capitalism as a "universal" value. He added that "the role of the state [was] changing" and that countries all over the world were "making room for the dynamism of the private sector."[97] The message was clear. Governments could only provide the institutional setting to allow business to thrive; economic growth was the business of the private sector. Adding that market capitalism faced "no major ideological rival," he outlined a classical liberal rationale drawing from Kant as well as Smith and Schumpeter, according to which poverty constitutes a threat to political stability and justice is the guarantor of prosperity and peace.[98]

The theme was reiterated at another World Economic Forum in January 1998, where Kofi Annan argued that the creation of wealth by the private sector and the promotion of "human security" by the United Nations were "mutually reinforcing goals."[99] "Thriving markets and human security go hand in hand," he stressed "without one we will not have the other."[100] He argued that the UN's universal values and global perspective supported the efforts of business by providing legitimacy and regulatory frameworks without which economic activities cannot be secured. But this address was even more significant for outlining the constructivist framework of values and principles that has since shaped the UN's outreach to the private sector. Values, Kofi Annan argued, are "a pillar of the global economy. Markets are also a reflection of values. Markets do not function in a vacuum. Rather, they arise from a framework of rules and laws, and they respond to signals set by governments and other institutions."[101] Among the values and rules that support markets, he cited the rule of law, property rights and contracts, transparency, and "a fair degree of equity."[102] Again, these values provided the foundation of political liberalism well before they were translated into liberal economics, but the purpose of the speech was to remind business leaders that agreement on values, and the rules and regulations that emerge from them, form the basis of thriving markets.[103] This conceptual outlook received a fuller exposition in his proposal for a "Global Compact of shared values and principles" made at Davos in January 1999 (see chapter 2).[104] The 1998 address also acknowledged the rising concern for corporate social responsibility. In line with a constructivist framework, corporate responsibility illustrates the effort by the private sector to promote and help embed in the global economy the very values that establish and strengthen economic activity.

Getting Started

Back at UN Headquarters, the new secretary-general was ready to apply his new thinking and the imperative of change to ongoing UN reform. In July 1997, less than seven months after his appointment, Kofi Annan unveiled a long-awaited reform proposal that was the result of a team headed by Maurice Strong, a Canadian national, former CEO of several large corporations, who had headed the preparations of the Rio Conference a few years earlier.[105] While the report did not devote a specific section to the UN-business relationship, it emphasized the role of civil society as not only a disseminator of information or provider of services but also as a shaper of policy.[106] Civil society referred to nongovernmental organizations, academic and research institutions, parliamentarians, and corporations. Indeed the report stated openly that the relationship of the UN system with the business community was "of particular importance." It added that "it would be timely to develop better means of consultation between the United Nations and the business community."[107] The secretary-general also announced that he would avail himself of the mechanisms proposed by the International Chamber of Commerce and the World Economic Forum (the organizer of the annual Davos conference) to facilitate such consultations.

The need for a forum to facilitate consultations between the UN and the business community led to the recommendation to create a United Nations Enterprise Liaison Office, modeled after the existing Non-Governmental Liaison Office.[108] The proposal soon encountered the opposition of member states, however, as they perceived the institutionalization of relations between nonstate actors and the United Nations as a direct challenge to their sovereignty and monopoly on policymaking. At the same time as they are willing to discuss the involvement of nonstate actors in UN debates, most member states seem unable to reconcile the conflict between reforming UN policymaking and preserving state sovereignty. As civil society and the private sector are more developed in the North than in the South, developing nations also perceive the attempt to raise the participation of NGOs and corporations in UN debates as a strategy by the industrialized world to increase its influence by other means. In 1997, discussions with governments regarding the creation of the Enterprise Liaison Office therefore hit a stalemate that UN reassurances could not break. Defenders of the reform proposal stressed that the creation of that office within the UN Secretariat did not require intergovernmental consensus, a reality that was more likely to raise fears than allay them.

The UN bureaucracy did not welcome the proposal with much more enthusiasm. UN agency heads saw the proposed office as a threat to the decentralized approach to corporations that had prevailed thus far. Agencies and professionals that have succeeded at establishing ties with large corporations are unwilling to share either contacts or experience, as the ability to strike partnerships is a specialized knowledge jealously guarded by a few specialists. Facing opposition on two fronts, the UN Secretariat found a solution through communication technology: the creation of a "virtual liaison service" in the form of a website on UN-business issues to which all UN agencies could provide content on a decentralized basis. The idea itself relied on another recommendation of Kofi Annan's July 1997 reform proposal, namely "to create an electronic United Nations."[109] Launched in early 1999, the website is the most comprehensive source of information available on the types and modalities of partnerships between UN agencies and the private sector.[110]

The recommendation to include the features of UN conferences in the debates of the General Assembly was turned down for reasons similar to those analyzed above.[111] UN conferences in the 1990s had called for the increased participation of the private sector. The extension of the "features" of these conferences to the political debates of the General Assembly would therefore have implied an indirect role for corporations in that forum. Predictably, member states are unwilling to share their prerogatives in that political body. Recent discussions point to some evolution in governmental thinking, as member states realize they will be unable to affect development issues without engaging the primary agents of economic change, namely global corporations. As of this writing, however, the involvement of the private sector in policy discussions is limited to specific issue areas in ad-hoc forums. The participation of Wall Street bankers in hearings held in October 1998 by the General Assembly's Second Committee on the impact of the Asian financial crisis provides an example of such fleeting involvement.

In the area of fund-raising, the reform proposal recommended the creation of an Office for Development Financing to partially remedy the steep decrease in ODA financing of development activities through corporate fund-raising and access to private capital markets.[112] This idea also elicited suspicion from various quarters. The UN did not want governments to believe that a structural and permanent reduction of their financial commitments to the organization would now be taken for granted. UN development bodies also doubted whether the anticipated conditionality of corporate grants would be compatible with the UN's long-term development objectives, as well as the political sensitivity of most UN activities. In the end, the Office for Development Financing did see the light of day, but its mandate was transformed into elaborating policies and generating ideas as to how corporations could support UN development activities rather than actually tapping them for money.

With hindsight, it is difficult to understand why UN officials expected the private sector to bail out UN activities that member states were no longer willing to support. But the $1 billion gift to the UN made by Time Warner Vice-Chairman Ted Turner in the fall of 1997 led to high expectations of corporate philanthropy to benefit UN causes.[113] It soon became evident, however, that a gift of that magnitude was unlikely to be replicated, and that UN fund-raising would have to rest on specific issues and professional skills available in only a few UN agencies.[114] In any case, the private sector signaled early on that the purpose of its rapprochement with the UN was not to be taken for a fund-raising ride.

Reviving the Dialogue

Beyond his appearance at Davos three years in a row, the UN secretary-general has engaged in a continuous dialogue with business leaders facilitated by business associations, nonprofit organizations, and chambers of commerce in the United States and Europe. The initial objective of these encounters was to overcome the suspicions inherited from the 1960s and 1970s and revive the spirit of collaboration that had prevailed at the UN's creation in 1945.

Meetings held since 1997 have been too numerous to be listed exhaustively here. This section seeks essentially to analyze the content of this ongoing dialogue and to highlight the new dynamic that has evolved out of it. In Europe, two organizations have played a key role in facilitating and hosting meetings between the secretary-general and business leaders. Headed by Maria Cattaui, the Paris-based International Chamber of Commerce (ICC) remains the UN's leading policy counterpart on the issue of UN-business relations. As will be recalled, the ICC was the first and only business association to be accredited to the UN in 1946. Rich of a worldwide network of chambers of commerce, the ICC is able to bring to the UN table the CEOs of all leading global corporations. After reading the 1997 UN reform proposal, the ICC wrote to Secretary-General Kofi Annan to offer help in implementing those aspects of his plan that related to the role of the private sector in future UN activities.[115] In the fall of 1997, a first meeting took place in New York between Kofi Annan and Maria Cattaui, which paved the way for a larger gathering between an ICC delegation and the secretary-general's senior staff in February 1998. The objective of the first 1998 encounter was to "lay the basis for closer consultation between the UN and business and to strengthen cooperation in specific areas of mutual interest."[116]

The meeting established the cornerstone of the policy of rapprochement subscribed to by both the UN and business. This policy recognizes that "political stability is essential for business to grow in today's interconnected world, while prospering markets are a precondition for spreading more widely the benefits of globalization and for integrating developing countries into the world economy."[117] A joint statement issued by the ICC and the UN on February 9, 1998 stated openly the "potential for the goals of the United Nations . . . and the goals of business . . . to be mutually supportive."[118] A second meeting held in Geneva in September 1998 was not attended by the UN secretary-general, but included the heads of several UN agencies such as UNCTAD and the UN High Commissioner for Refugees (UNHCR), as well as the World Trade Organization (WTO). The Geneva Business Declaration issued at the end of the conference affirmed open support for the supportive role of multilateral organizations in the context of globalization and foreign investment. It went one step further in accepting the necessity of a global framework of rules no longer as "concessions to foreign investors," but as "a win-win proposition" in the pursuit of the business interest to sustain globalization.[119] The declaration also called for continuing dialogue with international organizations stating: "we need effective global decision-making and institutions. . . . Global governance and the adequacy of international organizations is a priority consideration."[120]

Meeting again in July 1999 in Geneva, the ICC and the secretary-general issued a statement that reiterated the themes of mutual interests and mutual benefits from cooperation. The ICC also welcomed the secretary-general's Global Compact announced at Davos in January 1999 and offered its readiness to cooperate in implementing it. Both parties repeated the need to embed global markets in global rules, recognized the "capability of companies to create wealth," and called for increased collaboration between governments, civil society, and business in the aftermath of the emerging market crisis.[121] Moreover, the statement represented full adherence by the United Nations to trade liberalization, as it stressed the importance of the Third Ministerial Conference of the World Trade Organization (Seattle,

November 1999) in launching a new trade round to "reinforc[e] the economic momentum generated by liberalization and [build] a stronger rule-based multilateral trading system."[122] The latter was significant in demonstrating how far the UN had progressed in refashioning its approach to the private sector since the creation of UNCTAD in 1964. While the outcome of the UN's meetings with the ICC may seem to bear little impact on operational activities between the UN and business, their contribution to altering the dynamic between these long estranged partners cannot be underestimated.

Another nonprofit organization supported by international corporations is the London-based Prince of Wales Business Leaders Forum (PWBLF). The PWBLF held its first meeting with the secretary-general in October 1997 in New York to review "areas of common concern" and discuss possible partnerships.[123] The discussion focused on the unevenness of foreign investment, the need to support good governance, and the urgency of job and enterprise creation in the next generation of emerging markets. The discussion with members of The Prince of Wales Business Leaders Forum has in many ways been more operational than consultations between the ICC and the UN. However, UN collaboration with the PWBLF fits within the policy context codefined with the ICC and indeed seeks to translate these concepts into UN projects and partnerships. The October 1997 meeting also signaled the beginning of a discussion between the PWBLF and the UN Staff College on the design of a course aimed at training UN staff members for future work with private sector firms. Subsequent meetings in 1998 focused on misperceptions between UN staff members and corporate representatives, potential areas of collaboration, and the publication of case studies on successful partnerships.[124]

In the United States, meetings between the UN secretary-general and the business community have received less publicity. In April 1997, the secretary-general met with a group of business leaders, members of the Business Council for the United Nations (BCUN), a New York, nonprofit organization that has lent corporate support to the United Nations since its creation in 1958.[125] Another New York association, the Business Council for International Understanding (BCIU), organized a briefing with the secretary-general and numerous business leaders in July 1998. Neither organization has held another meeting since then, but both remain active supporters of the UN's outreach to the business community. Because he is based in New York, the secretary-general enjoys more direct and informal access to American business leaders whom he meets at dinners, receptions, and other events not specifically targeted to the issue of UN-business collaboration.

In June 1999, the secretary-general went to Washington to deliver his first address to the U.S. Chamber of Commerce which, with 3 million member corporations, is the largest trade association in the world. To help dispel the myth of an inherent incompatibility between the UN and business, Kofi Annan addressed the audience in a direct, matter-of-fact manner. He stated squarely that "the United Nations needs the world's businessmen and businesswomen: as promoters of trade and investment; as employers and entrepreneurs; as experts on globalization; in short as full partners in our global mission of peace and development."[126] Kofi Annan also called for corporate support of full payment of U.S. dues to the United Nations, a common theme of his addresses to American corporate audiences. In touching upon that theme, he has repeatedly appealed to the corporate sense of fair play and respect of one's word, without which business contracts could not be trusted.

The new wind of public-private partnership has also blown on UNCTAD, transforming this "child of the 1960s" into a think tank on globalization, trade, and investment.[127] The appointment in 1995 of Rubens Ricupero as UNCTAD's new secretary-general was in itself an expression of a new outreach to international business and finance. A former minister of finance of Brazil, Ricupero earned the respect of international bankers in 1994 after he stabilized Brazil's economy and launched a new currency, the *real*, to staunch Brazil's run-away inflation. His recent speeches have emphasized rule-making and good governance as the institutional requirements of development in the context of globalization.[128] In November 1998, UNCTAD convened a week-long conference in Lyon (France) to address the role of corporations in helping UNCTAD define a relevant agenda of development partnerships suited to the specific conditions of global markets and communications. Named Partners for Development, the event was attended by hundreds of business, government, and civil society leaders and offered day-long workshops on UN-private partnerships in such areas as microfinance, African development, electronic commerce, commodity financing, and biotechnology. The follow-up to this event is suffering from a UN-wide lack of operational guidelines applicable to UN-business partnerships—a topic fully developed in chapter 3. In a January 1999 report, Rubens Ricupero noted that successful implementation of the ideas reviewed in Lyon would require changes in UNCTAD's administrative rules, clear guidelines for the selection of corporate and civil society partners, and a clarification of legal issues pertaining to UNCTAD-business contracts.[129]

But the lack of operationalization at this stage should not overshadow the psychological impact of encounters between UN officials and business leaders and the role they have played in altering the negative chemistry inherited from the time when the UN and business worked at cross-purposes. It has taken three years of intense consultations with corporate leaders to establish a dialogue based on mutual trust and interest. The stage is now set for more concrete projects between the UN and business, although that road is also strewn with obstacles.

• • •

This historical review began in the fifteenth century, and some will undoubtedly see the Renaissance as a strange starting point for a history of UN relations with the private sector. The dangers of historical parallels come to mind in current attempts to read contemporary Russian events in the light of the Russian or Soviet past.[130] Yet the "longue durée" is a source of inspiration for the future and comfort in the present.[131] If the Italian Renaissance provides some guidance in the current context, it is in supplying a model of eminently successful partnership between private and public actors, as well as the image of an era that thrived on the multiplicity and diversity of power. As citizens around the world fear the unitary reductionism of some aspects of globalization, the Renaissance offers the paradigm—possibly mythical— of bustling diversity concurrent with international integration.

At the beginning of the new millennium, no other institution better embodies global diversity than the United Nations. A universal organization based on the principle of equality between states, it provides the ideal setting for integrating all participants in the pursuit of openness without raising Orwellian fears of identity loss. Among these participants, the private sector is an unavoidable, and indeed a most desirable partner. After all, globalization is a creation of business, not an invention of states. It has taken the UN the better part of 50 years to return to the spirit of public-private partnership that animated its founders in 1945, and the current rapprochement with the business community may not have happened had Kofi Annan not been selected as secretary-general in 1997. His charisma and understanding of business and economics have persuaded international business leaders to resume an alliance with the United Nations. In their encounters with corporate representatives, UN staff members have found at times suspicious, at times eager counterparts. Corporations are now counting on the UN to deliver real possibilities of partnership. The challenge of operationalization cannot be understood, however, without a closer look at what each side is hoping to get out of the relationship.

CHAPTER 2

Creating the Future

The political conditions of the twenty-first century provide a context in which the original partnership between multilateral institutions and corporations finds a stronger rationale than ever. Key to this recovered alliance is an understanding of the differences and comparative advantages of both actors, and the acknowledgement that their respective interests do not negate the fundamental motivations of each party. Corporations are profit-making entities, and the current UN outreach to the private sector does not question the fact. Indeed, it assumes that the continued prosperity of global corporations is an unmatched opportunity for development. It is precisely to sustain global economic expansion that the UN secretary-general challenged business leaders to adopt his Global Compact in January 1999. Multilateral organizations are by definition political creatures. Their membership is constituted by nation-states, which continue to wield ultimate decision-making power. At the same time, these states have lost the capacity to rule single-handedly on an array of issues critical to the future relevance of the multilateral system. The United Nations therefore needs to find acceptable ways to engage nonstate global actors—civil society and the private sector—in its activities and programs. In this new political equation, global corporations are a key variable.

It would be erroneous to portray the business world as a homogeneous group. It clearly is not, and its attitudes toward the UN vary widely by industrial sector and geography. Overall, Silicon Valley is more prone to establishing relations with multilateral agencies than Detroit or Appalachia. Within the corporate hierarchy, CEOs show greater understanding for and interest in corporate citizenship than mid-level managers. The latter, of course, are judged on their sales performance and cannot afford the luxury of long-term strategic thinking. Finally, European firms, with their annual or biannual reporting formats, have longer-term views than American corporations, which face quarterly financial reporting requirements. A tradition of government intervention in the economy and the exigencies of cooperation imposed by proximity and dependence on neighboring states have also made European business leaders more amenable to exchanges with global policymakers than their American counterparts. But only a minority of European businesses has made corporate responsibility as consistent and innovative a strategic activity as American firms have. Furthermore, recent encounters between U.S. corporate executives and the secretary-general give reason to believe that American business is overcoming the bias inherited from the 1960s and 1970s.

A review of the respective interests of UN and corporate actors demonstrates that their partnership is built on a strong foundation of overlapping motivations and shared aspirations.

I. The View from the 38th Floor

The 38th floor of the UN's main building on New York's First Avenue is home to the office of the UN secretary-general. While his views are not binding on the entire UN system, I refer to the 38th floor symbolically here as the nerve center of UN policymaking toward the business community. Of course, many UN agencies in and away from New York are steadfastly pursuing a similar rapprochement with the business community. The reference to the 38th floor of the UN building is therefore metaphorical: it aims at portraying the UN's motives and rationale for seeking a new relationship with the private sector.

In defining this rationale, the UN has addressed and sought to convince several constituencies. The first group is the private sector itself. The UN must fight the legacy of suspicion inherited from the antiliberal era that began with decolonization and persuade business that it has become not only a bona fide partner but a necessary one. The UN's arguments are also aimed at governments and representatives of civil society. UN member states see the UN's rapprochement with the private sector as the formalization of their loss of monopoly on policymaking. Even as they realize that corporations cannot replace sovereign states in political decision-making, governments remain wary of sharing the limelight with nonstate actors on global issues. While they no longer possess all the tools necessary to regulate a global world, states are still reluctant to rely on the tools and power of those they perceive as rivals. Civil society organizations, on the other hand, share a point in common with private sector firms. Both are nonstate actors seeking to increase their influence on global policymaking. Yet nongovernmental organizations have often been suspicious of corporate objectives and continue to find them at odds with such causes as the promotion of human rights, environmental control, and labor rights.

Finally, UN policymakers must also persuade the internal UN bureaucracy in New York and at other UN headquarters, as well as in the approximately 175 countries in which the UN carries out various types of operations. UN officials in executive positions, typically in their late-40s to mid-50s, often originate from their national foreign ministries. Many have divided their professional lives between government, international organizations, and civil society groups, and few have ever worked in the private sector. Business degrees are rare, as the political nature of UN work leads to the assumption that management techniques are irrelevant to the UN's success. The prevalence of government or NGO experience at times implies a suspicion for the profit motive and a lack of exposure to the pace of corporate life, its communication style, and its focus on outcome as opposed to process. Again, there are many exceptions to this generalization and attitudes have changed markedly, especially as a new generation of executives is groomed for the future. But the cultural gap cannot be denied and the UN's task of bringing the troops on board is not yet completed.

A Conceptual Framework for
Multilateralism in the Twenty-First Century

The UN Charter, it will be recalled, was drafted in the aftermath of a devastating five-year world war, which itself unrolled in the wake of a decade-long economic depression of great proportions.[1] The international order built in 1945—the United Nations and the Bretton Woods institutions—took for granted a consensus favoring government intervention that had evolved out of the nadir of depression and war. In this Keynesian vision, the state was expected to promote, if not provide, full employment, price stability, and social safety nets during recessions. The ability of the state to act on behalf of national economic interests was facilitated by the existence of mostly national corporate actors whose transactions with foreign firms or nations took place within a framework of decidedly national and separate economies. In this context, point-of-entry barriers to international transactions constituted acceptable and efficacious tools of economic policy. At the same time, the sheer size and power of American economic resources guaranteed the prevalence of an open and nondiscriminatory approach to international economic relations—until the Cold War entered its full bloom and unraveled the consensus. The absence of openness to trade and financial exchange during the Great Depression became a key explanation for the rise of fascism and Nazism, with its accompanying political and economic closure symbolized by Hitler's autarkic policies.[2] The postwar settlement therefore included a return to the liberal credo of openness as the maiden of international security, even if the tragic experiences of the 1930s had mitigated the inherent optimism of liberalism in favor of social-democratic principles.

This consensus of "embedded liberalism" was threatened time and again during the subsequent 50 years. The influence exercised by the Soviet Union over newly decolonized nations in the 1950s and 1960s, and the embodiment of a neo-Marxist analysis of international economic relations in such UN bodies as UNCTAD, questioned the liberal side of the consensus. Conversely, beginning in 1980, the liberal reaction to the ideological landscape of the previous decade consciously sought to promote the liberal values inscribed in the consensus at the expense of the Keynesian legacy. Yet, this alternating discourse between openness and intervention remained central to the entire period, until globalization transformed the conditions of the international economy, making some of the assumptions of the old discourse obsolete.

Globalization and Its Effects

Globalization, it should be noted, is a process more than a reality.[3] As much as the economic and political discourse highlights the internationalization of exchanges, 80 percent of the national production of the world's leading economies is still consumed domestically.[4] The process of globalization also contains an inherent contradiction between openness and closure, internationalization and localization, universalism and tribalism. The microeconomic nature of globalization is evinced by trade and international production statistics. Sales by foreign affiliates in both domestic and international markets totaled $11 trillion in 1998, while total world exports amounted to only $7 trillion. Of total world trade, one third takes place within multinational firms and another third is accounted for by arms-length transactions associated with those firms. The capital base of multinational corporations represents four times the stock of foreign direct investment emanating from the developed countries—a stunning demonstration of the financial power of these corporations.[5]

This face of globalization, which highlights its local, firm-level manifestations, is contradicted by a centrifugal movement of outward expansion and seemingly uncontrolled openness that threatens the economic and cultural security of workers and individuals. This aspect of globalization has disconnected networks of production and finance from their traditional national institutional settings, sending them off on a "spatial and temporal trajectory" of their own.[6] While it has created unparalleled economic expansion, this explosion of national economic borders has introduced new disequilibria that jeopardize its sustainability. For one, globalization has mostly benefited the developed nations of Western Europe and the United

States as well as the Asian tigers of the 1970s. Such emerging markets as Malaysia, Thailand, and Indonesia have no doubt risen to economic prominence on the wave of globalization. But even there, social dislocations and the absence of institutional and regulatory mechanisms to accompany growth constitute serious threats to the continued integration of these nations in the process of globalization, as well as to political stability. "Chaotic uncertainty," write Keohane and Nye "is too high a price for most people to pay for somewhat higher levels of prosperity."[7] Particularly left-out of the benefits of openness is the African continent, whose multiple intranational conflicts provide tragic evidence of the absence of a stake in peace as the foundation of economic development. "The process that has come to be called 'globalization,'" writes Dani Rodrik "is exposing a deep fault line between groups who have the skills and mobility to flourish in global markets and those who either don't have these advantages or perceive the expansion of unregulated markets as inimical to social stability and deeply held norms. The result is severe tension between the market and social groups such as workers, pensioners, and environmentalists, with governments stuck in the middle."[8]

Globalization evinces a second disequilibrium, this one affecting domestic policies and the capacity to enforce them. Because globalization has taken place within firms rather than between nations, governments have lost the capacity to regulate a vast array of economic transactions in the context of a global world. In particular, they have lost the ability to tax the proceeds of global transactions, impairing the national commitment to funding the safety nets of the Keynesian compromise.[9] Because "trade becomes contentious when it unleashes forces that undermine the norms implicit in domestic practices,"[10] globalization will only be sustained if the metanational economic space it has defined becomes embedded in a broader framework of shared values and institutionalized practices.[11] While "rule-making [in the past decade] has been primarily concerned with constructing a supportive context for global markets,"[12] other global phenomena such as environmental degradation, human rights abuses, and the marginalization of the poorest have not benefited from similar regulatory efforts.

"A key challenge for the international community, therefore, is to devise for the *global* economy the kind of institutional equilibrium that existed in the postwar *inter-national* economic order."[13] In the wake of the Asian crisis of 1998, calls for a new economic architecture reflected this quest, although the construction of institutions may be less effective than a reinterpretation of the mandates and constitutive texts of the multilateral system, including the UN Charter and the UN's functions.[14] The secretary-general's effort to include the private sector and civil society in UN policy-making activities may be seen as such an interpretative adjustment of the

UN's role in the context of globalization—one that does not require the design of new institutions or amendments to the UN Charter.

NGOs and Multinationals: David and Goliath?

The conditions of globalization have brought market and society in direct contact through the interactions, and clashes, of NGOs and global corporations. While the question is as old as economic activity itself, civil society is again asking whether "the business of business is merely business, or is it something more?"[15] As demonstrated during the Third Ministerial Meeting of the World Trade Organization in Seattle in November 1999, the fight between the potentially divergent interests of global corporations and NGOs is being fought in the arena of trade. What is at stake, specifically, is whether the global trade regime should accommodate a variety of social agendas in such areas as human rights, labor rights, and the environment, or whether such concerns ought to be managed separately. For those defenders of the latter view, the challenge is to devise such a separate mechanism to handle societal concerns while not jeopardizing the expansion of global trade.

The Diversity of the NGO World

Accredited to the United Nations since its creation, NGOs have long played a role in international affairs.[16] In 1948, the number of NGOs accredited to the UN stood at 41. That figure reached 700 by 1986 and has more than doubled since then. Today more than 1,500 NGOs have consultative status to the UN and hundreds still await accreditation. No event, however, captures better the recently acquired power of civil society than the signing of a ban against landmines in Ottawa in December 1997, an international agreement virtually imposed on the international community by the International Campaign to Ban Landmines. For this feat, the coalition of then 1,100 NGOs was awarded the Nobel Peace prize the same year.[17] In 1998, NGOs played a significant role in halting the OECD-sponsored negotiations on a Multilateral Agreement on Investment (MAI), bringing further evidence of their power of persuasion.[18]

NGOs are creatures of globalization too, as use of E-mail and the Internet has enabled them "to tap into broader social movements and gain media attention."[19] Following the lead of transnational firms in the 1970s, NGOs began internationalizing their structures. While their activism relies on decentralized, grass-roots tactics, some now boast global networks of organizations that take advantage of state-of-the-art communication technology to push issue-specific agendas. Because they capture the primary societal concerns of our era, NGOs will continue to exert an influence on global issues.

It is significant to note that of the 1,500 NGOs with cur
to the UN, more than 1,100 have an interest in the envirc
rights. Such NGOs as the World Wildlife Fund (Y
Amnesty International, and Human Rights Watch are ₅
power of these concerns and the ability of global NGO netwc.
around them. These predominant civil society interests, in turn,
bridge to the corporate concern for social responsibility, forcing corporatio..
and NGOs into an inescapable dialogue.

Corporate Responsibility: The New Imperative

Globalization is giving corporate social responsibility (CSR) a new salience
and meaning.[20] Because the consistent liberalization of global trade seems to
have provided multinationals with unlimited and unchecked increases in
bargaining power,[21] civil society has developed a new stake in correcting this
perceived imbalance. Convinced of the responsibility incumbent upon them
to supply the checks and balances of global economic activity, NGOs have
again relied on effective use of the Internet and the mobilization of the international media to expose the excesses of irresponsible firms. The naming
and shaming tactics that human rights organizations refined and levied
against governments in the 1960s and 1970s are now being used against
such corporate "sinners" as Nike, Rio Tinto, and Shell.

The countervailing power of civil society groups also feeds on the microeconomic nature of globalization. The intrafirm character of global trade
implies that the interface between producers and consumers is less mediated
than was the case under interdependence. Then, governments remained the
main interlocutors of corporations seeking to expand internationally, and
government-sponsored legislation regulated the interface between society
and business. The loss of national regulatory power over global transactions
has weakened the mediation capabilities of states, putting corporations face
to face with their consumers with no institutions to cushion the potential
blows. "The shift of power away from nation-states means that the public in
general requires more accountability from other powerful actors, such as
business, and expects them to respond directly to the demands of public
opinion rather than waiting for that opinion to be mediated by governments
in the form of legislation or regulation."[22] The geographical dichotomy of
globalization means that multinationals face their constituencies both at the
local and the global levels, and in both instances, governments can not be relied upon to provide the public good of mediation.

Exposure to the unmediated wrath of local communities has resulted, paradoxically, from such globalization strategies as global branding. The latter illustrates particularly well the unlimited opportunities and new vulnerabilities

d simultaneously by global firms. Globalization being as much a cultural phenomenon as an economic one, global corporations use a single advertising strategy and image to sell the same goods in Moscow, Paris, and Kuala Lumpur. It is estimated that such intangible assets as brand name and corporate image now constitute 40 percent of the market value of corporations.[23] Protecting such assets has therefore become a major challenge for the success of global marketing strategies, fostering an array of corporate responses ranging from private sector initiatives at the firm and industry level to private-public partnership approaches.[24] Such pioneers as British Petroleum and Shell have publicly broken rank with conventional views and embraced concerns for human rights, the environment, and labor in their mission statements, management practices, and annual reports.[25]

Multinationals also face internal needs. "Many have begun to confront the challenge of how to integrate into one global corporate culture the increasing number of diverse national cultures of their officers and employees."[26] As in the past, the definition of a corporate identity and culture has a direct impact on the bottom line. What is new, however, is the complexity of the task in a contemporary context that alternates between the respect of diversity and the universalizing proclivities of globalization, the nurturing of linguistic identity and the ubiquity of English, the gentle gait of cultural expression and the frenetic pace of economic efficiency. The corporate interest in business ethics reflects this concern.[27] Corporations must find common denominators between employees of various religious and cultural backgrounds—of which the "golden rule" of not doing unto others what one does not want done to oneself is an example.[28] Lest they adopt values around which employees can coalescence and with which they can identify, corporations cannot retain their best asset in the global economy: their workforce. Formed to foster some of the objectives of the Copenhagen Social Summit (1995) and accredited to the UN, the Harvard-based Triglav Circle confirms the search for a common source of ethics through the respect of diversity. Bringing together economists, political scientists, and UN practitioners "committed to a political, economic, ethical and spiritual vision for social development based on human dignity, human rights, equality, respect, democracy, mutual responsibility and cooperation, and full respect for the various religious and ethical values and cultural backgrounds of people," the Triglav Circle is another attempt at reconciling the uniformizing tendencies of globalization with the richness of culture, art, and civilization.[29]

Epitomizing the multicultural workplace, the United Nations could provide a source of inspiration to its corporate partners. Although it is dominated by bureaucratic culture, the UN has had some success in developing an internal narrative and behavior that values and celebrates cultural and linguistic diversity—a commitment reflected in the variety of national dress, official holidays, culinary events, and other physical markers of a multinational culture. A dialogue between UN and business leaders on how to resolve the quandary of local diversity vs. global uniformity in the workplace could prove a useful partnership between both parties

Fighting It Out over Trade

Multinationals have had an obvious incentive to support trade liberalization in the past two decades. Contrary to a commonly held myth, successive rounds of trade negotiations demonstrate that liberalization has elicited more rather than fewer rules as an expanding global trade regime has necessitated enforcement and dispute mechanisms. Globalization, therefore, rather than representing a battle of markets vs. states, has been promoted by the policy choices of Western industrialized nations.[30] The corporate stake in rule-making has grown accordingly, as the continued prosperity of global firms hinges on ever-expanding market access and supportive regulation. NGOs also see in the multilateral trade system a means to translating their values into new regulations and constraints on multinationals. Calls for a "level playing field" often conceal attempts to directly change the trading rules to accommodate social agendas. Predictably, "the relationship between trade, on the one hand, and social, environmental, or human rights issues on the other, has emerged as a flashpoint of controversy" between civil society and global firms.[31] The clash acquired worldwide notoriety as riot-control police attempted to clear the way for government officials and trade negotiators to join the opening ceremony of the Third Ministerial Meeting of the World Trade Organization in Seattle in November 1999.

Opponents of continued trade liberalization represent highly heterogeneous groups that pursue different goals often at cross-purposes with each other.

The spectrum covers a small minority motivated by ideology; single-issue groups in the mainstream who are concerned with the neglect of the environment, continued human-rights abuses, and growing income inequalities; trade unions who fear that structural adjustments are not offset by positive effects of globalization; grass-root movements of almost all colors; and powerful national and regional economic interests that seek government protection and oppose global integration.[32]

As pressure by civil society actors has intensified, various attempts have been made to appease their concerns by increasing the transparency of the WTO and by searching for compromises. At the 1999 WTO meeting, President Clinton echoed their calls for building a link between trade and labor, and went as far as proposing that the WTO sanction countries that did not meet minimum social standards. Earlier, former WTO Director General Renato Ruggiero had stressed the need for balancing global governance structures, culminating in his proposal for a World Environment Organization.[33]

Those who oppose linking trade with other concerns have pointed out that the trading system was not designed to solve labor, environmental, and human rights issues, and that burdening the trade regime with such clauses would only limit commercial exchanges while leaving social problems unresolved. "Moreover, opponents strongly suspect that the true motivation for establishing such links is protectionism."[34] A statement released by the ICC in April 1999 called upon governments to "be vigilant not to undermine the rules of the multilateral trading system when designing policies to achieve environmental objectives that such policies are not misused for protectionist purposes."[35] Seeing in global standards a scheme to undermine their comparative advantage, developing countries have rejected them, stressing that higher standards in such areas as the environment "can only be achieved through an incremental process of accumulating skills, capital, and technology."[36] Indeed, empirical evidence indicates that trade and investment have positive and mutually reinforcing consequences for human rights, development, and the environment, as well as on employment and wage levels.[37]

As became apparent during the November 1999 WTO meeting, the views of developing countries are increasingly converging with those of multinationals and other outward-oriented corporations to form a novel policy coalition. Ahead of the WTO meeting, a group of international trade economists headed by Jagdish Bhagwati issued a statement arguing that the attempt to impose a "trade-unrelated agenda" on the WTO was the result of an alliance between domestic protectionist groups in the developed countries and "morally driven human rights and other groups that simply wish to see higher standards abroad."[38] Calling the strategy "selfishly protective," the statement demonstrated that such measures were only aimed at lowering market access for the products of developing economies, thereby protecting inefficient industries in developed countries and compromising the development policies of poorer countries. Yet, acknowledging the good intentions of the morally inclined NGOs, the group offered an alternative strategy whereby violations to moral standards should be treated within the complex economic, political, and social contexts of all countries with "sophisticated and nuanced public policy programs . . . symetrically applied" to developed and developing nations.[39]

The presence of an effective institutional mechanism to define and enforce global rules on behalf of trade liberalization stands in sharp contrast to the institutional vacuum that prevails on behalf of such causes as the environment, development, human rights, and labor. The UN hoped that the international conferences it convened on an array of social issues in the first half of the 1990s might initiate a larger debate on the institutionalization of these issues in an appropriate governance structure. But as Kell and Ruggie point out, "at the United Nations, there is a wide gap between the ambitious goals and broad commitments embodied in various United Nations conferences on social issues and the degree to which governments are willing to honor such commitments."[40] This imbalance in governance mechanisms adds moral weight to the fight of civil society and carries with it a threat against sustained openness unless the causes of civil society become institutionally channeled. The business community is not insensitive to the threat, as will be demonstrated below. As a result, it has "begun to look to the United Nations to play a larger role in setting norms and standards that express not merely the functional values of direct interest to business, but also broader global social issues."[41] Because the United Nations provides a bridge between the private sector and civil society, it is in a position to propose a governance mechanism for regulating the normative no man's land of globalization without affecting the multilateral trade system.

The Global Compact:
Rephrasing the "Compromise of Embedded Liberalism"

The "Global Compact of shared values and principles" outlined by Kofi Annan at Davos in January 1999 represents an attempt at creating such a balanced governance mechanism by riding on the wave of corporate responsibility. The Compact also aims to renew the partnership that bound the United Nations and the international business community in 1945 and rewrite the consensus of "embedded liberalism" to fit the specific conditions of globalization.

The Global Compact is unquestionably supportive of globalization, and it sees the balance of its creative and destructive powers as positive. Indeed it is predicated on the assumption that globalization constitutes a potentially crucial opportunity for development—possibly the best chance for the "developing world" since the latter's creation as a unitary political construct in the 1950s and 1960s. But the rationale of the Compact is also motivated by a great concern for the risk of a backlash to globalization if the identity, human dignity, and basic social needs of all cultures are not secured. It is precisely because a backlash to globalization would represent a historically unmatched threat to economic prosperity and peace that the Global Compact urges international business leaders to take reasonable steps to secure the emerging values of global civil society in exchange for a commitment on the part of the United Nations to market openness.

The principles retained in the Compact are directly relevant to the UN's mandates, as well as suitable to global rule-making and corporate action. Nine principles fit within the three value categories of human rights, labor rights, and environmental sustainability. These principles are derived from the Universal Declaration of Human Rights adopted by the UN in 1948, the Rio Declaration adopted at the end of the 1992 UN Conference on the Environment and Development, and the Declaration on Fundamental Principles and Rights at Work adopted by the ILO in 1998.The legitimacy of these texts rests on governmental commitments—some of which are legally binding—to implement their provisions.

The Global Compact's Nine Principles[42]

Human Rights

1. Businesses should support and respect the protection of internationally proclaimed human rights within their sphere of influence; and
2. Make sure that they are not complicit in human rights abuses.

Labor

3. Businesses should uphold the freedom of association and the effective recognition of the right to collective bargaining; and
4. The elimination of all forms of forced and compulsory labor; and
5. The effective elimination of child labor; and
6. Eliminate discrimination in respect of employment and occupation.

Environment

7. Businesses should support a precautionary approach to environmental challenges;
8. Undertake initiatives to promote greater environmental responsibility;
9. Encourage the development and diffusion of environmentally friendly technologies.

The embodiment of these principles in UN activities, and in UN partnerships with private sector firms, constitutes a reinterpretation of the compromise between liberal and Keynesian policies contained in the UN Charter. In this framework, the values on which the sustainability of global expansion are likely to hinge in the twenty-first century have come to replace the Keynesian goals of full employment and safety nets relevant to the post-depression era.

While acknowledging that governments continue to play a major role in the maintenance of universal values, the Compact assumes that, in the context of a global economy, corporations can wield critical influence in enforcing such values in their production systems as well as their relations with consumers, clients, and partners. The Global Compact is not designed as a code of conduct. Rather, "it is meant to serve as a [frame] of reference to stimulate best practices and to bring about convergence around universally shared values."[43] Because it relies on principles rather than such material capabilities as technology or capital, the Global Compact cannot be said to discriminate against poorer nations. It assumes responsibility and mutual interest and is predicated on the existence of absolute gains to accrue to multilateral institutions, civil society, and international business. If such abuses as child labor or child prostitution have become unacceptable to the world community, corporations are in a better position than most governments to root out such practices from their operations. As employers, they can commit to not resorting to child labor. As sub-contractors, they can impose similar standards on their business partners. And as investors, they can pressure governments to enforce socially responsible legislation. As partners of the UN in operational partnerships, they can also fund or implement efforts to provide alternatives to such practices—by supporting education and poverty reduction, for example.

The Compact cannot be segregated from a new UN attitude toward the multilateral trade regime. Although the WTO is not a UN agency per se, it is often referred to as "de facto UN agency." At the time of the WTO's creation, a fierce debate took place within the United Nations—and between the UN and its partners—as to the wisdom of making the WTO a UN body. Plans for an International Trade Organization (ITO) had been shelved in 1946, as governments could not agree on a liberal platform for the promotion of free trade. A multilateral trade regime, the General Agreement on Tariffs and Trade (GATT), remained outside the UN's purview and never became a true organization. In 1992, as they debated the institutional linkage of the future WTO to the UN, governments differed on the position to take. Business remained wary of including the WTO within the UN as the latter had not yet demonstrated an unquestionable commitment to market openness nor a desire to reach out to the international business community. Finally, the WTO remained outside the UN system, although some analysts believe that if it were created today the WTO would likely have the status of a UN specialized agency.[44]

It is precisely because the WTO cannot be seen as the appropriate mechanism for the enforcement of such values as human rights and environmental responsibility that the United Nations provides an alternative venue for the proper inclusion of these values in global exchanges. Secretary-General Kofi Annan made his offer public in an editorial that appeared in the *Wall Street Journal* on the eve of the WTO meeting.[45] Calling the WTO meeting "pivotal" to set the twenty-first century on a course of economic expansion and peace, he wrote that "the WTO must not be distracted from its own vital task: extending the benefits of free trade fully to the developing world;" adding that "it is hardly surprising if developing countries are suspicious of those who claim to be helping them by introducing new conditions or restrictions on trade," he insisted that because "trade is cheaper than aid" it constitutes the best chance for development.[46] Responding to those who are concerned about human rights, labor rights, and the environment, he reiterated his invitation to multinationals to work with United Nations agencies to embed these values in their activities and global corporate cultures.

The various UN agencies concerned by the Global Compact are developing ways to operationalize its provisions in programs and projects, and the challenge is a long-term one. Through their partnerships with corporations around the world, UN agencies have access to noncoercive methods of promoting these values and changing attitudes and behaviors. While decisive results will require time, no other institution than the United Nations (including its Bretton Woods affiliates) is better positioned to advance the adoption of universal values to accompany rather than stall globalization without damaging the trading opportunities of developing nations. How the Compact was received by the business community and is being applied by UN agencies is examined in chapter 3.

Rules and Norms: Providing the Regulatory Infrastructure of the Global Economy

One of the key services performed by the United Nations on behalf of business is often overlooked: namely the provision of the public good of governance and regulation. While regulation is typically presented as anathema to business, recent exchanges between UN officials and business leaders demonstrate that the latter appreciate the merit of UN regimes, norms, or rules that lower transaction costs, ensure the rule of law, define common standards, and guarantee property rights. The UN regulatory role affects a myriad of exchanges and relationships whose sustainability is often taken for granted out of ignorance of the "soft infrastructure" that makes them possible.[47] Following is a list of the UN's regulatory functions and the agencies responsible for developing the corresponding norms and rules:

- Promoting agreements on states' jurisdictional rights (General Assembly, ICAO, IMO);
- Promoting accords on intellectual property rights relevant to international commerce and fostering creativity and development in all countries;

- Standardizing definitions and measurements of economic concepts (UN Statistical Commission, UNCITRAL, WMO, WHO, FAO, and other bodies);
- Standardizing and harmonizing rules for international commercial transactions (UNCITRAL);
- Developing standards for technologies and procedures employed in international commerce (ICAO, IMO, ITU, UNCTAD, UPU, ECE);
- Preventing damages to goods and services that are traded internationally (ICAO, IMO, ITU, UPU);
- Assuring compensation for losses from accidents, pollution, and crimes (UNCITRAL, IMO, UPU, ICAO);
- Reducing transborder damages that could provoke harmful actions against international firms (UNEP, IMO, ICAO, WHO, FAO);
- Assuring that the promotion of labor standards does not impede international commerce (ILO);
- Preventing international "money laundering" (UN Commission on Crime Prevention and Criminal Justice and affiliated bodies); and
- Gathering and disseminating economic information that facilitates international accords (WMO, UNCITRAL, UNCTAD, ICAO, and others).

(Excerpted from *The United Nations and Global Commerce,* by Mark Zacher, page 11.)

UN rules and norms perform critical functions but also promote values central to global commerce. The central value of openness, for example, is upheld by UN agreements on navigation rights that guarantee "the freedom of the high seas, innocent passage through territorial seas, and free transit through international straits."[48] Similarly, a UN convention on air space ensures the "freedom of the air" as well as "the right to cross the territory of other countries without landing and the right to land for emergency and technical reasons."[49] Property rights, without which a liberal market economy could not function, are guaranteed by the registration of patents, trademarks, and industrial designs with the UN World Intellectual Property Organization (WIPO). Although the World Trade Organization has become involved in the protection of intellectual property rights, WIPO still received 4.8 million national applications for patents in 1998. It has also made recommendations on ways to defend Internet domain names, a matter of increasing concern to communication and Internet firms, the majority of which are incorporated in the United States. Yet other UN specialized bodies are involved in standardizing economic measures and statistics, agreements under private commercial law, or the contents of such products as vaccines.

The requirement of standardization to ensure modern commercial exchanges dates back to the creation of money in the early Renaissance. Money is nothing more than a standard convention on value required by post-barter economies. Standards play two essential roles in a market economy. Their universality and equal applicability allow the development of trust in economic relations, a sine qua non of exchange. It is because standards are the same for all parties to a market that strangers can exchange all types of goods and services across borders without fearing deception or theft. Here standards serve to promote a value without which relations between economic parties would be seriously impaired. Standards also play a more instrumental function in lowering transaction and information costs, which in turn lowers the general level of prices and fosters economic efficiency. The negotiation and promulgation of standards by UN bodies imply that corporations do not face negotiation and research costs of their own when considering an economic exchange or agreement. As a result, transactions are cheaper, which lowers the prices of goods and services to consumers. They are also faster, an ever-growing requirement in the global economy of E-commerce and instantaneous financial transfers.

Keeping in mind the definition of multilateralism as a system of relations in which universal concepts apply universally and equally to all members, the UN advantage in the negotiation of universal standards becomes readily apparent. Because the United Nations was erected on the principle of equal membership for all states in the international system, it is ideally suited to negotiate universal principles that apply equally to all parties. In this sense, universal standards are a quintessential UN product and the organization provides the cheapest and most effective way to negotiate such standards. To quote Ruggie, "the performance of this task on a multilateral basis seems inevitable in the long-run, although in fact states appear to try every conceivable alternative first."[50]

In its regulatory and normative functions, the UN therefore provides an environment that enables and sustains open economic exchanges. Other arguments in favor of the UN's enabling role focus on the UN's multifaceted operational activities in the areas of peace and security, humanitarian assistance, and economic and social development.

The Opportunity Cost Argument:
The Link to the Corporate Bottom Line

Opportunity costs measure economic loss and missed opportunities. The concept applies to the UN's work in two ways. UN intervention to secure peace and security through peacekeeping operations or humanitarian missions addresses a negative: the disruptions caused by wars, internecine conflicts, and natural or man-made disasters. The loss of economic activity, the destruction of physical infrastructure, and the displacement of populations represent some of the real costs of wars and humanitarian crises. UN economic and social development activities, however, are aimed at creating positives. They seek to eliminate the opportunity cost of poverty, illiteracy, or institutional vacuum through the creation of economic opportunities. The UN role in landmine removal illustrates this double definition of opportunity cost particularly well. The presence of landmines in approximately 60 countries around the world has real costs on local populations, which include the total expenditure of medical and psychological care required by landmine victims. At a minimum, UN demining programs seek to eliminate or alleviate the burden of these costs on the poorest developing countries— a negative value. More importantly, however, landmines prevent economic development by making the land unavailable for agriculture, infrastructure development, trade, and transportation. It is precisely because landmines paralyze a country that parties to conflicts lay them indiscriminately. In this instance, the opportunity cost of landmines amounts to poverty and lost economic activity and UN demining activities become part of development programs—a positive value.

Both real and opportunity costs provide the UN and the private sector with a common interest and the basis for additional partnerships. The UN needs the private sector to participate actively in post-conflict reconstruction, mine clearance, and the resettlement of refugees, among other security-related activities. Arguably, the UN must rely even more so on corporate responsibility to invest in the development of the poorest developing countries, many of which also happen to be recovering from protracted conflicts, humanitarian crises, or a combination thereof. The opportunity cost rationale therefore provides a natural link between the interests of international organizations and those of business and it captures the conditions required for creating win-win situations between them.

The academic debate on public goods can be read as a rephrasing of the opportunity-cost argument.[51] Public goods are defined as nonexcludable and nonrival. Nonexcludability refers to the fact that no party can be excluded from the consumption of the good; nonrivalry implies that consumption by one party does not deplete the good for consumption by others. The most public of all goods is the air we breathe. National parks are also cited as a typical example of public goods, although the nonrivalry clause is questionable, as sustained consumption of national parks may degrade their natural environments and reduce their enjoyment by subsequent generations. Global public goods are those nonexcludable and nonrival goods that are consumed by people around the world and belong to the international community. Typical examples include the world's oceans, international architectural treasures,

UN peacekeeping, and UN development programs. Because their enjoyment can accrue to the entire international community and they create positive externalities that are nonexcludable and nonrival, all the examples listed above fit the definition of a public good

The presence of positive externalities makes a case for the UN's involvement in the production of global public goods. Positive externalities present the international community with the problem of free-riding. The creation of a positive value for which the producer of the good is not remunerated implies that a private, profit-making entity has no incentive to produce the good. Assuming that it took the initiative of producing the good, the private producer would be incurring a cost on behalf of others, who would free-ride on the supply of the good by the generously minded producer. Since paying for other people's way is not a rational economic decision for a private sector actor, the free-riding problem makes it difficult to engage private sector firms—domestic or global—in the production of public goods. Because they embody the public interest and can channel the energies of multiple actors in a single direction, governments have been the suppliers of public goods in the modern era.[52]

Indeed, the creation of the modern state can be seen as a means of supplying larger and more complex societies with the public goods necessary to ensure their survival. Defense and the creation of national armies to replace mercenaries were the original public goods produced by the nation-state. Education, health, and infrastructure are relatively modern additions. In a global context, states have either insufficient incentives or insufficient capacity to produce the global public goods of environmental responsibility, international peace, and poverty reduction. Moreover, an international system of 188 states poses a collective action problem, as coordinated action by so large a group of actors is difficult to organize. In the context of a global system facing global threats and problems, multilateral organizations supply the collective action mechanism to engage states and nonstate actors in the production of global public goods. If they choose to provide the lead for such production, these multilateral bodies can attract private sector firms to participate in the production of global public goods based on the anticipation of future profits. Integrating the least developed countries in the global economy is an example of a global public good that presents both unquestionable peace and security benefits and profit opportunities, thereby providing a formula for UN-business partnership based on mutual interest. As confirmed by Richard McCormick, former CEO of US West and president-elect of the ICC:

We seek stable markets and prosperous trading partners, both of which are likely in countries at peace. . . . UN peacekeeping has helped quell violence and provide countries with the breathing room needed to move from civil unrest to function-

ing states. Areas once held together by UN peacekeepers are now places where we find stable economies and growing markets.[53]

II. The View from the Corporate Ladder

As described in the introduction to this chapter, business attitudes toward the United Nations vary among industries, levels on the corporate ladder, and geography. After two years of sustained outreach to the business community, however, it is fair to say that the relationship between the UN and the business world has now entered a zone of trust and mutual respect that will allow both parties to deepen their partnership in the coming decade.

The corporate views quoted in this section emanate from speeches, articles, and personal interviews. Overall, they demonstrate the prevalence of common interests between the UN and corporations and the availability of mutual gains in cooperation. First and foremost, business leaders understand the risk of a backlash to globalization and the consequences that such an occurrence would have on global growth. The Asian and Russian financial crises of mid-1998 have sharpened the perception of this risk, although the recovery of Asia quickly lowered pressure for regulatory reforms. Informed corporate executives understand the arguments in favor of the UN's rule-setting and policymaking roles as sources of legitimacy for openness. The corporate need to project an image of good citizenship matches the UN's reliance on corporate responsibility to implement the Global Compact. Here too, a common interest supports further collaboration. But corporations would be failing their raison d'être if profit making did not motivate in part their collaboration with the UN. As stated above, the opportunity costs of poverty and war represent a substantial economic loss that corporate involvement in development and post-conflict reconstruction can dramatically reduce. Corporate assistance to the UN's operations in the poorest developing countries is also the surest way of bringing into the world economy the next generation of emerging markets in Asia, and above all Africa. Corporate executives also argue that they have and can continue to make a contribution to UN reform by proposing their values of efficiency and their management methods as models to be emulated by UN bodies. Here the UN and business tread on more contentious terrain as mythical constructs and suspicions inherited from the past rear their heads again.

Supporting the UN: Recovering the Spirit of 1945

Defending the UN's role in defining and guaranteeing the rules and norms of the global era has become the leading corporate argument in favor of the

United Nations. Senior corporate leaders understand only too well that the guarantee of a liberal economy lies paradoxically in the quality and enforceability of the rule of law. Corporations must face equal conditions in principle to have the freedom to avail themselves of various opportunities in practice. In a global context, these rules must be defined and applied globally by global policymakers. States Richard McCormick: "The UN provides us with an arena to resolve disputes and to uphold the rule of law."[54]

The need for business support of international policymaking is not a development of globalization. An ICC paper dated from 1977 demonstrates that interdependence had already made it imperative for the private sector to become involved in, and indeed seek to influence, the "international cooperation" debate.[55] Globalization has rekindled the business interest simply because the rules that prevailed in the 1960s and 1970s no longer fit the conditions of a global world, thereby making necessary the construction of a new regulatory and normative apparatus. The corporate support of global rule-making appears unequivocal in an ICC statement "on behalf of world business" issued in May 1998. "Government and business" the declaration stated, "must also work more closely together to design the multilateral rules for the worldwide marketplace which will be increasingly necessary for the smooth functioning and good management of globalization."[56] "Globalization," the authors of the statement added, "is a business-driven phenomenon, and business is the natural partner of intergovernmental bodies to help them in agenda-building, decision-making, and implementation." Far from contradicting liberalization, the business view stems from the recognition that "like freedom, markets only work within an appropriate framework of laws, rules, and institutions."[57] "The particular contribution of business to this task," added the ICC a year later, "is to help governments strike the necessary balance between freedom and rules that maximizes the scope and stability for business to work productively to create wealth and employment."[58] Because the governmental role in global rule-making is increasingly embedded in multilateral institutions, "the ICC strongly supports the . . . work of the UN system . . . to tackle the complex and frequently interrelated problems emerging in the global economy at the dawn of the new millennium."[59]

Since 1997, various ICC policy statements have stressed legitimacy as the requisite underpinning of well-functioning markets. Because the regulatory apparatus of interdependence based on national sovereignty and government mediation has become obsolescent, a new system of rules must be devised to legitimize the activities of global firms in a global economy. Because it gives all governments an equal voice and provides civil society and the private sector with a forum for discussion, and increasingly for policymaking, the UN system offers the best mechanism for the coordinated construction of the regulatory framework of globalization. "Multilateral rule-making" state ICC business leaders, "has to adapt itself to the faster pace of change in a global marketplace in order to keep the rules aligned with rapidly evolving business realities and requirements."[60]

In the weeks preceding the November 1999 WTO meeting, the ICC gave its strongest endorsement yet to the UN's role in designing a system of rules to legitimize globalization without impairing trade liberalization. Arguing that "governments must resist being sidetracked by a single array of single-issue activists who have joined forces in an anti-trade campaign called 'mobilization against globalization,'" ICC President Adnan Kassar wrote in a statement to be distributed to governmental delegations at the Seattle meeting that "the right place for addressing [human rights, labor, and environmental] issues is the UN and its appropriate agencies. The most productive way forward is to enhance the authority, effectiveness, and the resource base of these UN bodies."[61] Although it did not name the Global Compact, the statement was a resounding endorsement of the Compact's proposal to allow the UN system to develop rules in the three areas of human rights, labor rights, and the environment, in order to salvage the multilateral trade system from resurgent protectionism cloaked as social empathy.

The call for increased funding of UN bodies is not the least striking rearticulation of the mutual interest that multilateral institutions and the private sector had correctly perceived at the UN's creation but had ignored until recently. If the new alliance between the UN and the international private sector is to be maintained thanks to a recognition of the values and functions of both parties, the spirit of 1945 will not only have been recovered but indeed expanded.

Looking Good:
The Rewards of Corporate Responsibility

Corporate responsibility was discussed above as providing a basis for common action between corporations and the United Nations in the context of the Global Compact. This section illustrates the salience of reputation to multinationals in a global economy, and their interest in obtaining from the United Nations statements of recognition for their good behavior.

Human rights organizations have long known that reputation matters. In the absence of international enforcement mechanisms for human rights, such organizations as Human Rights Watch and Amnesty International have for decades relied on the tactic of embarrassment to generate changes in countries with poor human rights records. As was stated above, globalization has increased the salience of corporate social responsibility and the appeal of good reputation. A UN survey of UN-business partnerships conducted in the fall of 1998 found that more than anything, corporations want the UN to confer "good corporate citizenship awards."[62] The representative of an American management consulting firm that worked at DPKO in the 1990s stated in an interview: "We're very proud of our work for the UN. We gave them the best service we could and a special treatment."[63] One does not treat the UN as any other client: such intangibles as pride and the satisfaction of making a contribution to peace and social values are part of the reward of service. Based on this understanding, the Geneva-based UN program against AIDS, UNAIDS, has elicited very positive corporate responses to its Award for Business Excellence, a title bestowed annually on a corporation for the quality of its AIDS prevention and information policy.

The recognition of corporate social responsibility, however, is not new. The author of a paper published in 1977 by the ICC quoted a 1964 statement issued by the International Organization of Employers according to which private enterprise has a:

> *Responsibility [toward the community at large] of contributing to its orderly development by ensuring a balanced general economy with monetary stability, in particular by fully satisfying stated or apparent needs, and by ensuring together with a fair distribution of the results of production, the highest possible level of employment consistent with demographic growth.*[64]

The same report quotes an ICC member, Sidney E. Rolfe, as stating in 1969 that "the responsibilities of the international corporation are above all to be a good corporate citizen. . . . This means not only respect for the host country's laws and regulations, but also identification as far as possible with its economic, social, and human aims and policies."[65]

In a global economy where multilateral organizations have assumed some of the regulatory functions of nation-states, it is natural that multinationals would turn to the United Nations to obtain legitimacy and various forms of endorsement. The annual conference of Business for Social Responsibility (BSR) in November 1999 provided a timely illustration of this developing relationship.

Attended by over 700 participants including such Fortune 100 companies as Texaco, Ford Motor, and Fannie Mae, the conference addressed the needs for successful partnership formulas between business and civil society and offered workshops to learn the ropes of brokering such alliances. In a keynote address, UN High Commissioner for Human Rights Mary Robinson stated that "business is increasingly interested in the issue of human rights," so interested in fact that the UN Office for Human Rights was working with BSR to create a UN award for good corporate behavior in the area of human rights, to be conferred annually on a deserving corporation.

The award would additionally include a cash prize to be granted to NGOs involved in human rights advocacy and projects. While the operational details of this potential UN-business partnership were far from being ironed out at the time, the idea pointed to the corporate interest in, if not obsession with, reputation management. But as Robinson stated herself, "ad hoc approaches [to corporate support of societal concerns] risk being short-lived."[66] As a remedy to this short-term focus on rewards and PR techniques, she advocated corporate support of the Global Compact.

The conference demonstrated that the interaction between NGOs and multinationals around the issue of CSR is highly dynamic and evolving rapidly.[67] While numerous NGOs continue to pursue confrontational approaches, applying a wide range of campaign tools such as provocation, consumer boycotts, litigation, and direct protest, a growing number recognize that corporate-change leaders can become effective role models or advocates for broader societal concerns. [68] The BSR event pointed to the embryonic stage of these partnerships as well as the lack of development of operational arrangements for ensuring their success. Many such alliances still require the sponsorship of a neutral broker, such as a government agency or business NGO.[69] The United Nations has also begun to emerge as potential broker as well as partner. In a speech that vaunted adoption by the Gap of vendors' codes of conduct, Robert Fisher, CEO of the Gap Division, acknowledged the complexity of a business environment in which he must negotiate with vendors, employees, civil society groups, host countries, the media, and consumers all at once. The United Nations provides an obvious one-stop shop for the global CEO. Yet the novel corporate function of reputation management will have to be broadened if UN-business partnerships on behalf of social values are to be deepened and institutionalized.

The Profit Motive

As the UN approach toward the private sector is predicated on the prevalence of a win-win formula between both actors, I would be remiss not to acknowledge that corporations hope to turn their partnerships with UN agencies into profit. This reality in no way contradicts the UN's own interest in working with business. The UN mandate to integrate, say, the African continent into the global economy matches the business interest in expanding into this untapped market. Only if such mutual gains can be derived from UN-business partnerships will the relationship be sustained in the coming decades.

The most elementary way in which the private sector has benefited from working with the United Nations in the past is through the award of UN procurement contracts for products as varied as food rations, computers, water purification equipment, vaccines, and condoms.[70] This UN market, however, hovers at around $3 billion a year and shows no sign of growth. The reason is simple. It was not the original intent of the UN to substitute itself for governments and business in developing nations, except for an initial period after the accession of these countries to independence. The test of the UN's success therefore is not in operating on behalf of nations, but rather in building the national capacities of countries to act for their own sake. In keeping with the spirit of "helping the developing countries help themselves," the UN's major mandate is to transfer knowledge and power to the countries in which it is involved. Managing projects, purchasing equipment, and contracting services are only three of a myriad of functions that developing nations must internalize within their own institutions. The dwindling UN procurement market therefore does not constitute a future avenue of corporate interest in the UN.[71]

The concept of partnership, however, presents the potential of long-term financial benefits to those corporations that respond to the UN's call for engagement on behalf of UN values and causes. The UNCTAD Partners for Development conference in November 1998 and the Aid & Trade 2000 event in May 2000 outlined the realm of possible partnerships in microfinance, Internet linkages, post-conflict rehabilitation and reconstruction, mine action, etc. Although it requires refinement and substantiation, the concept of partnership proposes a model in which the UN's operational roles are passed on to the private sector while the UN itself acts as guarantor of values and principles and provider of advisory services. Partnerships recognize that corporations are better armed to invest, transfer technology, build infrastructure, and, in some cases, train workers in developing countries. The UN's comparative advantage lies in enlisting the support of civil society and governments around the world in favor of their sustained integration into the global economy, as long as business respects their identities, rights, and environments. The benefits to the private sector are obvious. Instead of competing for $100,000-UN contracts—and these are the big ones—corporations can invest in and obtain million-dollar, multiyear contracts from nations with virtually unlimited needs for equipment, communication technology, and training. In the long term, these communities will turn into sustainable markets that will add hundreds of millions of consumers to the global economy.

It is clear that corporate representatives understand the potential, even if they often lose patience over the pace at which these partnerships are being concretized. In defense of the UN, it is fair to say that the short-term orientation of business—especially strong in the United States—remains an obstacle to building lasting partnerships. These differences in chronological perspectives and other cultural issues are analyzed in chapter 4.

One area of past partnership has been UN reform. The corporate contribution to reforming the UN Department of Peacekeeping Operations was described in chapter 1. Although it receives little publicity, the business input in UN processes and methods filters through the UN system whenever corporations and UN bodies work together in field projects or at UN headquarters. The recruitment of consulting firms to conduct studies on internal reorganization and communication strategies, to cite two common themes of UN reform, represents an entry point for the introduction of corporate methodology in UN bodies. The resistance to such processes, however, remains high among UN staff members.

The ICC supports sustained funding of multilateral organizations in general and the UN in particular, "but the proviso must be that institutional reform tackle bureaucracy and the duplication of tasks and responsibilities . . . A more effective involvement of business in the activities of the UN system and other intergovernmental organizations must form part of the reform process."[72] When asked in a private interview whether the UN would need to borrow some values from the business world to ensure the success of their partnership, Secretary-General of the ICC Maria Cattaui did not hesitate to reply that this was "inevitable."[73] When interviewing UN staff members, replies to the same question rarely elicit so categorical a "yes." UN staffers insist on the specificity, complexity, and sensitivity of the UN's political mandates to justify the UN's insulation from corporate methods. The theme is familiar to those who have tried to "reinvent" government or build public-private partnerships at the domestic level. It seems doubtful, however, that UN relations with business can thrive in the long term if the private sector is expected to promote the values of the UN Charter without some recognition of corporate values on the part of their UN partners.[74]

• • •

The United Nations and the private sector have embarked on a significant rapprochement since 1997, one that holds the promise of a long-lasting partnership based on mutual interests in cooperation. Given the quality and regularity of this dialogue, and based on the unqualified endorsement of UN rule-making functions by the ICC, it is pertinent to ask whether business is apt and willing to use its influence to support the UN politically. Although a creation of American policymakers in the 1940s, the concept and values of the United Nations have suffered unprecedented attacks in the United States in the past decade. While other countries have called for UN reform and pointed to waste and redundancies, none has questioned the necessity for a universal multilateral body to help address intergovernmental and global issues. The stridency of the critique that has emerged in some American quarters was matched by U.S. arrears to the UN totaling $1.6 billion at the end of 1999 according to the world body, of which the U.S. acknowledged only $926 million.

According to Maria Cattaui, European business leaders are more likely to support the UN politically and argue for the continuation of the course set by Secretary-General Kofi Annan. She points to the proximity of European countries to one another and a history of almost 50 years of European unification as conditions favoring corporate support of multilateral cooperation and action.[75] After all, the history of the ICC demonstrates that private sector support of the League of Nations originated among senior European business leaders with liberal leanings, of which Etienne Clémentel, and later Jean Monnet, were illustrious examples. While American business leaders have spoken in favor of the UN's role within such organizations as the United Nations Association of the U.S.A, the Business Council for the United Nations, or the Business Council for International Understanding, they have not used their clout to influence the erratic course of American policy toward multilateralism in the past decade. Isolated efforts at speaking up on behalf of the United Nations can be recalled. In March 1998, the U.S. Council for International Business sent a letter to Senator Newt Gingrich stating: "Our businesses depend on international stability, which the UN promotes. The UN provides us with an arena to negotiate our differences, as well as to uphold the rule of law."[76] In October 1999, the U.S. Chamber of Commerce, the Business Roundtable, and the National Association of Manufacturers sent a letter to President Clinton and several senior members of Congress arguing for payment of the U.S. debt to the UN without linking the financial settlement to "unrelated issues." Sponsored by the Better World Campaign, the letter stated that "by increasing economic security in poor nations, supporting the establishment of democracies and helping war-torn countries to achieve peace, the UN helps to build emerging markets where the private sector can grow and prosper." Such efforts, the heads of the three organizations added, are "vital to American interests."[77] At the same time, the Better World Campaign released a survey showing that 98 percent of export business leaders had favorable impressions of the UN and that 92 percent of the same group opposed linking payment of the U.S. dues to family planning issues.[78]

Still, no nationwide business group or coalition of Fortune 500 corporations has played at the domestic level the policy role of the ICC in demonstrating the importance of multilateral institutions to business interests. Many reasons can be conjectured to explain this discrepancy in behavior. Still prey to much of the suspicion inherited from the 1960s and 1970s, American business has adopted a wait-and-see attitude toward the changes implemented at the UN since 1997. American corporations are also less dependent on cooperation than their European counterparts, either because their clout allows them to prevail internationally or because the American economy has enjoyed its longest period of sustained growth in decades. Finally, while liberalism remains a minority political movement in most European countries, its tenets form the basis of the American consensus—except for some marginal departures on both left and right.[79] The argument in favor of UN rule-making seems to contradict the American tradition of governmental nonintervention in the economy, and American business leaders have not paid enough attention to recent developments to notice the UN's change of tone on globalization and openness.

The fact remains, however, that as corporate leaders and UN staffers struggle to flesh out a wide range of multifaceted UN-business partnerships—the subject of chapter 3—the UN will require the support of the private sector to defend the new approach and convince the reluctant parties. If it is true that a mutual interest exists in favor of cooperation, business will have to overcome its guardedness and fight actively to prevent a reversal of this budding UN version of perestroika.

CHAPTER 3

First Steps

Good theories make good policies. This applies to the political analyst as policies and programs remain the inescapable tests of theoretical cohesion. It is even truer when working with corporate partners who expect action, results, and tangible benefits. The emerging UN-business partnership is therefore now facing the test of operationalization. As UN bodies grapple with the objectives and modalities of their collaboration with the private sector, they are relying on a set of guidelines in various stages of development and dating back, in some cases, to the creation of the UN. The first order of duty is to dust off the regulations inherited from 1946 and draft a new UN policy framed within the conceptual approach of the Global Compact and aimed at enabling rather than stifling cooperation.

This chapter is essentially descriptive. It begins with a review of the guidelines currently used by various UN agencies to steer their collaboration with the private sector. It then lists and describes a series of UN-business activities in four functional areas: policymaking; fund-raising; awareness and advocacy; and operations. These categories are themselves refined into subcategories, particularly in the operational realm. As will be seen, a number of partnerships—possibly the most successful and promising—cross over several, if not all, categories. UN collaboration with the private sector varies greatly among UN bodies. Such agencies as UNICEF have reached out to corporations since their inception. Others, having recently warmed up to the trend, are catching up rapidly. In final analysis, however, UN collaboration with the private sector is far more widespread and far-reaching than generally assumed, and it is fair to say that every UN organization is currently involved in multiform private sector partnerships. For that reason alone, the cases presented below cannot be exhaustive. They mean rather to illustrate and set the stage for an evaluative and normative review of collaboration in chapter 4.

I. Guidelines for Cooperation:
The Test of Time

When this book went to press, a Working Group on Operational Guidelines formed at UN Headquarters in New York was working on a new set of guidelines for UN-private sector collaboration, aimed at modernizing rules established in 1946 and providing a policy suited to the new objectives and the great variety of UN-business partnerships. By then, the recent experience of UN collaboration with business had already demonstrated the need for a clear definition of the objectives and modalities of partnerships as a prerequisite to their success. Lessons learned were already pointing to the failure of adjusting means to ambitions and engaging all relevant stakeholders as some of the prohibitive errors of the early days of UN-business partnering. Hence the decision to specify the aims and methods of partnerships in a set of common guidelines that could serve as reference manual and preparatory checklist in the early stages of partnership formulation.[1]

The working group's raw materials were a series of draft guidelines designed by each UN body independently of each other. One task therefore was to bring some unity to these policies without curtailing the plurality of forms of partnerships, nor stifling the creativity of each organization. The section below reviews the state of UN guidelines at the agency level prior to the adoption of a common policy in 2000.

Definition of the "Private Sector"

The first element of note to emerge from a cursory reading of UN guidelines on private sector collaboration is that the UN system has yet to agree on a common definition of what constitutes the "private sector." Several UN organizations have narrowed their definition to the activities of privately held, profit-making commercial entities. According to this view, the profit-making nature of corporations makes these actors fundamentally different from not-for-profit entities, even when the latter are private organizations relying on private funds that often engage in fund-raising. Some UN agencies such as UNDP, however, accept to include foundations and private nonprofit organizations in their definition of the private sector. Focusing on the nongovernmental nature of private sector actors, UNCTAD also acknowledges some overlap between corporations and NGOs, even if these two types of organizations maintain very different relations with their UN partners and indeed have at times rather opposite views of each other. Stressing that the rationale of profit creates a stark distinction between the corporate and the NGO worlds, UNICEF restricts its definition of the "private sector" to profit-making corporations. According to UNICEF, civil society is a "programmatic partner" of the organization, whereas at this stage corporations have not been relied upon to help define and implement UNICEF programs. Similarly, the World Bank applies the term "private sector" only to the business world.[2]

In agreement with the latter two organizations, the definition I have retained in this book applies to privately held commercial enterprises engaged in profit-making activities, be they in the manufacturing or service sector. The responsibility of a corporate CEO to increase the value of a corporation's share price and the net worth of its shareholders gives rise to a set of motivations and behaviors that differ fundamentally from those of NGO leaders. While it is true that the new imperative of corporate responsibility has altered the calculations of many a global corporation, it remains that these considerations enter the corporate planning process through the door of profit. Such novel business activities as reputation management and the adoption of voluntary regulations are always measured against a strict cost-benefit analysis. Moreover, the constant fluctuation of share prices and the velocity of global transactions impose a pace on corporate life that is unknown in the NGO world. The conditions under which corporations function translate into a result-orientation that gives UN collaboration with the private sector a unique character and poses a slew of cultural and attitudinal problems for civil society and governmental actors. More will be said on the matter in chapter 4.

What Is a Partnership?

Still more surprising than the lack of consensus on a definition of the private sector, UN guidelines offer no definition of the term "partnership," even as they dwell at length on the objectives and benefits of such agreements. Only the World Bank's guidelines provide the following definition. According to the World Bank, a partnership is:

> An agreement to work together, for common goals, with all parties committing resources (financial, technical, or personnel) to agreed activities, with a clear division of responsibilities and distinct accountabilities for achieving these goals.

The World Bank stresses that partnerships are multi-stakeholder activities involving government and civil society actors, which it clearly distinguishes from for-profit corporations. To succeed, partnerships must be transparent—they must provide equal access to information by all participants. Concerned with conflict-of-interest issues, the World Bank devotes two paragraphs to competition and unfair advantage. To ensure that partnerships do not lead to skewed competition and unfair advantages for a select few corporate partners, the World Bank insists that any corporation must enjoy the opportunity to present a partnership proposal to the Bank. Indeed, it encourages competition for partnerships among potential corporate partners. When, for example, the Bank and a corporate sponsor convene a meeting on an economic or development issue, competitors of the corporate sponsor must be invited. The Bank also includes a disclaimer in partnership agreements stating that such partnerships do not constitute an endorsement by the Bank of its corporate partners.

Two experts on the "partnership alchemy" and often-partners of the UN have proposed a well-thought-out definition that focuses on the key ingredients and the potential pitfalls of partnerships. They define a partnership as:

> *People and organizations from some combination of public, business, and civil constituencies who engage in voluntary, mutually beneficial, innovative relationships to address common social aims through combining their resources and competencies.*[3]

This statement is broader as it does not apply to the sole realm of UN-business partnerships. It stresses the importance, however, of three fundamental aspects of successful partnerships: their voluntary, noncoercive nature; the presence of mutual benefits; and the achievement of common goals. Mutuality of benefits and commonality of goals are requirements of so-called "win-win situations," without which any private-public partnership is meant to fail. One additional requirement of such agreements is the ability of each partner to claim credit for its contribution and for the joint production of the partnership's output, whatever its format. Recognition and reward for one's work are the unquestionable requirements of productivity and the most basic incentives to action. Because reward and credit facilitate the development of a "we-feeling" in the context of joint action with partners, they enable a team leader to enlist support for the partnership from within the ranks of his/her own organization.

Keeping these elements in mind, this author's own definition of a UN-business partnership reads as follows:

> *A UN-business partnership is a mutually beneficial agreement between one or more UN bodies and one or more corporate partners to work toward common objectives based on the comparative advantage of each, with a clear understanding of respective responsibilities and the expectation of due credit for every contribution.*

The Objectives of Partnerships

Because they differ in their mandates, all UN agencies do not aim toward similar objectives in their relations with corporate partners. UN bodies with policy or research mandates are likely to look to corporations for expertise, research capabilities, secondment of expert personnel, or simply an exchange of views. Operational agencies look at corporations as providers of goods and services or sources of management advice. Recent developments in UN-business partnerships, however, point to a great diversity of objectives, as even the most operational UN bodies have moved beyond the traditional consideration of procurement as the basis for UN relations with business. For the sake of description, partnerships can be ordered in four major categories: policy-related activities, awareness and advocacy, fund-raising, and operations. This division will often seem arbitrary, however, as the majority of partnerships straddle more than one area of collaboration.

Policy-Related Activities

Partnerships are often placed in a conceptual context, stressing policy and value expectations. The World Health Organization (WHO), for example, stresses that a "partnership should contribute to clear health gains" and "enhance WHO's role and image as the leading international public health authority." The World Bank's guidelines place partnerships within the context of globalization, which it sees as "a world in which the public sector can never determine development outcomes by itself." According to the Bank, a policy partnership aims "to improve the business environment, solve market failures or broker solutions to conflict, through different combinations of meetings, conferences, workshops, and training."

Policy-related activities include the joint convening of, or corporate participation in expert meetings; the publication of reports; the organization of expert panels on global economic issues or health problems; as well as the secondment of expert staff to advance the policy work of UN bodies. The latter has obvious operational implications when corporate staff actually works in UN offices; yet it also has policy ramifications.

The UN Conference on Trade and Development (UNCTAD) and the UN Development Program (UNDP) are the UN agencies that most regularly call upon business to coorganize or participate in meetings on economic issues. UNDP states that corporate relationships can add value by "involving significant stakeholders in a policy dialogue with local policymakers and public authorities." UNCTAD enters into partnerships with private sector entities to organize meetings, carry out research, and publish material as long as these activities "promote the objectives of and [are] relevant to the program of work of UNCTAD." UNCTAD cautions that an arrangement for exchange of information with a private entity "will not involve the formation of a formal association of a legal nature." When cosponsoring a meeting, seminar, conference, or training course with a private sector firm, UNCTAD insists on having control over the arrangements, including setting the agenda, the choice of speakers, the working languages, and the publication of the final report. Invitations to such meetings and conferences may be sent jointly by the cosponsor and UNCTAD.

Even as operational an organization as UNOPS has entered into a partnership agreement with a conference and trade show organizer to convene Aid & Trade 2000 in New York on behalf of the UN system. In signing this agreement, UNOPS demanded to retain control of the substance of the conference program, leaving all logistical arrangements to the trade show partner. This agreement was seen as fitting UNOPS's role as service provider to the UN system, the "service" consisting in this case of providing a forum for a high-level policy discussion of UN-business partnerships.

Conflict of interest issues can arise when a UN agency and a corporation jointly convene expert meetings, and UN bodies have given the matter some thought. WHO's guidelines, for example, allow exhibitions organized by corporations to be held at WHO meetings as long as the exhibition takes place in a separate room. To avoid conflict of interest, WHO does not cosponsor or jointly organize scientific meetings with pharmaceutical companies, although it accepts to participate in meetings cosponsored by pharmaceutical firms when the logistics of the meeting are subcontracted to a separate conference organizer.

Corporate support of policy work can take unexpected forms, however. Any corporation that transfers funds to the UN Population Fund (UNFPA) through UNFPA's foundation in the United States, for example, supports the organization's role in facilitating family planning techniques and programs around the world. That is particularly true of the UN Foundation, which allocates many of its project funds to UNFPA activities. Resource mobilization therefore has indirect policy implications as it funds and supports a myriad of UN policy mandates. UNICEF also engages in policy activities when it enlists business associations to co-sign statements against or help combat child labor and the sexual exploitation of children for commercial ends. Policy considerations entered the procurement process when UNICEF was the first UN body to exclude from bidding exercises any corporation having any relationship with a manufacturer or exporter of antipersonnel landmines and landmine components.

Finally, exchanges of expertise and technology and secondment of staff are two additional activities with policy implications. Virtually every UN body with a scientific mandate carries out its activities in partnership with corporations in its respective scientific or technological field. WHO, UNICEF, and UNFPA have long worked with pharmaceutical firms to develop products and procedures. While this type of activity is clearly operational, it has important policy implications, as it may alter the way in which these agencies approach their mandates and carry out their programs. Often, UN-business scientific collaboration entails the secondment of corporate staff to a UN body. In this case, a number of regulations have been adopted against conflict-of-interest situations. Corporate personnel seconded to WHO, for example, are exchanged for a fixed duration. Such personnel operate under WHO regulations and authority, must respect WHO confidentiality rules, and are precluded from receiving instructions from any outside entity—particularly the staff members' own employers.

Awareness and Advocacy

Aside from WHO's, few UN agency guidelines cite awareness, the improvement of an organization's image, or raising the profile of an organization with the public as separate objectives of partnerships. This is surprising when considering the number of UN-business partnerships that exhibit educational or advocacy goals or result in raising the profiles of specific issues as a by-product of partnership. Recent initiatives such as Netaid (see below) seem to be evolving naturally out of practice rather than resulting from deliberate plans. The reach of the Internet promises to increase advocacy and awareness campaigns by UN bodies on behalf of their substantive mandates. But such activities are not considered as conscious objectives of private sector collaboration.

Awareness and advocacy provide perfect illustrations of the difficulty of analyzing the objectives of partnerships along unidimensional criteria. They are embedded in and result from other activities such as fund-raising, policy projects, and joint operations. The thorny issue of corporate use of the UN name and logo has also made advocacy and awareness partnerships difficult to structure legally. The matter is dealt with at length below.

Fund-Raising

Most UN guidelines view fund-raising as a potential benefit of collaboration with the private sector. Fund-raising is also the type of activity that overlaps the most extensively with advocacy and awareness campaigns. Indeed, UN fund-raising is turning into a technique of advocacy rather than an end in itself. UN documents often refer to fund-raising as "resource mobilization." The expression is useful inasmuch as it includes in-kind donations and the acquisition of pro bono services or staff.

It is important to note at the outset that corporate fund-raising carried out by UN bodies is not meant to fund regular UN activities or to pay the salaries of the UN's own staff, be it permanent or of fixed duration. These budgetary lines are financed by the regular or extrabudgetary contributions of governments. Corporate fund-raising (or resource mobilization) is therefore aimed at financing specific projects in which corporate sponsors may play a role, and from which they usually expect to derive reputational benefits.

As the veteran of UN fund-raising, UNICEF has developed multiple partnerships supported by corporate sponsors. UNICEF's guidelines are remarkably open in considering fund-raising as a dominant objective of collaboration. UNICEF has ranked the scope of its corporate partnerships according to the level of corporate funding. UNICEF enters into an international alliance with any suitable corporation contributing $1 million to UNICEF. National or cross-border alliances must bring UNICEF $250,000 per annum per country (in the first case) or per territory straddling two or more borders (in the second case).

Concern over conflict of interest is prevalent in fund-raising activities. To limit such risk, WHO accepts contributions not earmarked to specific projects only if they cannot further the commercial interest of the donor. Financial support for travel of WHO staff to scientific meetings is accepted as long as other participants obtain identical privileges. In cases where WHO undertakes specific projects funded by corporate sponsors, it has established a separate set of guidelines to address conflict-of-interest issues (see below). With similar concerns in mind, UNCTAD has adopted the following rules: a contributor to an UNCTAD activity may not stipulate the conditions of use of the contribution; decide the planning and outcome of the activity; use the UNCTAD logo and name in a manner suggesting endorsement by UNCTAD; or influence UNCTAD's policies.

In-kind donations come accompanied by problems of their own, particularly when they involve medications and vaccines, of which UNICEF and WHO are the largest UN recipients. WHO requires donated medicines and vaccines to meet a number of criteria. Evidence of the efficacy and safety of a drug must be demonstrated before the product is donated to WHO. There must be "objective and justifiable criteria for the selection of recipient countries, communities, or patients." A supply system must be in place that guarantees the prevention of waste, theft, and leakage. A training and supervision program must also be available at field locations in the recipient country to ensure proper use and storage of the donated medicines. Drugs must not be donated for promotional purposes, and a phase-out plan for the donation must also be agreed upon with the recipient country.

Alone among UN bodies, UNOPS is precluded by its institutional status from receiving any funds from outside the UN system, including from the private sector. This apparent constraint can in fact turn into an advantage when UNOPS approaches private sector partners. The inability to engage in fund-raising immediately removes a measure of suspicion from partnership discussions. When considering the comparative advantage of a corporate partner, UNOPS cannot stress corporate wealth but focuses rather on expertise and technology. The current shift away from pure fund-raising partnerships to joint substantive activities, to which corporations contribute funds as well as less tangible assets, demonstrates that the rest of the UN system understands the need to give its corporate partners a more even-handed role in shaping the message and showing a reputable face to the world.

Operations

As was discussed above, operational activities may overlap with other categories of partnership objectives. Operational collaboration ranges from the joint implementation of projects to procurement, technical cooperation, the exchange of expertise and management techniques, and the secondment of staff. UN agencies with operational mandates are the most accustomed to working directly with business, usually in field projects, but also at headquarters in such areas as product development or information systems restructuring, to cite only two examples of operational collaboration. UNICEF, the World Food Program (WFP), and the UN High Commissioner for Refugees (UNHCR) have long relied on corporate donations and outsourcing of goods and services to intervene in humanitarian crises. WFP is the largest recipient of food commodities in the world, receiving annually approximately 3 million tons of food staples from governments and private sector companies. The Department of Peacekeeping Operations relies on the logistics of private contractors to deploy and maintain its peacekeeping missions. UNOPS has had more extensive outsourcing relationships with the private sector than any other UN body. As a result, its procurement regime can be seen as forming part of its operational manual for private sector collaboration. But even the most policy-focused among UN bodies are now developing operational types of partnerships with private sector firms. UNCTAD's guidelines, for example, state that the organization may enter into arrangements with corporations for the implementation of technical cooperation projects approved by a recipient country or an NGO. Specifically, "UNCTAD may take initiatives to establish Cooperation for Development Clusters to facilitate the financing and implementation of projects."

Possibly the result of the great diversity of UN operational mandates and operational modalities, UN guidelines remain very general on the operational objectives of UN-business partnerships—and this may be for the best. The sticking points of partnership agreements are not specific to operational activities but rather run across the spectrum of UN-business collaboration. These are reviewed below.

Selection Criteria

How to select corporate partners suitable to the UN's values and responsibilities has already emerged as the central issue in the elaboration of UN
guidelines on private sector collaboration. Among the categories of criteria
under discussion is the performance of individual corporations vs. sectoral
behavior. The Global Compact's approach favors the latter and a set of such
criteria could be derived from its nine principles. Indeed, the UN's internal
need to define selection criteria arises from value concerns. The UN must
ensure that the objectives of the UN Charter are compatible with those of
profit-making entities, and it must be ready to respond to criticism from
within its own ranks and civil society. Many UN agencies have drawn a list
of what they consider beyond the pale, and a general value consensus seems
to be emerging.

Most agencies (UNDP, UNCTAD, WHO, UNICEF, UNOPS) will not
enter into partnerships with tobacco companies and weapons manufacturers. Some, such as UNICEF and UNCTAD, will exclude corporations that
derive the bulk of their profits from the production or sale of alcoholic bev-
erages. WHO expects corporations to "follow WHO public health policies."
UNICEF will not associate with any corporation engaged in pornography.
Some agencies cite corporations linked to gambling, illegal financial transactions, and drug trafficking as unsuitable partners (UNDP, UNCTAD,
UNICEF).[4]

In recent years, resort to child labor and practices that threaten the environment have also been added to the list of unacceptable corporate behaviors (UNDP, UNICEF). In the area of labor practices, poor gender policies
as well as other forms of discrimination (racial, sexual, ethnic, etc.) are cited
by some UN agencies as strong considerations against the selection of a corporate partner (UNDP, UNCTAD).

A number of UN bodies, including UNDP and UNICEF as well as the
World Bank, provide their representatives with a checklist of items meant to
facilitate the selection of corporate partners. UNDP invites its resident representatives in the field to determine the acceptability of a partner based on
ethical and normative behaviors, the value of the potential partnership to
UNDP, and the capacity of a corporate candidate to carry out its end of the
bargain financially and technologically. Credit reports are run on potential
partners, a practice also followed by UNOPS as part of in-depth background
checks on companies.

The most thorough in the UN system and exhibiting a long-term experience with private sector collaboration, UNICEF's guidelines reflect a general concern for the ability of corporations to commit to UNICEF's "core
values." A corporate alliance must help UNICEF to "pursue its mandate to

advocate for the rights of children and women, and to helping meet their basic needs." Under the authority of the Private Sector Division, UNICEF's screening process is assisted by the services of ethical research agencies retained under UNICEF contracts. After filling out various forms that answer questions of concern to UNICEF, staff members submit requests for alliances to the Private Sector Division, which approves partnership proposals in agreement with UNICEF's executive director.

As leaders in their fields, desirable companies must have influence on the public, governments, or specific market sectors. They must be socially responsible and exhibit a history of philanthropy, community involvement, and commitment to the development of their employees. Their management style must be open and transparent. Preferred partners present a potential for functional alliances, of which media organizations and water distribution companies provide two examples. Additionally, UNICEF does not enter into partnerships with any manufacturer of breast milk substitutes. The latter point illustrates the difficulty of defining UN-wide selection criteria. While UNICEF considers breast milk substitutes as contradicting some of its policies, they surely do not endanger the lives of infants around the world and cannot be lumped together with landmines, tobacco, and child labor. UN selection criteria must therefore focus on a set of broad ethical values, but they cannot dictate the acceptability of every single corporation for 40 UN bodies with multiple mandates and differing objectives.

Use of the UN Name and Logo

Even more contentious than the issue of selection criteria, the use of the UN name and logo by corporations associated with the UN touches a sensitive nerve. Here too practices vary widely and the matter is not as complex, nor its solutions as elusive, as some would like to portray. The document regulating the use of the UN name and logo was adopted by the General Assembly in 1946 and has since never been formally revised. GA resolution 92(I) of December 7, 1946 recommends that governments take measures:

> *To prevent the use, without authorization by the Secretary-General of the United Nations, and in particular for commercial purposes by means of trade marks or commercial labels, of the emblem, the official seal and the name of the United Nations, and of that name through the use of initial letters.*

In its above form, the rule is rather innocuous, particularly as it gives the UN secretary-general ample leeway to determine actual practice. As always when confronting legal issues, however, the crux of the matter lies in the interpretation of the text. Charged with setting legal policies based on UN resolutions, the UN Office of Legal Affairs (OLA) has interpreted the 1946 rule to mean that "the use of the UN name and emblem, as well as any abbreviation thereof, is reserved for official purposes of the Organization; commercial use, as such, is prohibited." OLA has not defined "commercial use" but refers to *Black's Law Dictionary*, which defines the term "commercial" as "use in connection with or for furtherance of a profit-making enterprise."[5] In 1999, OLA advised to maintain the policy of "prohibiting commercial use of the UN name and emblem" without supplying a new definition of "commercial use."

If the UN were to follow *Black's* definition, use of the UN name and logo by a corporation would be precluded whether or not the corporation derived a commercial profit from such use. Moreover, under *Black's* assumption that a "commercial" relationship includes "connection with . . . a profit-making enterprise," the very principle of UN-business partnership could be threatened, as UN agencies that partner with corporations are obviously working "in connection" with them. As is not uncommon, UN jurisprudence has evolved far from the text and OLA's interpretation of it.

OLA's caution regarding use of the UN name and logo is based on the protection of these assets from all financial and other forms of liability under the Paris Convention for the Protection of Industrial Property. Loss of that privilege through a "privatization" of the UN name and logo, if the latter were used for commercial gain, would result in financial costs to the organization. These costs would result from the fact that, in order to protect its name, the UN would need to enter into national agreements in each country where such use by or in connection with a commercial entity were permitted. Moreover, the privatization of the name and logo would expose the UN to litigation risks like any private corporation.

In fact, early in UN history, use of the UN name was granted to nonprofit entities as long as such use did "not imply official connection with the United Nations." The United Nations Association and the Business Council for the United Nations were the early beneficiaries of this policy. In addition, these nonprofit organizations were allowed to use the UN logo in conjunction with their own name and activities. Indeed, their names and logos, which include the UN's own, are displayed on stationary and promotional material, some of which serve fund-raising purposes. At a minimum, these organizations therefore use the UN name and logo to raise the funds that enable them to remain in business.

Other departures from the official interpretation of the 1946 rule soon followed. In the past two decades, whenever the UN has dedicated a year to a special concern, a symbol incorporating some portions of the UN logo has been designed for advocacy, awareness, and fund-raising purposes.

Such logos were designed for the International Year of the Child in 1979 (for which UNICEF was lead agency), the International Year of Disabled Persons in 1981, the International Year of the Family in 1994, the International Year of Older Persons in 1999, and the UN's own anniversary in 1995. The following typical arrangement was established in each case. A secretariat was set up, usually linked to the lead agency for each International Year (IY). The secretariat could approve requests for use of the IY logo, including use for "commercial purposes." Alternatively, the secretariat established national committees in participating countries, the latter deciding in turn to grant use of the IY logo to commercial entities. Contracts signed between the users and the national committees included language that preserved the UN from liabilities and litigation risks. Most importantly, these contracts were signed between two private entities rather than between a private entity and the UN. The UN's assets were thereby protected.

A similar arrangement was retained for the UN's 50th anniversary in 1995. A special UN50 emblem was designed for exclusive use during 1995. Although UN texts stipulated that the emblem "should not be used in connection with commercial activity," the secretary-general himself granted use of the UN50 logo to a few global sponsors for fund-raising efforts aimed at supporting UN50 educational and communications activities. Use of the UN50 emblem for noncommercial purposes was also permitted in exchange for large donations. All use was subject to clearance by the UN 50 Secretariat. Linked by a formal agreement to the UN, a UN50 Foundation was established to receive tax exempt contributions from private donors approved by the UN. The practice has therefore evolved toward an understanding of "commercial use" implying direct profits from use of the UN logo by corporations or the sale by corporations of items bearing a UN logo. WHO's guidelines confirm this interpretation, stating: "No commercial company shall be authorized to use the WHO name for the marketing of its products." Along the same lines, UNCTAD affirms that the name and logo of UNCTAD "cannot be offered for use in exchange for a voluntary contribution" but may be used "to express support for the policies, aims and activities of the United Nations or UNCTAD."

UNICEF has stretched the limits of jurisprudence even further. It has openly set financial benchmarks for use of its logo by corporate sponsors associated with UNICEF activities. A contribution of $50,000 is expected for use of the UNICEF logo in conjunction with a national alliance. The benchmark reaches $100,000 for a cross-border alliance and $250,000 in the case of an international alliance. Alliances that permit use of the UNICEF name or logo are formalized through written partnership agreements, memoranda of understanding, or other legal documents. Such agreements preserve the privileges and immunities of the UN; establish a dispute resolution procedure through arbitration; require the corporate sponsor to acknowledge that use of the UNICEF logo does not permit use of the UN name and logo; and include warranties that neither the corporation nor any of its affiliates resort to child labor or are involved in the manufacture of landmines. Finally, UNICEF also reserves the right to license some of its registered trademarks, such as "Change for Good," for example.

The Recognition of Contributions

In contrast to the case reviewed above, there is no formal policy regulating the recognition of corporate donations by the UN. According to OLA, the publication of contributions is acceptable "if such action itself is consistent with the policies, aims and activities of the Organization." Such written acknowledgments should not, however, promote products or services nor solicit business activities. In practice, most UN agencies have adopted various formats for recognizing contributions while staving off the risks of commercial exploitation by corporate donors.

WHO, for example, acknowledges the contributions of donors in publications related to the activities for which corporate funding was obtained. While permitting the listing of such donations in corporate literature including annual reports, WHO's guidelines state that corporations "should not" seek commercial gain from the publication of their gifts. UNCTAD recognizes corporate donations in its own material and allows the publication of such donations by corporate donors themselves, but reserves the right to approve the language of public documents. UNDP also acknowledges corporate contributions "in an appropriate manner." Donors may announce their contributions through press releases, as long as such statements do not imply UNDP's endorsement of the activities and products of said corporations. Moreover, UNDP expects to review the texts of corporate announcements, as does UNOPS. Because it does not involve the use of the UN name and logo, the issue of recognizing corporate gifts in UN or donor publications is less charged than the former. When it does involve such use, the two issues merge, demonstrating that UN policy challenges lie with the use of the UN name and logo rather than the principle of recognition of corporate gifts.

Conflict of Interest

Although conflict of interest is on the minds of all UN officials working to establish UN-business partnerships, UN guidelines devote remarkably little attention to ways to solve the problem. Indeed, with the exception of WHO, hardly any UN agency addresses those concerns directly.

The sensitivity and real-life implications of WHO's health activities may explain the organization's awareness of conflict-of-interest issues. WHO must rely on pharmaceutical companies for help in product development, clinical trials, and in-kind donations—activities from which these corporations can derive real market advantages. To protect itself against conflict-of-interest situations, "the concerned WHO offices and departments must establish procedures which ensure that the establishment of norms and standards is based on science and evidence and not on commercial interests." Additionally, "any interaction with commercial enterprises must be audited and monitored."

WHO cautions against accepting funds from companies that have a direct interest in the outcome of a project. This is more easily said than done, however, and the oligopolistic nature of the pharmaceutical industry makes it difficult to cooperate with a corporation without creating a market advantage. When such direct interest cannot be avoided, as is often the case in clinical trials, WHO allows cooperation to go forth if it meets the following conditions. Collaboration between WHO and the corporate partner must serve the interest of public health. Moreover, research carried out in a particular clinical trial must be performed by WHO, and, it can be demonstrated that if this were not the case, the research would either not be undertaken or would be undertaken under internationally unacceptable scientific and ethical conditions. In such cases, it can be argued that WHO guarantees the integrity of clinical trials.

In the case of joint product development between WHO and a corporation, an agreement stipulates that the jointly developed product will be made widely available, including at preferential prices in developing countries. Once a corporation has agreed to such conditions, WHO accepts to receive funding to support a clinical trial, the rationale being that the public benefits derived from the activity outweigh the risks associated with or the potential damage arising from a conflict-of-interest situation. When a corporation works toward developing a product in conformity with WHO specifications, WHO accepts to provide technical assistance as long as other companies having an interest in the product "have been invited to collaborate with WHO in the same way."

Solutions to conflict-of-interest issues lie in open disclosure, transparency, and competition. Because the UN is a political organization, transparency is not embedded in its culture, which may account in part for its anxiety toward conflict of interest alongside the surprising absence of guidelines to address it. Expertise to solve such matters is available, however, and in this area corporations may be able to contribute their skills and experience to their UN partners.

II. UN-Business Parnerships:
An Illustrative Review

As stated earlier, the following provides a selective, yet representative, review of UN-business partnerships in the four areas of policymaking activities, fund-raising, advocacy, and operations. The purpose of these examples is to inform the reader on the format and extent of collaboration between UN bodies and corporations and provide the raw ingredients of the evaluative analysis presented in chapter 4.[6]

Policymaking and Related Activities

UN-business collaboration to define the norms and rules of the global economic and political system of the twenty-first century has barely begun. It is at once the most important, promising, and potentially difficult area of collaboration. While such cooperation is essential to construct a framework suited to the new world, and while recent exchanges between the UN and the business community show signs of a strong mutual interest in this enterprise, the road ahead is paved with political hurdles, psychological roadblocks, and cultural chasms. No matter, the parties are plowing ahead, animated as they are by a sense of urgency and mission at a time of historical transition. Initiatives in this area are limited to few UN bodies, as the majority of them continue to devote their resources to operational activities. They involve the secretary-general's office, the International Organization of Labor (ILO), the UN Conference on Trade and Development (UNCTAD), the UN High Commissioner for Human Rights (UNCHR), and the UN Environment Program (UNEP).

Policymaking at UN Headquarters

The ICC remains the UN's leading policy partner, both because of the global representativeness of its corporations and the significance of the statements it has codefined and signed with the United Nations since 1998. As they were amply quoted in the two preceding chapters, excerpts from these statements will not be reiterated here. Suffice it to recall that the objective of these policy declarations has been to call for a UN role in setting the necessary norms and rules of the global system within the framework of the Global Compact, and to support the process of globalization and open trade inasmuch as it is accompanied by UN normative functions. These policy statements therefore point to a mutual under-standing of both the opportunities and the threats inherent in globaliza-tion and a common interest in addressing the latter together. While an international business organization and an intergovernmental organization retain separate mandates and responsibilities to their members, the UN and the ICC have chosen to focus on their common concerns and strengths as a basis for cooperation. Conceptually, their approach rests on the three pillars of political liberalism, including the link between eco-nomic openness and political stability, the presence of absolute gains to ac-crue from cooperation, and the more largely debated link between democratic regimes and peace.[7]

As of this writing, no other organization has demonstrated the capacity to complement and enhance the policy work of the ICC on behalf of the UN and more generally to support the role of multilateralism in a global world. While the quality of the ICC's thinking is difficult to match, the support of other policy organizations would only strengthen the case of multilateral institutions in ongoing foreign policy debates around the world.

The Follow-Up to the Global Compact

Efforts to promote the Global Compact and translate it into action began in earnest in the summer of 1999. The UN posted the Global Compact's nine principles on a specially designed website, accessible from the business side of the UN's home page.[8]

Early on, the London-based Prince of Wales Business Leaders Forum of-fered its assistance in reaching out to its corporate members and inviting them to adopt its recommended good practices. Relying on its long experi-ence in brokering partnerships between public and private sector actors, the PWBLF proposed to:

1. Help "interpret" the Compact for the benefit of corporations;
2. "Identify and communicate useful examples of good practice" as il-lustrations of potential corporate actions aimed at implementing the values of the Compact;
3. Help broker cross-sectoral partnerships involving corporations, UN agencies, and civil society;
4. Facilitate increased exchange of knowledge and skills between UN and corporate partners relying on the comparative advantages of both; and
5. "Create a learning network" to ensure a dynamic implementation process by drawing lessons from the evolving UN-business relationship.

The PWBLF has outlined four conditions favorable to the success of cross-sectoral partnerships. These include:

1. The presence of a common agenda between partners;
2. The development of skills in partnership methodology and management;
3. The existence of a transparent dialogue between partners that values the respective capacities and motivations of each; and
4. A shared commitment to the enterprise.[9]

In November 1999, the ICC also joined the implementation effort by dedicating a portion of its website to documenting the good practices of international corporations in the areas of human rights, labor rights, and environmental responsibility. Working jointly with the secretary-general's office, the ICC has called for written contributions from socially responsible firms, and offered reciprocal links between the Global Compact section of its website and the sites of the corporate participants. The initiative signals the beginning of a voluntary normative effort on the part of business through the establishment of a database of good practices.

The same month, the president of the Geneva-based International Organization of Employers (IOE) sent a letter to the association's members seeking their support and asking for their views on the Global Compact. Inviting members to write to ILO Director-General Juan Somavia to document actions taken on behalf of labor rights and good practices, he suggested that corporations not only "support the broad thrust of the Global Compact" but also "give some practical examples of initiatives in which your organization and/or its members are involved."[10] A rejoinder issued by the IOE secretary-general in December 1999 stated: "The downsizing of the state has not only meant more influence in society for the private sector, but also more of a presence and involvement in global issues. The Global Compact provides us with an opportunity to tell the world that employers are capable of meeting the challenges of the modern economy in a way which accommodates the fundamental expectations of society. . . . It is our belief that it is in the best interests of employers that they embrace the concept [of the Compact] as part of the process of globalization."[11]

In December 1999, the World Business Council for Sustainable Development began to campaign on behalf of the Global Compact by organizing and facilitating a meeting in London between the United Nations and 24 high-tech and global corporations, such as Total, Shell, Ericsson, Novell, and Microsoft. A meeting between the secretary-general and the International Confederation of Trade Unions also took place at UN Headquarters in January 2000. In the wake of the WTO meeting, the gathering aimed to invite trade unions to see in the Compact a positive approach to their social concerns, and enlist their constructive support in getting corporations to adopt the Compact's nine good practices.

Following a seminar held at Tallberg (Sweden) in 1998 where corporate CEOs and UN officials discussed ways to include human rights in corporate plans and publications, the office of the UN High Commissioner for Human Rights is pursuing discussions with corporate responsibility groups and corporations to enlist their support on behalf of human rights. In November 1999, UN High Commissioner for Human Rights Mary Robinson addressed the annual conference of Business for Social Responsibility (BSR), an American business NGO that supports such initiatives. Her office and BSR were considering an original proposal for the creation of a human rights award to be bestowed annually on a forward-thinking and well-behaved corporation, accompanied by a prize to be distributed by participating corporations to human rights NGOs to help fund their work.

Keeping with the spirit of the Global Compact, the International Labor Organization (ILO) also devoted its 1999 Enterprise Forum to issues of corporate responsibility in relation to labor rights, and was expected to focus on this topic again at its annual conference in May 2000. Collaborating with PWBLF and the UN Staff College, the ILO is also involved in the design of a course on private sector partnerships to be disseminated to UN staff members engaged in this new type of UN activity.

At UNCTAD

UNCTAD offers various ad hoc forums for the discussion of an array of economic issues that have a bearing, and provide opportunities for, UN-business collaboration. Written with the input of business, academia, trade unions, and consumer groups, UNCTAD's annual *World Investment Report* is a reference on investment trends and flows. The 541-page 1999 edition made a substantial contribution to the definition and quantification of globalization and echoed the UN secretary-general's call for "a global compact of corporate responsibility."[12] While recent UNCTAD statements, as well as the report, exude a lukewarm attitude toward the overall benefits of openness, the organization remains engaged in a positive discussion with multinationals on the inclusion of the poorest developing countries in the process of globalization and FDI allocations.[13]

UNCTAD also convenes and invites corporations to ad hoc expert meetings on various technical issues dealing with trade, transportation, insurance, and accounting standards, among other topics. The largest international accounting firms belong to UNCTAD's Group of Experts on International Standards of Accounting, and provide technical support on accounting training in economies in transition. None of these forums, however, has become institutionalized, and the private sector has no standing membership in any of UNCTAD's divisions, committees, or expert groups.

At the invitation of the UN secretary-general's office, UNCTAD and the ICC have also embarked on a project to encourage investment in Africa, traditionally a poor recipient of FDI. The project, which has both policy and operational implications, was launched in July 1999 with the release of UNCTAD's Foreign Direct Investment Guide in Africa and a factsheet on investment in Ethiopia jointly produced by the ICC, UNCTAD, and PriceWaterhouseCoopers. The publications showed that contrary to common assumptions, returns on FDI in African countries have been high and that Africa as a whole is suffering from a stereotype of instability fostered by ethnic conflicts in a limited number of countries. A statement sounding like an advertising campaign and signed by the senior executives of such firms as Coca-Cola, Citibank, and Marubeni told prospective investors not to "miss out on Africa" as their "competitor may well be there already."[14] A month earlier, UNCTAD and UNDP had sponsored a workshop in South Africa aimed at strengthening the skills of the least developed countries in trade negotiations "so that they can more effectively participate in the WTO's Third Ministerial Conference" (November 1999). Taught by trade advisors from UN agencies and private sector firms, the workshop exemplified the shift of UN activities from implementation to training aimed at increasing the benefits of openness to the developing countries. Reflecting the new form of partnership between business and UN agencies, this activity was not structured around the exchange of goods or services but premised on supporting common goals and cooperating in achieving them. Finally, although it began as a policy initiative, the follow-up to the UNCTAD Partners for Development conference is discussed under "Operational Activities" below.

At UNDP

Issued annually, UNDP's *Human Development Report* provides comprehensive data on the state of development and poverty in the world. Proposing an alternative to the quantitative definition of development seen as being favored by the World Bank, UNDP has developed a Human Development Index based on such qualitative measures of progress as education, health, and access to clean water. Although politically more sensitive, human rights and good governance criteria are being defined for inclusion in the Human Development Index.

The 1999 *Human Development Report* sparked an immediate controversy when it advocated a global tax on Internet access to fund poverty reduction programs. The outcry over the proposal forced the newly appointed administrator of UNDP Mark Malloch Brown into immediate crisis management aimed at dissociating UNDP from the "independent" authors of the report.[15]

UNDP's Bureau for Development Policy attempts to remain on the crest of the policy wave by issuing regular publications on topics related to growth and development. In 1999 it made an original contribution to the contemporary debate on development policy with the publication of *Global Public Goods,* a book that recommends shifting the work of aid organizations from its project approach to the provision of such international public goods as health, peace, and environmental cleanup and protection.

Examples of UNDP policy initiatives that also bear operational implications include the Money Matters Institute, a UNDP think tank supported by private banks and financial institutions aimed at turning the least developed countries into emerging markets by attracting private foreign investment. The Public-Private Forum, another initiative cofunded by Yale University and Citicorp, promotes the exchange of information on best practices in public-private sector cooperation worldwide. The forum offers a newsletter, a website, a reference library of key articles, and other publications. Also in collaboration with Yale University and Citicorp, UNDP's Public-Private Partnership (PPP) Program carries out research with faculty, students, and others on best practices resulting from the collaborative work of public and private institutions in the specific area of urban environmental problems. The PPP has set up a Global Learning Center at Yale to help developing countries get access to state-of-the-art information on good environmental practice. Finally, with the collaboration of AT&T, British Petroleum, the Ford Foundation, and Interface, UNDP has launched a research program to investigate the feasibility of issuing tradable pollution permits. The list is again not exhaustive, but it illustrates the corporate contribution to UN policy activities, as well as the policy and advocacy aspects of many an operational project.

Fund-Raising

As was stated, although it may be the oldest form of collaboration, fund-raising does not constitute the UN's main interest in partnering with the private sector. Under this heading are included a wide array of activities, such as sponsorships, cash grants, in-kind donations, matched giving, and point-of-sale activity. In addition, this section describes the follow-up to the largest grant ever made to the United Nations: a $1 billion gift to be disbursed over ten years made by Time Warner Vice-Chairman and CNN founder Ted Turner in September 1997.

Traditional Fund-Raising Activities

The UN's own involvement in corporate fund-raising began in earnest with the preparations of the UN 50th anniversary in 1995. An exceptional interpretation of the 1946 rule (discussed above) was agreed upon to allow use of the UN name and logo by corporate donors. According to the UN Department of Public Information, over $8 million was raised from various foundations and firms authorized to use the UN 50th anniversary logo on products and direct mail marketing pieces. Sponsors included the Korean firm Gold Star and Swiss Corp. for Microelectronics, as well as several lesser-known private foundations.

UNICEF, however, had long pointed the way in fund-raising activities. To facilitate the acceptance of tax-exempt private funds, UNICEF has set up local committees in 37 countries. The U.S. Committee for UNICEF transferred $146 million to UNICEF for the biennium 1998–99.[16] In November 1999, the U.S. Committee secured for UNICEF its largest private contribution ever—a gift of $26 million made by the Gates Foundation for the eradication of neonatal tetanus worldwide. Each committee works independently and is subject to local financial and tax regulations. UNICEF's "Change for Good" program, under which passengers on certain airlines are invited to put their loose change in UNICEF envelopes and hand them in to flight attendants, has added $18 million to the Fund's coffers since the inception of the program in 1987. "Check Out for Children," another fund-raising initiative supported by 154 Sheraton Hotels worldwide, invites hotel guests to donate $1 toward UNICEF programs at checkout time. An initiative of the U.S. Committee for UNICEF, "Trick or Treat for UNICEF" is cofinanced by Warner Brothers, Turner Network TV, and Coinstar. It raised $3 million in 1998 through the distribution of orange buckets for children trick-or-treating, paid for by the corporate sponsors. UNICEF's greeting cards operation dates back to 1949. As UNICEF is the sole beneficiary of card sale receipts, the use of the UNICEF logo on these cards is deemed to serve "official" as opposed to commercial purposes.

Following UNICEF's lead, UNHCR has also stepped up its fund-raising activities, now the responsibility of its Public Affairs Unit. UNHCR has established a group of "Friends of UNHCR" in Geneva and a U.S. Association for UNHCR in Washington, both authorized to receive private donations. UNHCR also receives in-kind or cash donations on an ad hoc basis. A gift of $430,000 made by U.S. oil company UNOCAL in 1997 to support UNHCR's shelter project in Azerbaijan and a gift of $200,000 by U.K.-based Glaxo-Wellcome for the construction of health centers in Rwanda in 1997–98 are only two examples of such donations.

Similar moves were made by UNFPA in 1999 when the agency established a U.S. Committee for UNFPA, a not-for-profit organization that advocates U.S. funding of UNFPA and facilitates the collection of corporate and private contributions. In an effort to give its campaign a public face, UNFPA has named Time Warner Vice-Chairman Ted Turner and Jane Fonda its "Goodwill Ambassadors."

WFP established its own not-for-profit organization in the United States in 1995 under the name "U.S. Friends of WFP." The American tax-exempt status of that organization allows WFP to collect and acknowledge the donations it receives from private sources, as well as list the donors in the U.S. Friends of WFP's Annual Report. WFP is trying to set up a similar system in Japan, although the legal environment makes it more difficult to obtain tax-exempt status. The agency is also examining ways to earmark private funds for specific activities, such as landmine or regional programs. Examples of ad hoc gifts include an in-kind donation of fortified soy milk valued at $1 million, made by U.S. food giant Archer Daniels Midland in 1997 to support WFP's relief work in North Korea. WFP acknowledged the donation through a press release, the circulation of pictures documenting the use of the gift, the distribution of press clippings on the gift, and a follow-up report. WFP's use of the Internet for both fund-raising and advocacy purposes is discussed below.

Established in 1995 with five UN parents and a small budget, the UN program against AIDS has had to display creativity to secure the resources necessary to publicize its message. UNAIDS's brochure on private sector partnerships is rich in examples of corporate philanthropy.[17] Many of these contributions did not go directly to UNAIDS but to its implementation partners, exemplifying UNAIDS's role as a catalyst for global action on AIDS. Examples include:

- A cash grant of $16,000 made by Levi Strauss to a Brazilian research center for an AIDS awareness program in Sao Paulo;
- The sponsorship of California AIDS Ride, a bike ride between major cities, by the U.S. subsidiary of United Distillers, exporters of Tanqueray Gin to the U.S.;
- The distribution by Chevron in Angola of disposable syringes to limit the spread of HIV in communities close to production and refining facilities;
- The donation by Apple Computers of $1 million worth of computers to HIV-AIDS agencies in the U.S.;
- The donation of advertising time and services by Levi Strauss and Coca-Cola;

Stores of the U.K.-based Body Shop have sold AIDS ribbons and placed collecting tins by their cash registers to encourage AIDS donations by the general public.

Most UN agencies benefit from in-kind and cash donations. WHO and other health and humanitarian agencies rely on donations of vaccines in emergencies. Donors include the largest pharmaceutical companies around the world, such as SmithKline Beecham. In 1992, UNDP received V-SAT equipment valued at $1.5 million to establish the first satellite-based communication network in the former Soviet Union. In 1996, UNDP estimated the total private funding it had received at above $3 million, to which must be added computer equipment and software valued at $1.7 million donated by Hewlett-Packard to initiate a networking program on sustainable human development. The company also provided training to equip field staff with the skills necessary to use and support the equipment. UNEP has received equipment and systems from IBM for the construction of an environmental information network.

Following Up on Ted Turner's Gift

The largest gift ever made to the United Nations, a $1 billion donation made by Ted Turner in 1997, is likely to remain unique in UN history. The donation was motivated by Ted Turner's belief that in a world that is slowly shrinking to a "single global neighborhood," the "UN alone provides the machinery to help find solutions to international challenges, and to deal with pressing concerns facing people everywhere." [18] The support of the UN is premised on the need for greater international cooperation, as well as tighter and more numerous partnerships between the UN, civil society, and the private sector—an objective strongly supported by the donor. The gift itself was made in the form of Time Warner stock, the number of which is capped at 18 million shares whatever their dollar value over the course of the gift. The gift is being disbursed in ten annual installments of $100 million each. When he made his gift, Ted Turner "promised" to raise awareness of the UN funding crisis among other senior international business leaders and encourage them to follow his example.

As guardian of the gift, the UN Foundation was established by Ted Turner to set programmatic priorities and allocate money to UN projects and agencies, support the United Nations and its causes, tell the story of the UN, and help raise additional funds for UN programs and purposes. Headquartered in Washington D.C., the UN Foundation is headed by Timothy Wirth (former U.S. environment secretary in the Clinton administration) and a board of directors of eight prominent international leaders including Ted Turner and former U.S. Representative to the UN and Atlanta mayor Andrew Young. The foundation's sister organization, the Better World Fund, is charged with educating the public about the United Nations, supporting its funding, and arguing for the UN's role in "addressing global issues and forging international cooperation." Its Better World Campaign is a multifaceted education and advocacy effort aimed at all constituencies, including the U.S. Congress and the business community.

The foundation receives grant proposals through the UN Fund for International Partnerships (UNFIP)—a department of the UN Secretariat over which UN Deputy Secretary-General Louise Fréchette wields final authority. As the foundation does not accept unsolicited proposals, UNFIP provides a screening mechanism for directing to the foundation the UN projects that best meet the foundation's criteria. At this stage, the foundation has set the following four areas of programmatic priority:

- Women and population, with a special focus on empowering women in developing countries and providing adolescent girls with good reproductive health services;
- Children's health, including supporting the implementation of the action plan of the World Summit for Children and the Convention on the Rights of the Child;
- The environment, with particular attention to climate change and biodiversity issues; and
- Humanitarian causes, which overlaps with human rights initiatives and focuses on the prevention of conflict as well as its effects (landmines, for example).

Selected recipients of UN Foundation grants are listed below for illustrative purposes:

- Women and Population Grants: UNFPA and UNHCR have received a three-year grant of almost $6 million to strengthen reproductive health services in communities in crisis. UNDP was granted $300,000 for a program to eradicate female genital mutilation in Kenya. UNICEF and UNFPA are recipients of a $3 million, 4-year grant to increase bilingual literary (Quechua-Spanish) for reproductive health in Bolivia;
- Environment Grants: UNESCO has received a $4 million grant to address invasive species in the Galapagos. FAO has received $500,000 to produce a UN Atlas of the Oceans. UNCTAD's plan to launch a plurilateral greenhouse gas emissions trading system is funded by a $1.25 million grant over a two-year period;

- Humanitarian Causes: a number of landmine-related projects have been funded, including the production of a landmine safety handbook and training activities ($440,000 to DPKO and UNDP) and a priority-setting program for mine clearance ($3.8 million to UNDP). UNICEF has received $1.1 million to assist the demobilization of child soldiers in Sierra Leone; and
- Children's Health: the foundation earmarked $1.5 million to WHO for a two-year media project promoting "A Tobacco Free World." UNICEF will receive over $3 million for the eradication of polio in African war-afflicted countries. And UNAIDS was granted $1.9 million for a three-year program aimed at slowing the spread of AIDS among African youth.

The UN Foundation-UNFIP mechanism remains a unique example of UN-private sector collaboration based on philanthropy. It is evident from this brief review, however, that philanthropic partnerships quickly acquire policymaking as well as operational characteristics. In setting funding priorities, the UN Foundation plays an indirect policy role by assigning salience to specific UN mandates. The foundation's grants must also be turned into effective projects, which presents the UN recipients and UNFIP with the challenges of operationalization, monitoring, and evaluation. The analysis of the Turner gift therefore demonstrates that it is difficult to categorize UN-business partnerships under a single objective as many, and indeed the most successful ones, have multifaceted impacts.

Awareness and Advocacy

UN fund-raising activities are often linked to awareness and advocacy campaigns aimed at supporting UN causes such as the reduction of poverty, environmental responsibility, and humanitarian assistance. Indeed, UN agencies have slowly but surely understood that fund-raising efforts linked to a specific issue and delivered through a powerful media campaign are the most successful. This approach also has the merit of advancing various UN mandates, thereby making a substantive contribution to UN-business collaboration beyond the short-term objective of raising money. Because these awareness and advocacy campaigns can run the entire gamut of UN issues, it is more useful to describe them according to modes of delivery.

The Traditional Media

A few UN agencies resort to advertising and awareness campaigns through the press and television. The attention given to UN issues by the broadcasting media is also a form of free advertising and advocacy for the UN.

UNHCR demonstrated the power of advertising during the Kosovo crisis when it published in the *New York Times* in the spring of 1999 a striking two-page advertisement displaying a large blood mark on a white
background along with the logos of UNHCR and United Colors of Benet-
ton.[19] The ad called for donations to be made to the UNHCR American
office on behalf of the Kosovar refugees. Following the launch of the Netaid website (see below), UNDP and CISCO also released a full-page ad on
November 1, 1999 in the *New York Times* to invite the general public to
visit the sight and fight poverty through donations. The ad bore the logos
of both organizations. Using the medium of television, UNESCO has
signed contractual agreements with broadcasting companies to produce
such promotional films as Treasures of the World, which educate the public about World Heritage sites. Private-sector publishers also collaborate
with UNESCO to produce such materials as a 12-volume encyclopedia on
the World Heritage.

Television programs focusing on the UN are few and far between. Available on CNN International, CNN's *Diplomatic License* is a weekly program
that reviews the UN's most salient political stories of the week. Its off-peak
broadcasting time slots, however, prevent the program from reaching many
viewers. Overall, CNN remains the most engaged media organization on behalf of UN issues, which are woven into such programs as the *CNN World
Report* and benefit from special features on peacekeeping or other themes.
The UN's own TV program, *The UN Chronicle,* is also broadcast on selected
international channels with relatively low viewership.

The Worldwide Web: The New Favorite Medium

The web is a dream come true for advertisers and advocates of all stripes, and
its unlimited possibilities have not escaped UN agencies. Indeed, the UN
business website has greatly facilitated the UN's outreach to the business
community and remains a virtual meeting place for UN agencies and their
corporate partners.

Of all recent UN website initiatives, the launch of Netaid by UNDP
and CISCO Systems in the fall of 1999 is clearly the most ambitious.
Seeking to raise awareness of and funds for the elimination of utter
poverty, Netaid was launched on September 8, 1999 with President Clinton, U.K. Prime Minister Tony Blair, and former South African President
Nelson Mandela as its first users. Three rock concerts concurrently held in
the United States, the United Kingdom, and Switzerland on October 9
subsequently aimed to raise the interest of Generation X advocates and
their baby-boomer parents. The first objective of Netaid is indeed to facilitate advocacy and raise awareness of the plight of the poorest people in

the world. Relying on the Internet enables UNDP to reach an unprecedented number of people around the world, as well as to cast the image of a reformed, "information technology-savvy, less risk averse UNDP" that can broker partnerships with recognizable and cutting-edge businesses.[20] The website, of course, is also a fund-raising mechanism, and it remains to be seen how the monies will be translated into UNDP field projects that impact people in the least developed countries. In the spring of 2000, Netaid began raising money for specific projects via its website, focusing on the plight of refugee communities in Rwanda among other target groups. While highly publicized by both CNN and Time, these initiatives were too recent at press time for conclusions to be drawn as to their efficacy. Lastly, Netaid has policy implications as UNDP seeks to make it one of the world's most authoritative sources of information on poverty and development policies, as well as a forum for reinvigorating the North-South dialogue on these issues. Netaid therefore embodies the four objectives of UN-private sector partnerships: policy, fund-raising, advocacy and awareness, and ultimately operations—even if the evaluation of actual projects will require some time.

Although of lesser media appeal, the Hunger Site constitutes another web-based initiative developed by a non-UN entity but benefiting WFP.[21] Aimed at raising money for humanitarian food relief, the site also provides statistics and information on the situation of hunger around the world and seeks to sensitize the public to the plight of the hungry. Visitors are invited to make donations online and the proceeds of donations go to WFP. It is unclear at this stage what level of response the Hunger Site will elicit, as advocacy initiatives are highly dependent on the intensity and quality of media campaigns to strike a cord in the public. The quality of the Hunger Site in no way compares with that of Netaid, and its launch did not receive wide press coverage. It remains that use of the Internet as a means of enlisting private actors behind various UN agendas is likely to increase.

Organizations that are not official members of the UN family yet work on its behalf are also developing advocacy websites aimed at raising both consciousness and money. UNA-USA's landmine website provides an example of such a double objective on behalf of UN demining programs. Its Adopt-a-Minefield program raises money from the public, which it then turns to UN agencies engaged in mine clearance, retaining for itself an administrative overhead fee. The program pairs donating communities around the world with the recipients of the funds and organizes visits by sponsoring communities to beneficiaries of UN demining activities. The site also supports and advocates ratification of the landmine ban by nations that did not sign the Ottawa treaty in December 1997.

Advocacy Statements and Awards

Other advocacy initiatives, no less successful and critical to the UN, are not linked to fund-raising activities but seek rather to promote the adoption of standards through statements and the sheer power of moral persuasion. The granting of awards is also a means of rewarding those corporate partners that advocate UN values and goals. Testimony to the central importance of child labor issues within the context of the UN's normative activities, in 1997 the ILO and UNICEF signed with the Pakistani Chamber of Commerce and Industry an agreement aimed at eliminating child labor. While such declarations are unlikely to result in immediate changes, they are important to officially enlist business organizations behind the UN's normative objectives. Such declarations also bear a policymaking aspect, as they advance the goals of the Global Compact in the specific area of labor rights.

UNEP's work with the banking and insurance industries on behalf of environmental standards dates back to 1992. UNEP has obtained the signature of 100 banks in 25 countries to its Statement on Banks and the Environment. Similarly 71 insurance companies in 25 countries have signed on to the UNEP Statement of Environmental Commitment for the Insurance Industry, launched in 1995. On the advocacy level, these statements acknowledge the principle of sustainable development and include commitments to increasing environmental management. They also contain a normative dimension as corporate signatories commit to adopting "best practices in such core areas as credit risk management, energy efficiency, and environmental impact assessment."[22] The interest of the banking and insurance industries in promoting such standards stems directly from the financial risks they incur in environmental damage and disasters caused by their corporate clients. Under another advocacy project entitled Tierramerica, a number of Latin American corporations and press organizations sponsor a pro-environment newspaper supplement in exchange for publicity and logo recognition in the paper. These partnerships also have operational characteristics, as will be seen below.

Recognizing the power of charismatic historical leaders as advocates of global agendas, UNAIDS has established a Global Business Council on HIV-AIDS under the chairmanship of U.K.-based Glaxo-Wellcome and the honorary presidency of Nelson Mandela.[23] The council gathers a diverse group of international corporations involved in advocacy and partnership programs on HIV-AIDS. The participating corporations exchange views based on their respective corporate experiences and their CEOs offer advice at the highest level on how to cope with the pandemic. President Mandela has spoken on behalf of the council at the Davos World Economic Forum. In 1998, the council bestowed its first Award for Business Excellence, which reflects the quality and efficacy of a corporation's response to the challenge of AIDS. The 1998 winner was South Africa-based Eskom, an electricity generating company that has adopted internal proactive information and education programs toward HIV-AIDS but also acts as an opinion leader on this issue in South Africa.

In the same vein, UNESCO has established the Helena Rubinstein Award for Women in Science with the support of cosmetics firm L'Oréal/Helena Rubinstein to promote the role of women in science and technology and engage in joint activities toward this objective. In 1995 and 1996, Euro-Disney cosponsored with UNESCO two Children's Summits aimed at sensitizing children and their parents to the imperative of environmental protection.

Operational Activities

The realm of operational partnerships between UN and business organizations is multifaceted and quasi-unlimited. As has already been shown above, many policy and advocacy initiatives have operational implications, and vice versa. Operational partnerships do differ from the examples described above in two significant ways. They imply actual joint implementation of projects between UN and corporate partners. And they involve such concrete business activities as the procurement of goods and services, the recruitment and secondment of staff, financial transactions, the sharing of expertise and skills, and many others that come with the territory of working together. As a result, operational activities tend to be physically observable and palpable sooner than, say, advocacy or policy initiatives. It is important to note that the term "joint venture" has not been retained below. While the term can be heard in UN circles, it is used loosely to refer to the joint production of outputs. In the business world, however, a joint venture implies shared investment responsibilities and shared profits between partners. Inasmuch as no UN agency has entered into a profit-sharing arrangement with a corporation to date, it seems preferable to eschew the term "joint venture" so as not to confuse the business reader.

The list of examples cited below is once again illustrative. Many of these initiatives are described on the UN's business website, as well as on the websites of the respective UN agencies. Published by The Prince of Wales Business Leaders Forum, *Business as Partners in Development* describes 150 case studies of international public-private partnerships in the field of development, although not all involve UN organizations. The discussion below has retained the objectives of operational partnerships as the main criteria for separating and analyzing various UN-business activities. It will be readily apparent that such separations are not airtight and that overlapping objectives are common.

Knowledge-Based Partnerships

Most UN agencies rely on corporate input to gain knowledge, technology, and skills. The contribution of a management consulting firm to solving the challenges facing the Department of Peacekeeping Operations in the early 1990s (mentioned in chapter 1) provides a perfect example of exchange of knowledge and methodology between a corporation and the UN. Such partnerships aim not only at increasing capacity within the UN but also at transferring knowledge and skills to developing countries. They thereby fall within the increasingly favored approach to development policy that seeks to help developing countries acquire the mechanisms of development through the transfer of knowledge, as opposed to increasing their dependence through actual UN implementation of projects.

Among UN health organizations, WHO has a long-standing and far-reaching experience of cooperation with virtually all international pharmaceutical companies. Under its Expanded Program on Immunization, WHO works with the world's largest producers of vaccines in the elaboration of vaccines and delivery supplies. WHO also receives private funding to carry out some of these immunization activities ($20 million was received from Rotary International in 1996–97). Collaboration with pharmaceutical firms in the area of tropical diseases has resulted in the development of successful tools to control the appearance and spread of some of these diseases.

UNEP has also collaborated with such organizations as IBM and the European Space Agency to develop information systems in such areas as geographical analysis, environmental data acquisition and dissemination, and the creation of a global communications network for UNEP offices worldwide.

UNDP is particularly active in exchanges of knowledge and skills. Under the UN International Short-Term Advisory Resources (UNISTAR) private sector experts and advisors drawn from large corporations are assigned on loan to country programs on a short-term basis. In October 1999, UNDP and the American Bar Association (ABA) signed a partnership agreement to create a joint Legal Resources Unit to be housed by UNDP. The unit's objective is to provide developing countries with pro bono legal services in order to strengthen their governing institutions and legal infrastructures. Estimated at $1 million, the annual cost of running the unit is to be shared by UNDP and the ABA. The unit focuses on assisting the democratic processes of developing countries by providing these countries with advice on how to create electoral commissions, draft electoral laws, fight corruption, train their judiciary, and build or reform their institutions.

Secondment of personnel is often linked to knowledge-based partnerships between the UN and corporations. Many organizations have engaged in such exchanges, among them WHO in the context of joint product development and clinical trials carried out with pharmaceutical firms. UNDP has also resorted to such measures and its now stalled Global Sustainable Development Facility project (see below) was likely to make such exchanges still more necessary. The UN Environment Fund (UNEP) has also signed an agreement with Dupont for the secondment of staff to its Atmosphere Unit.

Business Creation and Investment

Any UN organization with a mandate in economic development is concerned with increasing investment flows to developing countries and facilitating small and medium-size business creation. Chief among them are UNDP and UNIDO.

Mandated to assist the development of small industry in developing countries, UNIDO pioneered an International Business Advisory Council in the mid-1990s and entered into cooperation agreements with specific companies or business associations. The Alliance for Africa's Industrialization, which has expanded into 20 country-based industrial partnership councils, is an example of private sector collaboration aimed at creating small and medium-sized industrial firms in Africa.

UNDP is active in business creation through microfinance mechanisms and the development of public-private companies in developing countries. Its Micro-Start Program invites microfinance practitioners to provide expertise and share best practices with organizations involved in UNDP microfinance projects around the world. UNDP's Enterprise Africa contributes to the development of small and medium-size enterprises in Africa through partnerships with local business associations, banks, and private consulting firms. With Argentinean business associations UNDP is identifying opportunities for venture capital initiatives in two provinces of Argentina. The Soros Open Society Institute and other private sector partners are supporting business creation in countries of Eastern Europe and former Soviet republics by transferring legal, accounting, and other skills, and developing business incubators. UNDP's Public-Private Partnership Program seeks to turn urban environmental challenges into viable business opportunities through partnerships between cities and private firms. Under this program initiated in 1995 with the support of the World Business Council for Sustainable Development (WBCSD), actual companies jointly owned by private and public entities are formed in recipient countries to invest in such areas as waste management, water and sanitation, and energy efficiency. The program aims to create up to 50 such companies worldwide. Finally, in November 1999, UNDP and the State of Arizona cosponsored a conference devoted to business development in regions of Africa, such as the Sahel, that share similar climatic and topological conditions as Arizona. Businesses in the southwestern American state were invited to avail themselves of investment opportunities in those African regions, while the latter in turn highlighted their success stories and showcased their products. This cross-investment program has now been expanded to Connecticut and New Jersey.

Again these UNDP private-sector partnerships in the operational area of business creation and development bear policy as well as advocacy characteristics. They rely on the expertise of partners—experience with desert climates in the case of the State of Arizona partnership—and often lead to policy changes or adjustments. Additionally, through their sheer involvement in these activities, private sector partners necessarily become advocates for UNDP and developing country causes.

Complex Partnership Approaches

The concept of UN-business partnership having taken root, several UN agencies are now venturing into multitiered partnership formulas bearing policy, advocacy, and operational aspects. Furthermore, by putting business at the center of growth and business creation in developing countries, these forms of cooperation are seen as crucial to renovate and make more effective the development assistance activities of the UN system. While such an orientation will appear obvious to any business leader, it took the end of the Cold War and the recognition of free market enterprise as the only viable vehicle of economic growth to impose on the UN system and others a reassessment of traditional development policy. In this respect, the emergence of the complex partnership approach between UN and corporate partners cannot be divorced from the historical evolution and the conceptual framework outlined in chapters 1 and 2, respectively. Three UN agencies stand out as having made the greatest strides thus far in the direction to all-encompassing UN-business partnerships. They are UNDP, UNCTAD, and UNOPS, and their new partnership formats are presented below.

1. UNDP's Global Sustainable Development Facility (GSDF)

Undergoing an in-depth review, a UNDP proposal to launch a Global Sustainable Development Facility (GSDF) represents thus far the most ambitious general partnership approach between a UN agency and the private sector. The complexity of the proposal, as well as the controversy generated by some of its features, led the new UNDP administrator to reconsider its launch. While the outcome of this review was unknown at press time, it is useful to look at the detail of its intended arrangements as they provide an indication of current thinking and future directions at the UN.

The facility was to have both for-profit and not-for-profit activities. As plans stood in mid-1999, the GSDF was to be incorporated outside the UN system as a not-for-profit enterprise that would reinvest its own profits. The GSDF's three key missions were stated as follows: 1) maintain a "project bank" and seek project partners; 2) vet projects that fulfill GSDF purposes and guidelines; and 3) "assist in the translation of ideas and concepts into business plans to be reviewed by potential corporate funders."[24] The GSDF's staff was to be recruited directly or seconded from corporations. The not-for-profit activities were to focus on the creation of enabling environments for project implementation by addressing such issues as governance, transparency, diffusion of best practices, and education. These not-for-profit projects were to be funded on a grant basis and managed by governments, foundations, and corporations.

For-profit activities, on the other hand, were to focus on two areas: project definition and management, and the creation and management of investment funds. Corporations participating in the GSDF would fund the projects themselves, as well as propose projects to the GSDF. The financial risks associated with the projects would be borne by the corporations—one of the factors that contributed to putting the proposal on the shelf. With the intention of combining capital investment with community development, the Investment Fund modality would provide corporations with the opportunity to invest in sector-focused commercial funds dedicated to large-scale infrastructure projects in such areas as electrification, water, and transport. The funds would be opened to investment by financial firms, corporations in the sectors mentioned above, as well as governments and development banks. The GSDF was to act as a catalyst in the creation of the funds and advisor in project design.

Selection criteria for participating corporations proved to be the most sensitive issue standing in the way of the GSDF's launch. Initially, UNDP had indicated that candidate corporations should enjoy a good public relations record (arms manufacturers and tobacco companies were ruled out), have significant international operations, and be willing to invest in long-term market development. A concern for corporate social responsibility, expressed through a commitment to sustainable development and the growth of emerging and yet-to-emerge markets, was of course a key selection criterion. Geographical and sectoral distribution would also figure among UNDP's selection variables. Finally, support of the three value areas of the Global Compact was also cited as a condition of membership, initiating an outcry from several NGOs when the latter claimed that a number of firms initially approached by UNDP had poor human rights records.

The GSDF was to be financed by the participating corporations—another bone of contention. The "entrance fee" to the GSDF amounted to $50,000 for each corporation. The partnerships between UNDP and the participating firms was to be formalized through a Memorandum of Understanding signed with each one. When the review was ordered in July 1999, 16 companies were said to have committed to the project, although none had committed any funds. Among them were ABB (Sweden/Switzerland), South Africa's Eskom, Sweden's furniture maker and distributor IKEA, U.S.-based Owens Corning, mobile phone company Ericsson, and U.K.-based Rio Tinto. The supervisory and management functions of the GSDF were to be handled by new structures in which UNDP, other UN agencies, and the participating corporations would have joint membership.

The GSDF offers undoubtedly a fascinating and exciting image of the future at the United Nations. It in fact proposes the first joint venture between the private sector and a UN agency, one that does not shy from engaging in profit-making activities, joint management, and joint decision-making. No other UN proposal has displayed such ambitions thus far. But its very daring nature and the lack of internal skills to match its ambitions have stopped the GSDF dead in its tracks. Its future fate will provide a good indication of how far UN-business partnerships can go in the coming years, and what reforms UN agencies are willing to implement to ensure their success.

2. UNCTAD's Partners for Development

UNCTAD's week-long Partners for Development conference held in Lyon (France) in November 1998 marked the entrance of the "child of the 60s" in the new era of UN-business partnerships. With the creation of its Trade Points in 1992, UNCTAD had already taken a more concrete, pro-trade orientation. The Trade Points aimed at facilitating access to export markets by providing firms in developing countries with a computer database of resources and information on trade. Among the services provided are advice on how to conduct international trade transactions; the provision of trade information, counseling, and banking services; access to customs and shipping services; and access to potential trading partners, buyers, and other partners around the world. A plan to provide a worldwide database of international procurement opportunities has not materialized, although it would constitute a powerful central source of information for developing countries seeking to increase their share of public markets. Of the 147 Trade Points established so far in 121 countries, 46 are deemed operational. UNCTAD is now focusing on increasing the impact of this program in Africa.

Facilitating the participation of developing countries into global trade through greater access to electronic information was one of the many topics tackled at the Partners for Development summit, in which local and national government representatives, CEOs, members of the UN and other international organizations, and representatives of NGOs participated.

Among the proposed areas of partnership were microfinance, African development, electronic commerce, commodity finance and risk management, transportation, and new technologies. Among the partnership ideas envisaged at the conference were the creation of associations between commodity producers, banks, and other financial institutions to help developing countries extend new engineering tools to commodity markets. Banks, asset management firms, and microfinance institutions were to be engaged in the launch of investment funds to channel private resources to microbanks and NGOs that finance micro and informal enterprises in developing countries.

In a follow-up report issued in January 1999, UNCTAD Secretary-General Rubens Ricupero stressed that progress on the implementation of the partnerships envisaged at the summit would require a reconsideration of administrative procedures to facilitate private sector funding of UNCTAD's activities; clear guidelines for the selection of private sector and civil society partners; and a clarification of legal issues pertaining to contracts between UNCTAD and private sector firms. At press time, concretizing the proposals of the Partners for Development summit was suffering delays attributable to the definition of UNCTAD's final guidelines on private sector collaboration—an exercise in which all UN agencies were then engaged.

3. UNOPS's Aid & Trade 2000 and Other Private Sector Partnerships

Convened by UNOPS in New York in May 2000, Aid & Trade 2000 was the first event on UN-business partnerships ever held by the UN itself in the United States. This multifaceted event included a policy conference entitled "The UN and Business: A Partnership for the New Millennium," partnership workshops, a procurement seminar, and an exhibition of goods and services by vendors to the UN system and the development banks. Gathering leading CEOs, UN officials, and representatives of governments, NGOs, and business associations, the conference provided the first opportunity for the UN system at large and its corporate partners to make the conceptual case for a renewed UN-business relationship in the context of the Global Compact. In two separate workshops, concrete new partnerships linking NGOs, UN agencies, and corporations were unveiled in the areas of conflict prevention, post-conflict rehabilitation, and mine action. For the first time, the private sector played an active and substantive role by providing input in, and indeed initiating several partnership proposals. Examples of partnerships included:

- Local investment and job creation in Guatemala by New York-based corporation PeaceWorks in support of the national reconciliation process and the promotion of human rights in that country, with the backing of the UN and Guatemalan investors associated in Industrias Para La Paz;

- Consultations between multinationals in Africa and the UN on corporate responsibility in several African peace processes;
- Job and export training adjusted to the conditions of mine victims in Mozambique with the assistance of U.S. NGO Aid to Artisans, the UN, the government of Mozambique, and local and international investors; and
- A partnership between Sweden's Ericsson and the UN system at large to improve the speed and efficiency of disaster relief.

Aid & Trade was itself the product of a UN-private sector partnership signed between UNOPS and the Winchester Group, a trade show organizer and publisher of trade directories based in England. Reflecting the comparative advantage of each partner, the partnership agreement exemplified the normative objectives of UN-business collaboration. The UN agency, which did not receive any fee for its services, played the role of conceptualizer and convener of the conference. To ensure the respect of UN values and interests, UNOPS also retained a veto on any material published in relation to this event. The private sector firm managed the logistics and the marketing aspects of the event, including the registration of conference delegates. The benefits of this partnership to both organizations are obvious. As a UN agency, UNOPS facilitated the promotion of a UN agenda and guaranteed the conceptual quality of the conference. As a private sector firm, the Winchester Group expected to derive a profit from a venture that is part of a new diversification strategy. By providing a forum for UN discussions with corporations, NGOs, and governments, UNOPS fulfilled its mandate of service provider to the UN system. UNOPS was also likely to benefit from the venture through the execution of some of the partnership proposals adopted at Aid & Trade. Because it combined conceptual and operational characteristics and promised to benefit both partners, the Aid & Trade event was a clear example of a "win-win" situation.

In 1999, UNOPS signed two additional partnership agreements with private sector firms—and new potential partners seemed to be knocking on UNOPS's doors on a weekly basis. Under an agreement signed with the French satellite imagery firm Spot Image, UNOPS promised to increase its own and the UN's access to this technology in a number of projects where satellites images are increasingly used. Applications of this technology range from humanitarian and relief operations, where satellite images permit better tracking of large refugee movements, to rural development projects and environmental data gathering. Under this partnership, UNOPS has entered product development inasmuch as its brokering role between UN agencies and Spot Image will lead to the creation of new technological applications and improved UN access to high-technology images—a role that goes beyond UNOPS's traditional outsourcing responsibilities.

A few months later, UNOPS was again at the center of a quadripartite partnership agreement involving medical laboratories in Vietnam, Carribean governments, and UNESCO. The innovative project allows Vietnamese drug rehabilitation medicines to be delivered to drug addicts treated in specialized facilities located in the Carribean, under the technical supervision of UNESCO—whose mandate includes science and technology—and the watchful eyes of UNOPS project managers on the ground. By benefiting several parties and constituencies, this agreement was another model of complex UN-business partnership. It served the development of the economies of Vietnam and the Carribean, matched UNESCO's substantive mandate, and capitalized on UNOPS's management experience. UNESCO's involvement was further needed to transfer project funds to UNOPS, the latter being legally precluded from raising its own funds. Of course, UNOPS did not grant exclusivity to any private sector partner in any of the agreements described above.

• • •

The flurry of activity that has characterized UN-business relations since the middle of the 1990s gives reasons for hope. In just a few years, UN organizations serving all types of mandates have had tighter and more frequent interactions with private sector firms than in entire UN history. These achievements deserve notice and praise, particularly as the UN-business relationship has now moved well beyond traditional commercial ties to encompass policymaking activities, advocacy of the UN's causes, and complex implementation of multipartite agreements. On the other hand, the progress made thus far has created high expectations and awakened the appetites of companies all over the world. Aid & Trade is only likely to feed the desire for additional and stepped-up partnerships. If the UN keeps claiming that it is open for business, business might well take the UN's word for it.

Much can be done to improve the quality and scope of UN-business partnerships. UN-wide guidelines on cooperation must be adopted; the UN's legal framework must be dusted off and revamped; opportunities for partnership must be increased and become a way of life; and the UN bureaucracy must change some of its ways to keep the relationship on an even keel. The experience of partnership is sufficient now to evaluate the results of the past few years and chart a course for the road ahead. As chapter 4 demonstrates, however, the UN is a political organization and it will, and indeed must, remain so. As one imagines the future, it is useful to keep its inherent limitations in mind.

CHAPTER 4

The Road Ahead

Before charting the course of future collaboration between the UN and its corporate partners, it is useful to draw lessons from the outreach that began in 1997 and the record of recent partnerships. Lessons apply at various levels. Firstly, as this renewed relationship fits in a specific conceptual framework, it is useful to revisit some of its underlying assumptions and check for their applicability and veracity. At an intermediary level, UN-business partnerships point to a set of lessons for UN policymaking on the objectives and modalities of partnerships. Finally, lessons can be drawn at the operational level, an area where progress will be critical to sustaining the interest of the business community.

Lessons, however, are useful only inasmuch as they facilitate charting future directions. In keeping with the conceptual framework of the Global Compact, the second part of this chapter therefore proposes ways for embedding its values in the global economy and translating them to the operational level of UN-business partnerships. The former implies developing a set of universal rules and strengthening such UN bodies as the ILO. As the UN embarks on this new regulatory challenge, however, it confronts the competition created by the sprouting of global reporting standards, as well as firm and sector-level codes of good behavior. How to reconcile so many competing standards without discouraging corporate responsibility finds no easy answer. The application of the Compact's framework to the UN's own activities has implications for UN reform, particularly in the area of human resources management, and assumes the creation of a UN culture favorable to business values and methods. The long-term significance of the Global Compact, however, is political. What is at stake is the formulation of a governance mechanism suited to the conditions of globalization and in which the participation of nonstate actors in UN forums and bodies becomes institutionalized. While the debate may generate the opposition of member states, failing to provide nonstate actors with an official representative status in intergovernmental organizations would put global governance and stability at risk in the new millennium.

I. Lessons

The lessons presented below point to the challenges that lie ahead of those committed to making the UN-business relationship work. At the root of these challenges are competing visions of the future global order, lingering suspicions as to the motives of the private sector, ideological differences, as well as seemingly smaller practical hurdles encountered in the legal and operational frameworks of partnerships. While those operational stumbling blocks may seem easier to address in the short term, so called "operational problems" may also disguise deeper psychological resistance and animosity toward the overall partnership approach.

Conceptual Lessons

Globalization, it was demonstrated in the previous chapters, is a process that owes its origins and persistence to the deliberate choices of nation-states.[1] At the root of the Globlal Compact, however, is the conviction that while states have not lost the authority to legitimize and initiate policies, they have lost the capacity to control many of the implications of the process of globalization. Included in this loss of control is the ability to regulate an array of global economic and financial transactions, to tax the proceeds of those activities, and to define single-handedly the social policies that ought to frame the process of globalization. The Global Compact therefore is neither based on the assumption that the state is dead nor that history has ended.

Because of the lasting authority and legitimacy of the state, defining the policies that will sustain or undermine globalization requires the support and participation of states. Providing a framework for UN action in the context of a global world, the Global Compact is based on the recognition that the United Nations remains first and foremost an intergovernmental body in which member states have rights unequaled by nonstate actors. As concerns the "end of history," the Global Compact is premised on the possibility of a potential backlash against globalization and an overall reaction against openness. If the riots that accompanied the opening of the November 1999 WTO meeting failed to impress those dogged optimists of the Internet revolution who believe that the Dow Jones can only go up, France's farmers setting McDonalds' restaurants on fire and the opponents of women's suffrage in Kuwait remind us that openness is not seen as a virtue by all. The paradoxical resurgence of localism and tribalism that accompanies the process of globalization evinces an inherent threat of global closure that cohabits with the promise of unlimited openness. Globalization, like the Renaissance before it, embodies elements of the Middle Ages and modernity. Which historical paradigm will dominate the twenty-first century is not a foregone conclusion.

Still, and while acknowledging the permanence of the state and the persistence of a historical dialectic, the rationale of the Global Compact acknowledges the limits of state control and the defeat of antiliberal and state-centered policies. As was recalled in chapter 1, the renewal of the UN relationship with the business community did require the end of the Cold War, the quasi-universal adoption of the tenets of both political and economic liberalism, and the onset of globalization. Support of the Global Compact both within and outside the United Nations should therefore lead to the expectation of an acceptance of these events and their conceptual implications. Adherence to and approval of the Compact's underlying assumptions should imply a recognition of the limits of governmental power and the applicability of market-based solutions to the problems of poverty, development, health, and other UN challenges. They might also lead to the understanding that private sector involvement in UN policies should increase rather than reduce the ownership of policies and their outcomes by developing countries, thereby giving these countries greater control on their development processes and decreasing their dependency on international organizations. In fact, the record of UN attitudes points to some measure of ambivalence toward the concepts and rationale underlying the policy of rapprochement with the private sector.

The State Is Not Dead

The comments of UN agencies on their interactions with corporations demonstrate their ambivalence toward doing away with the traditional roles of governments to the benefit of nonstate actors.[2] At the root of these concerns is the fear that increased corporate funding of UN activities will provide disincentives for continued and consistent government contributions. While the link between decreasing ODA and the UN's outreach to the private sector is conceptually incorrect, as I argue in the conclusion, UN officials are still focused on restoring ODA to its pre-1990 level, and see growing business support of their programs as potentially conflicting with that goal. UNICEF Executive Director Carol Bellamy and UNDP Administrator Mark Malloch Brown have both called for sustained government funding of development and other forms of international assistance. In a speech delivered at Harvard University in April 1999, the former called the decline of ODA in the past decade "a scandal." She added that private sector funding could not remedy the lasting decrease in ODA as "private capital seldom gravitates to the very neediest countries . . . [and] in those countries that it does reach, private capital often does little for the poor."[3] As he assumed his post on July 1, 1999, Mark Malloch Brown stated that "with only $6 billion more in annual spending, we could give a basic education to every child on earth"—a statement that assumes the virtual capacity of government funding to produce benefits irrespective of the quality of program implementation and the conditions needed for an efficient use of ODA.[4] In September, he proposed that "UNDP needs two things: organizational renewal and oxygen in the form of a campaign to rebuild political, and hence financial, support."[5]

According to UNCTAD, "member states remain ambivalent about inviting business to participate in 'their organizations' deliberative processes."[6] Governments show lingering suspicion about private sector involvement, even when they have fully liberalized and privatized their economies. Some governments are also concerned about corporate gifts coming with strings attached. While UNCTAD acknowledges that UN bodies must find ways to integrate nonstate actors in the activities of intergovernmental organizations, it admits that finding ways to do so "finds no easy answer." Partly accountable for the resistance of some developing countries to the growing role of business at the UN is their fear that the corporations of the developed world will dominate their economies. The corporate base of the developing countries is still too weak to reassure the latter as to the proper representation of their economic interests in the context of a stepped-up corporate presence at the UN. Two attitudes must change to generate greater support of the new policy by the developing countries. Firstly, those nations must de-link corporate and national identity: the idea that Microsoft is an American firm is obsolete and contradicted by the dichotomy between the domestic interests of states and the global concerns of corporations. Secondly, those corporations that have responded to the secretary-general's call for partnership with the UN must send the message that one of the fundamental objectives of this rapprochement is to improve the access of the developing countries to technology and markets. The developing world must know that it will be the primary beneficiary of UN-business collaboration and that global corporations have an interest in helping it eradicate poverty, catch up with the rest of the world technologically, and become an attractive investment option.

Indeed, several developing nations are adjusting positively to the UN-wide policy change. Because the aggregate power of the state in developing nations is smaller than in industrialized countries, some among the former are displaying an interest in capitalizing on the strength and wealth of the private sector. The existence of corporate social responsibility networks in Latin America, for example, demonstrates that firms in developing nations no longer rely on cheap labor and poor working conditions to gain a comparative advantage in trade.[7] Finally, because the outcome of forty years of international cooperation and development assistance is less than convincing, developing nations are keen to find alternatives to public sector approaches to development.[8]

Another argument against increased collaboration between the UN and business is that such relationships escape democratic control. Business executives, these critics point out, are not elected and seem accountable to no one. This argument suffers from equating democracy with representation, however, and it dismisses the possibility that increased ties between international organizations and multinationals may provide a map for making the latter accountable to the global public.

The official representation afforded by democratic elections does not guarantee the representation and the participation of all constituencies, nor necessarily that of the majority of voters. The growth and diversity of civil society organizations in the past decade is testimony to the fact that a multiplicity of interests in the global body politic are not properly addressed by elected officials. Civil society therefore provides a means for channeling the concerns and interests of groups left out of the formal political process. As it has evolved in the past decade, the debate on development assistance also demonstrates that governmental control of funds has not always resulted in local ownership of policies or actual improvements in standards of living, economic growth, and other measures of development. The focus of this literature on corruption and the sheer disappearance of ODA to benefit local rulers or corporatist interests provide the most blatant evidence of the limits of inter-governmental aid policies.[9] The consistent complaint that local communities have not owned the definition and outcomes of development policy further argues for the lack of representation of local interests in processes controlled by elected officials.[10] A vibrant democracy, as Tocqueville demonstrated, depends on the activism of a diverse civil society distributed in an array of social groups whose only legitimacy rests not on the electoral process but on the endorsement of their constituencies. There is little reason why what is true at the domestic level should fail to apply to an increasingly interconnected global world.

In this respect, there is reason to believe that corporate involvement in UN debates and activities will result in a democratic surplus rather than a democratic deficit. Because globalization has been driven thus far by global business, the continued exclusion of the private sector from UN policy processes would limit, if not stall, the UN's ability to assess correctly the dimensions of globalization and formulate solutions to its negative externalities. Such a conviction is, of course, at the center of the Global Compact. In a more operational realm, however, the involvement of the private sector at the local level is likely to improve the development process and increase its ownership by local communities. I see three reasons for such a prospect.

Firstly, UN agencies seeking operational formulas to translate the Global Compact to the local level are committed to selecting only socially responsible corporate partners. Chapter 2 stressed the role of corporate responsibility in the Compact's argumentation. UN-business partnerships therefore provide a recipe for enlisting the private sector behind the societal concerns of the global citizenry. Secondly, because economic efficiency has little tolerance for wasting money, the profit-seeking motive of corporations may provide a guarantee of efficiency and transparency in the provision of a new form of assistance through the partnership concept. Because the management of corporate funds usually falls under tighter scrutiny than the use of public money, corporations are likely to submit their partnerships with the UN to a serious cost-benefit analysis that may prevent the capture of development funds by political interest groups. This contention is not the product of some starry-eyed naiveté. There has been no dearth of corporate corruption, nepotism, and bribery in the past decade. But while public entities do not risk going out of business, the sword of Damocles of bankruptcy always reminds corporations of the limits of wasteful practices.[11] Finally, while corporate planners include macro considerations in their strategies, the daily operations of corporations take place mostly at the micro level of projects, partnerships, and local investment. Because they involve actors with local concerns, UN-private sector partnerships will often favor decentralized approaches. Being decentralized, these approaches will necessarily involve local communities at a deeper level than traditional country programs did, transferring to them larger responsibilities, control, and interests in the outcomes of partnership. Although corporations are not elected, their involvement in the realm of intergovernmental affairs may increase rather than reduce accountability and democratic oversight.

History Has Not Ended

The "end of history" argument made by Francis Fukuyama a decade ago assumed that the demise of the Soviet system would signal universal acceptance of political and economic liberalism. If true, such acceptance would facilitate, if not call for, public-private partnerships, as governments worldwide would subscribe to free markets, open trade, and creative competition. One would therefore expect to encounter little resistance to the role and relevance of the private sector in contributing solutions to the UN's challenges. Indeed, the policy contributions of the private sector were at the heart of the UN's own prescriptions to speed up the transition of Eastern European and post-Soviet countries to the free market in the 1990s.

As it turns out, resistance to the UN's outreach to business emanates from the UN's own ranks. Senior officials speak against "selling" the organization to business, and encounters between the secretary-general and CEOs are derided as "shareholders' meetings." In light of such internal opposition, one must appreciate the political courage of a secretary-general whose vision has yet to transpire to all levels of the organization. In her Harvard address in April 1999, UNICEF Executive Director Carol Bellamy stated that "it is dangerous to assume that the goals of the private sector are somehow synonymous with those of the United Nations, because they most emphatically are not."[12] She suggested that "in coming together with the private sector, the United Nations must carefully, and constantly, appraise this relationship." The persistence of internal pressures against UN collaboration with business led to the formulation of a course on private sector partnership for UN staff members (see below).

According to some, resistance to the private sector's involvement is also imputable to the fear of a single country imposing its values on the organization, as these may be reflected in the practices of its corporations. Namely, the global leadership of American corporations as well as the national American consensus on the superiority of free markets, competition, and entrepreneurship lead some to equate the American private sector with the American government, and to see in the involvement of the former the agenda of the latter. Such an argument is remarkably oblivious to the realities of a decade when the U.S. Congress has been in opposition to the very idea of multilateralism; when failure to pay U.S. dues to the UN in full and on time has noticeably impaired American influence in UN debates; and when the American private sector has been far less vocal in supporting the UN's roles and mandates than its international counterparts. No matter: in politics perceptions often structure reality.

Fear of job cuts as a result of efficiency gains is another explanation for fighting the influence of the private sector at the UN. The outsourcing of UN functions—such as catering, freight forwarding, or travel planning—as well as the secondment of private sector staff to UN bodies threaten both existing and potential UN jobs. Several years into the adoption of a hiring moratorium imputable to budgetary pressure, UN staff members can be expected to react against policies seen as infringing upon their professional territory. In this respect, zero-job growth is unlikely to promote the UN's objectives in creating additional partnerships with corporations. More will be said on the latter below.

The media has also exhibited an ambivalent attitude toward the UN's attempt to find a role for the private sector in shaping the policies of the global era. A number of positive reactions to the overall policy as well as the Global Compact can be quoted, and the European press has provided a faithful coverage of the secretary-general's speeches.[13] The leading international business daily newspapers, in particular, have demonstrated an understanding of and support for the Global Compact's rationale—at times providing major international CEOs with a forum in their editorial pages to express their own views on the policy. On the other hand, the fund-raising emphasis of some UN-business partnerships has led some representatives of the media to misunderstand and criticize the motivations of the UN's outreach to the business community. On December 3, 1999, ABC interviewed UNDP Administrator Mark Malloch Brown on the agency's mine-clearance programs. After reviewing the UN's recent alliances with corporate funders such as Time Warner and CISCO, the interviewer concluded that, "as the United Nations is asked to do more with less money, the financial purity the founders envisioned is being challenged by a need to pay the bills."[14] The underlying assumption that government funds are somehow "purer" than corporate money is always surprising, and rarely demonstrated. The contention that its financial crisis is forcing the United Nations to accept the funds of unscrupulous businesses also dismisses the basis of mutual interests and values on which UN-business partnerships are being elaborated. The rationale presented in chapter 2 demonstrates that the greatest benefits to accrue to the UN from private sector collaboration come in the form of advocacy for the Charter's values and goals, and corporate partners are submitted to ethical tests prior to qualifying for potential collaboration.[15]

The persistence of opposition to the new paradigm in several circles implies that the recovered UN-business partnership is still very fragile, and crossing the point of no return will require the strong commitment of senior officials for several more years.

Lessons on Partnering

Among the four policy lessons outlined below, the first two are related: corporations are not cash cows, and they care about their reputations. The last two address the need for UN legal standards and selection guidelines to frame the UN relationship with business.

The Limits of Fund-Raising

While some initial and current UN-corporate partnerships focus on fund-raising, most UN officials publicly claim that such is not the objective of their partnership with the private sector. They stress rather the desirability of "win-win solutions" benefiting both parties, as well as the conceptual and technological contributions corporations can make. According to UNICEF, "merely saying this is my funding partner is no longer an acceptable methodology for partnerships."[16] Recognizing that corporations want to have a role in determining the best uses of the funds, and even more so, in claiming credit and pride for their work, UNICEF states that "giving due credit to all partners is a key factor of success."

UNAIDS sees in the private sector its best advocate rather than a source of funding. Getting business to take on AIDS as a serious issue is "something that money can't buy," a UNAIDS official stated in a telephone interview in the spring of 1999. UNFPA similarly understands the benefits of helping corporations sell their products rather than donate their resources to UN agencies. In a December 1999 article, Corrie Shanahan, a spokeswoman for UNFPA, stated that the UN Population Fund is not "even asking for product donations. If the companies sell contraceptives to the middle classes in those [middle-income] countries, it will free up our supply for poor people."[17]

Legally precluded from raising funds from either governments or corporations, UNOPS approaches private sector partnerships from an ideal vantage point. This reality "reassured" many of the private sector firms with which UNOPS held talks in preparation of Aid & Trade 2000. It remains that the perception of a fund-raising motive has permeated both the media and a portion of the corporate community. It is essential that the UN correct this misrepresentation by presenting the overall rationale of the new policy, informing the media, organizing conferences on this topic for private sector audiences, and making sure that UN member states understand the purpose and the benefits of this policy to the UN and governments. The persistence of this misunderstanding would otherwise derail the longevity and spirit of the recovered partnership.

Reputation Matters

The reliance of the Global Compact on the prevalence of a deep corporate social responsibility movement seems to be borne out. The creation of a new and thriving niche in the business literature, a succession of international corporate responsibility conferences, and the emergence of voluntary corporate codes of conduct indicate that the compatibility of corporate activity with global societal concerns has become a sine qua non of success in the global economy. Moreover, corporate responsibility is not restricted to the largest multinationals, but has indeed penetrated many developing countries where social responsibility networks integrate progressive and outward-looking firms.[18]

Corporate interaction with UN bodies confirms the trend. As part of its 1998 survey, the UN found that corporations mostly want the UN to confer "good corporate citizenship awards." UNESCO concurs and sees a "desire on the part of the business sector to demonstrate 'good citizenship' locally and globally." UNAIDS stresses the appeal of its Award for Business Excellence, which each year rewards a corporation for its response to the AIDS crisis.[19] The attempt by San Francisco-based Business for Social Responsibility to obtain the UN's endorsement for a Human Rights Award provides additional evidence of the appeal of good reputation.

Two dangers accompany the prevalence of this trend. The first danger is that of regulatory capture by the private sector. The voluntary nature of newly adopted corporate standards and codes of conduct means that multinationals are in a position to structure these rules in ways that restrict them the least, fit the best their comparative advantages and operations, and evade pervasive control and monitoring mechanisms. Auditing systems are often devised by the organizations that author these standards in the first place, undermining the credibility of controls. Moreover, the multiplication of firm-level and sector-level standards creates confusion and does not guarantee the respect of a universal set of rules. While such decentralization has obvious advantages inasmuch as different sectors and different regulatory gaps call for different solutions, the premise of the Global Compact implies that a minimum set of norms in the areas of labor rights, human rights, and the environment must be universally adopted and respected. How to ensure such consistency in the interest of the sustainability of globalization without discouraging corporate responsibility and creating potentially counterproductive central auditing bodies is a conundrum that remains to be untied. The operationalization of the Global Compact must provide a partial solution.

A second danger is that the corporate emphasis on reputation and its accompanying rewards will divert UN-private collaboration onto a symbolic course that will fail to deliver real achievements—the latter being particularly expected by the developing countries. Here the risks seem more easily manageable. Business is likely to call for concrete results from collaboration, the more so if the corporate investment in time and other resources is high. The UN is developing a clearer picture of the benefits of the relationship, and budgetary pressure makes it less likely that time and money will be wasted in the effort. The challenge lies in an unambiguous articulation of the benefits and operational modalities of partnerships.

New Guidelines for Collaboration

The adhoc approach to private sector collaboration resulting from the absence of common guidelines setting clear objectives has set UN-business partnerships on a shaky course likely to lead to disappointment of one or both parties, if not outright failure. Guidelines must articulate the objectives and modalities of partnerships, the conditions of success and failure, and methods for integrating all stakeholders in sustainable partnerships. In this regard the failure to launch the GSDF (see chapter 3) is instructive. It can be imputed in part to the absence of clear objectives and tightly defined modalities, as well as a lack of consultation with NGOs that ultimately backfired on the authors of the project.

Additionally, the persistence of obsolete rules regarding corporate use of the UN logo and the recognition of corporate contributions make the negotiation of partnership agreements unnecessarily protracted, at the same time as it limits the benefits of collaboration to the private sector. All UN agencies agree that the legal impediments to corporate use of the UN logo must be removed while protecting the interests and values of the UN Charter. The inability to claim tax deductions, on the other hand, has been effectively addressed by agencies through the creation of tax-exempt NGOs, particularly in the United States.

In discussions of the UN Working Group on Operational Guidelines in the fall of 1999, opinions varied between the definition of UN-wide guidelines and decentralized approaches entrusting to each UN body the responsibility to choose partners and objectives respectful of the Charter's values. In line with the spirit of the Global Compact, the consensus seemed to favor the definition of macro principles of collaboration matched by a fair degree of agency-level autonomy. Addressing the selection criteria to be applied to corporate partners, UNDP spoke against establishing a list of "saints and sinners," but argued rather for a general agreement on values that would eliminate from consideration tobacco companies, weapons manufacturers, and corporations that resort to child labor, contravene fundamental human rights, or condone various forms of labor discrimination. Because different corporate partners are obviously suited to different partnership objectives, the issue of selection criteria partially overlaps with the definition of the objectives of collaboration. The working group therefore agreed that the drafting of new UN guidelines came down to solving two problems: 1) reinterpreting the 1946 rule on the use of the UN name and logo to allow wider use while protecting the UN's principles and assets; and 2) clarifying and defining the overlapping framework of partnership objectives and selection criteria. The UN Office of Legal Affairs (OLA), on the one hand, and UNDP and UNICEF, on the other, were asked to produce papers on these issues, respectively.

As it emerged from a draft paper circulated to members of the working group in the first quarter of 2000, OLA's interpretation of "the use of the UN name and emblem" by private sector entities has moved away from the strict interpretation of "commercial use" based on *Black's Law Dictionary* (see chapter 3). The new UN guidelines would authorize use of the UN name and logo by a private sector firm or NGO "to express support for the purposes and policies of the organization," "to assist in the raising of funds for the organization," and "to assist in the raising of funds for [non-UN entities] established to achieve the purposes and policies of the organization." If retained, the new interpretation would therefore not only authorize use of the UN name and logo by "a commercial entity even involving the making of some profit, as long as the principal purpose of such use is to show support for the purposes and activities of the UN," but also to raise funds for the organization.[20] The new policy also stresses that use of the UN name and logo should not be exclusive and should not be seen as endorsing the products or services of the user. While the interpretative shift was welcome, the new OLA guidelines amounted to bringing the law in line with the current, and in some cases traditional, practices of most UN agencies.

Also circulated in the first quarter of 2000, the UNDP/UNICEF paper emphasized the reasons and possibilities for mutual understanding and cooperation between the private sector and the UN in the context of globalization. Retreating from the brink of seeing fund-raising as a significant objective of UN-business collaboration, the paper stated: "There is little evidence to suggest that corporations are disposed to be major funders of the United Nations. Moreover, focusing on financial resources ignores the vast repositories of skills, technology, and know-how that these growing economic actors represent."[21] Touching upon the sensitive issue of selection criteria, the paper favored the exercise of "due diligence," as "there are few—if any—corporate saints."[22] Corporations whose activities are "fundamentally opposed to the principles of the United Nations Charter" were ruled out, including weapons manufacturers and organized crime as "obvious examples." The paper finally recognized the diversity of UN mandates as justifying the "different weighting of a possible ally's conduct," which could "lead to different selections of allies."[23]

In March 2000, a very preliminary text entitled "Draft Guidelines for Cooperation Between the United Nations and the Private Sector" defined the latter as "for-profit enterprises" and emphasized the need for a decentralized, case-by-case approach.[24] UN-business cooperation was framed in the historical context of business support for the UN Charter as it was expressed in 1945, and it was seen as "an integral part of the Secretary-General's reform to renew the Organization."[25] A section entitled "Terms of Engagement" listed the principles of cooperation as follows: "advanc[ing] UN goals;" exhibiting "a clear delineation of responsibilities and roles;" "maintain[ing the] integrity and neutrality" of the UN; providing "no unfair advantage" to any corporate partner; and promoting "transparency" on UN-business partnerships through equal access to information on partnerships by all UN agencies. Although the draft guidelines ruled out cooperation with corporations that are "complicit in human rights abuses" and "practice forced, compulsory, or child labor," UN organizations were "encouraged to develop their own criteria" to select suitable partners "in accordance with their specific missions and activities."[26] The nine principles derived from the Global Compact were cited as providing the normative map of UN-business collaboration and good corporate citizens were "encouraged to meet or exceed all principles by translating them into corporate practice."[27] A final set of UN guidelines for collaboration was expected to be finalized during the second quarter of 2000.

Operational Lessons

While the UN has made much progress on the alchemy of partnerships and was in the process of adopting new guidelines in 2000, operational inadequacies and outdated practices must be reformed to facilitate interaction with the private sector. Many of these hurdles can be overcome with the right commitment of resources—financial and human—and some cultural adjustments.

Committing the Resources

For all the partnerships that have been signed between UN bodies and private sector firms, few if any have led to tangible and quantifiable results that might be vaunted as evidence of the benefits of cooperation. The private sector is particularly keen to point to concrete achievements, as involvement in UN projects is often owed to innovative risk-takers who must justify their business decisions to their superiors in order to sustain the firm's engagement with the UN. While such individuals trust their visions and instincts to venture on a road that offers no guarantee of success, the environment in which they operate tolerates risk-taking only inasmuch as it produces financial benefits.

Among the signals the UN must send its business partners to convince them of the longevity of the new approach is the commitment of sufficient financial and human resources to the area of private sector partnerships. Agencies that have engaged in a serious outreach find their resources overstretched. As part of the survey carried out in the fall of 1998, UNFPA remarked that in the area of UN-business partnerships, "relatively substantial inputs . . . [must be] sustained over time . . . to have an impact." UNCTAD equally agreed that making progress in this work area requires serious budget commitments to fund, for example, new publications or travel to business conferences.

Committing the necessary resources also has implications for UN staff levels and skills. Firstly, the work that must be accomplished in this new line of activity is too burdensome to be appended to existing departments and project teams. Managing the specific responsibilities of private sector partnerships will require additional staff. Beyond quantitative needs, however, this new line of work will also demand a new set of skills that in many cases will have to be imported from outside the UN system. Here again the failure of the GSDF ought to serve as a lesson. The complexity of the GSDF's financial structure, the presence of business risks against which UNDP's corporate partners needed to be insured, and the demands of project management as the latter task is understood and practiced by the private sector were so many elements of the GSDF model for which UNDP had no matching skills. The GSDF could not possibly be launched and managed without recruiting business professionals trained to address the financial and legal challenges of such an enterprise. If the UN system is serious about jointly implementing operational partnerships with the private sector, it will have to recruit young professionals on business and law school campuses—a recruitment technique never yet practiced by the UN.

One additional problem concerns the turnover of staff committed to this new approach, both at the UN and within partnering corporations. Because the concept of the rapprochement with the private sector is not yet shared at all levels of the UN pyramid, the sustainability of private sector partnerships is highly dependent on the commitment and knowledge of a few individuals. Changes in personnel can simply stop a partnership dead in its tracks, and the best professionals are always the most likely to leave. The absence of employment incentives has long been the public sector's downfall, and innovative UN agencies might wish to think about remedial action. New business recruits will not be attracted and kept without appropriate performance recognition and reward—a potentially explosive topic in UN circles.

New Roles for UN Legal Departments

UN legal departments must play a significant role to create the institutional infrastructure of UN-business partnerships. In addition to overhauling the rules that apply to the use of the UN name and logo, legal expertise is now required to develop models of partnership agreements specifically suited to UN-business collaboration, risk management, and control mechanisms, and a predictable and clear definition of conflict of interest. In contrast to the work typically carried out by UN legal departments, what is required at this juncture is the creative formulation of new legal policies.

The types of agreements signed among UN agencies or between agencies and governments are not suited to partnerships with private sector firms. Such agreements often include a funding role for one of the partners. Conversely, UN partnership agreements with private sector firms do not always have financial strings attached to them. Unless fund-raising is their main objective, partnerships are based on comparative advantage, with each partner carrying and paying for its end of the work. As representatives of the UN and business craft a growing number of partnership agreements, they must also define common terms. The terms "joint venture" and "project" provide perfect examples of the definitional gap. Corporations assign detailed financial and operational dimensions to both terms, whereas the UN uses them more loosely to describe processes of joint activity that often lack precise budgetary and chronological schedules. At this stage, UN agencies and private sector firms are not signing joint venture partnerships in the corporate sense of the term. Joint ventures implying shared investment responsibilities, joint production, and profit sharing may develop in the long-term. The GSDF project hinted at such a model, but its crafters ran into definitional problems when they contrasted their understanding of the term "project" with that of the private sector. While real UN-business joint ventures will be long in the making—assuming they ever see the light of day—it may be useful for UN legal departments to think proactively about ways of making such agreements possible while keeping in mind the best interests of the United Nations.

UN agreements with corporations also reflect a more conceptual approach than do intra-UN agreements. It is unnecessary for a UN agency to require another to abide by the values of the UN Charter: such allegiance is assumed in the sheer status of a UN body. In the case of complex, multipartite partnerships, a clear definition of comparative advantage and respective roles is needed. Moreover, the possibilities of UN-business partnerships are as numerous and varied as the number and identity of the partners. UN-business agreements are therefore lengthier and more creative than the standard memoranda of understanding signed among UN bodies. UN legal departments therefore face a policy challenge, as they must craft original documents suited to unique situations. Within a few years, a new body of UN legal practice will have evolved, but some imagination is needed at this stage.

The conceptual aspects of UN-business agreements should not, however, conceal the need to address effectively and clearly the perception of business risks that is associated with UN collaboration. Such business risks, I must state at the outset, are not linked to the UN's ability to pay its bills. Despite payment delays attributable to the UN's financial crisis, the UN has never defaulted on its suppliers. While such considerations apply essentially to procurement contracts rather than more complex partnership agreements, the UN's payment record is essential in that it projects an image of trustworthiness that, if absent, would affect the UN's broader outreach to the private sector. The American management consultant involved with DPKO in the 1990s considers that the UN's "contractual culture" is different from that of industry. In a phone interview, a representative from that company stated that "there were times when we did not feel secure about the wording of the contract. The agreements are not tight enough. We took more risks with the UN than we normally would with other clients—private or public."[28] In addition to financial risks, the UN's corporate partners must also bear country risks, as most UN work takes place in countries rarely known for their financial or political stability. Addressing country risks provides an opportunity for an additional UN-business partnership, this one with the insurance industry and possibly countertrade firms that provide methods for guaranteeing payment by, or exchanging goods with, insolvent countries. The UN must therefore improve its financial forecasting and tighten the provisions of its legal documents, but lacking the internal capacity to solve larger country-risk problems, it should seek such expertise outside.

Finally, conflict of interest must cease to be the maligned and rumored-about threat it currently is, and become an openly defined notion with transparently applied remedies. Conflict of interest has acquired the well-known features of Beckett's Godot: everyone talks about it but no one has seen it face to face. The truth is that few UN agencies have developed a policy document stating when conflict of interest occurs and what can be done to prevent it. When asked to define it by their corporate partners, UN officials often illustrate conflict of interest with examples, but examples are arbitrary and do not constitute a policy. As in the case of operational guidelines for collaboration, the definition of conflict of interest and its remedial measures should probably be left to each individual agency. The discussion of WHO's conflict-of-interest policy in chapter 3 demonstrated the singularity of the problem in respect to each UN mandate. What is required is for agencies to specify in a public document—possibly accessible from each agency's website—the business situations it considers as conflictual. If and when such situations occur, UN bodies must have a set of publicly available guidelines spelling out ways to disclose and correct them. Staff members should be trained in detecting, disclosing, and correcting conflict-of-interest situations, and openness and transparency should be encouraged in this process, as conflict of interest thrives on secrecy and opacity. At UNOPS, such training programs have contributed to removing the taboo associated with conflict of interest. Full disclosure goes counter to the communication style of a political organization, however. Because information is power, the free flow of information has not been a traditional characteristic of UN communication policies. Wider use of the Internet and information technologies holds the promise of opening up UN communication practices.

The Cultural Gap

It was argued both in chapters 1 and 2 that the overall cultural gap that separated the UN from the private sector for the better part of the UN's history has now been closed. While this seems true at the conceptual level—when considering, for example, the respective functions of multilateral organizations and multinationals—many discrepancies remain in day-to-day behavior. Of course, the political nature of the UN system makes such divergent behavior predictable and in part immutable. The very comparative advantage of the United Nations lies in its function as a political body integrating all states and, increasingly, global civil society as well. As a result, the UN lacks a management culture. Such business functions as financial, human resources, and legal management are often approached from a political angle compatible with a political definition of efficiency. The prevalence of a management culture in the private sector implies an economic rationale guided by an economic definition of efficiency, which assumes best allocation of resources and lowest use of production factors. In a political organization, the definition of efficiency is driven by the achievement of political, and therefore often symbolic, goals—a focus that relegates to the bottom of the list concerns about costs and allocation of resources.

As political and economic rationalities meet in the context of UN-business partnerships, however, it seems infeasible that those UN departments directly engaged in this new line of work can escape changing some of their cultural assumptions and traits. Some rubbing-off of corporate attitudes and methods is bound to result from greater interaction, and will in fact be necessary to sustain the partnership. Long-term collaboration cannot prevail if people talk past each other. Departments charged with UN-business partnerships should be encouraged to develop a culture of their own, with matching policies and rules, in order to facilitate interaction with the private sector.[29]

The United Nations is a bureaucracy, and so are most corporations—the more so the larger they are. As bureaucracies go, however, the corporate kind operates faster than the UN. One cultural difference opposes the profit-driven focus on outcomes of the corporate world to the politically driven emphasis on process typical of the UN. Things move slowly at the UN and many a corporation loses patience over the delays. In addition to never starting on time, meetings do last longer than necessary or than would be tolerated in any corporate environment. Participants are allowed to speak at length in not always purposeful ways, rather than state a problem and chart alternative solutions in a few minutes—a technique business professionals are taught on the first day of business school. Memorandums share the same characteristics. One area of progress in the past few years has been the acquisition of information and multimedia technology throughout the UN system. While one can probably find better technologically equipped corporations, the UN is now compatible with corporate standards in such areas as video conferencing, use of E-mail and Internet, and the quality of computer equipment.

While the cultural details mentioned here are often trivialized in UN circles, there is little doubt that they stand in the way of more effective relationships between the UN and the private sector. Taking them seriously and figuring ways to address them is likely to prove a more fruitful attitude.

II. Future Directions

The work that lies ahead of the UN system and its partners in the business community is daunting in its breadth and diversity. As the lessons outlined above demonstrate, changes must take place at both the macro and the micro levels, in people's minds as well as in their professional habits. In line with the overall conceptual approach of this book, the following section will not address point by point the operational changes that must be implemented to make UN-business partnerships more tangible and effective. It falls upon UN operational departments to list these micro tasks and figure out ways to fulfill them. As is argued below, changes in human resources management can go a long way to addressing these operational challenges. The longevity of the UN rapprochement with the business community and the long-term success of the secretary-general's vision, however, lie in two larger issues. On the one hand is the conceptual and operational challenge of translating the broad values of the Global Compact to the global economy and those activities that are in one way or another influenced by UN action, be it at a policy or an operational level. Here the UN must find ways to leverage its relationships and influence on the world polity to embed the values of the Compact in global interactions and a new global governance system. The latter will hinge on the UN's ability to convince its member states to grant nonstate actors a representative status commensurate with their role in fashioning the global economy and responsive to their acceptance of the Global Compact's rationale.

Operationalizing the Global Compact

The competing pressures that prevented the successful ending of the November 1999 WTO meeting demonstrated the validity of the Global Compact's vision. In his editorial published on the eve of the Seattle gathering, Secretary-General Kofi Annan had outlined the only workable proposal for the week-long proceedings.[30] Unfortunately, the secretary-general was among several officials who never managed to reach the podium and deliver their speeches that week.

As a rephrasing of the "compromise of embedded liberalism," however, the Global Compact will only have an impact if its values and rationale become similarly embedded in the institutions and interactions of the global world system. The compromise of 1945 was the result of a wide consensus among and within governments, which in turn informed governmental action at both the domestic and the international levels and consequently the work of intergovernmental organizations such as the United Nations and the Bretton Woods institutions. It is because political actors, at least in the noncommunist world, shared the assumptions of that consensus that it provided a map for managing economic relations and their social consequences for several decades. Already threatened by the unraveling of the financial system after the dollar's status as reserve currency ended in 1972, the Keynesian compromise was buried by the end of the Cold War and the onset of globalization.[31] For the Global Compact to be equally successful, its assumptions must therefore filter through the global system and become the shared consensus of governments, multilateral institutions, civil society, and corporations.

How to ensure the translation of such a broad framework to individual actions at the global, national, and local levels is the challenge now facing the UN system, and it is a sizeable one. Against the background of regulatory hyperactivity that has characterized the past decade, the United Nations must play a consolidating role by facilitating the development of universal rules while not discouraging local initiative. UN agencies mandated to work on behalf of human rights, labor rights, and the environment—the UN Office of the High Commissioner for Human Rights, the International Labor Organization, and the UN Environment Program—are directly concerned by the Compact's agenda. Depending on the advancement and credibility of their normative functions, they will play more or less proactive roles in defining an effective UN contribution to global regulatory activities. The UN must also translate the values of the Compact to its own operations, partnerships, and global relationships. No UN work, be it on behalf of development, family planning, or post-conflict reconstruction, is devoid of considerations regarding human and labor rights. Part of the challenge of operationalization, therefore, is a relevant and well-adjusted translation of these values to each UN agency's work. Looking beyond these activities, however, the longevity of the Compact's impact lies in a restructuring of governance structures, and possibly of the UN's membership.

Advocating and Explaining the Global Compact

The WTO meeting demonstrated the need to explain the Compact's rationale to governments and civil society. While it is tempting to believe that the

UN is the world, it is erroneous to assume that what is pronounced within its walls necessarily reaches a wide audience.

UN policymaking bodies must take on the responsibility of publicizing the Compact's ideas to their partners all over the world. These organizations can become the UN's spokespersons on behalf of the Compact by explaining and disseminating it to governments, civil society groups, and corporations with which they interact regularly. Almost a year after the Davos speech, this author found that many missions to the UN had not read the speech, let alone understood its argumentation. Those organizations that have become counterparts of the United Nations in the Global Compact—the ICC, The Prince of Wales Business Leaders Forum, the International Employers' Organization, and the World Business Council for Sustainable Development, among many—are also engaged in the advocacy and explanatory phase of the Compact, and their efforts must continue. The websites of these organizations will become databases for good corporate practice that will supply models for other corporations to follow. Key to the success of this Internet-based campaign is facilitating the access of companies in developing countries to these websites. This challenge provides yet another opportunity for partnerships between the UN and information technology firms, in which the latter could lend their services and possibly donate equipment to ensure that the poorest countries are not left out of this debate.

As the UN takes on the challenge of advocating and explicating the Compact, NGOs and business associations must take the relay of UN agencies in disseminating the Compact to their members. As was stated in chapter 2, up to 80 percent of NGOs accredited to the United Nations act on behalf of the three value areas targeted by the Compact. These NGOs should feel particularly concerned by and become active in the advocacy effort. In the United States, such organizations as the UN Foundation, the Better World Campaign, and business groups such as BCUN, BCIU, and USCIB can act as significant relays of the Compact's message to the public, policymakers and scholars, Congress, and the business community. NGOs and business associations may devote a portion of their websites to a discussion of the Compact or decide to link with the UN's and the ICC's sites. Under a grant of the UN Foundation, the UN Wire, an Internet publication of the Washington-based *National Journal,* has designed and launched a UN Business Wire. In addition to supplying the business community with relevant pieces of information about the UN, the UN Business Wire could also become a designated forum for a discussion of the Compact with the business community and a source of information on best practices. In the developing world, such corporate social responsibility groups as Empresa could play similar roles.

Although it has thus far remained aloof from UN forums, the global financial industry must become a more committed partner of the UN in its search for a post-Seattle strategy. As the first global business and the creator of the phenomenon of globalization, the financial industry has a major stake in its sustainability. Because it provides the financial infrastructure of trade and development, this sector should also feel particularly motivated to help the resumption of multilateral trade talks by engaging in the search for solutions to societal concerns. Finally, any framework that helps to create the emerging markets of the twenty-first century by securing their access to free trade and improving their economic opportunities should obtain the support of global financial firms. Through a more sustained relationship, the UN and the financial industry could devise a delivery mechanism for the values of the Compact. As early investors, joint-venturers, investment advisers, and providers of financial infrastructure, financial corporations can wield unequaled power over the corporate activities of multinationals and local industry in developing countries and emerging markets. The UN, on its side, must find ways to articulate its message, clearly outline the benefits of cooperation to the financial industry, and propose concrete modalities for partnership. As little patience as the private sector as a whole displays for the absence of operational concreteness, the financial sector will only be more impatient.

The Regulatory Challenge

The implementation of the Compact's vision is first and foremost a regulatory and normative challenge. The difficulty lies in defining a unique and effective UN role against the richness of decentralized and global regulatory standards currently available. One starting point may be for the UN to suggest that sufficient efforts have now been expended in regulatory exercises and that the time has come to take stock of the standards that have been developed in the three value areas of the Compact. The current competition between standards could produce the achievement of the lowest common denominator, when the opposite ought to be the goal. It also results in higher information costs for corporations seeking to evaluate competing standards. Under the aegis of the secretary-general's office, the UN may consider convening a conference where such global regulatory bodies as the Global Reporting Initiative, the Sullivan Principles, the Center for Economic Priorities Accreditation Agency (CEPAA), and the ISO mechanism, as well as corporations and industrial sectors that have developed their own standards, would discuss the possibility of a joint consolidation exercise.

Pending such a gathering, and in order to facilitate the exchange of views and experience between regulatory bodies, UN agencies, and the private sector at large, the UN has chosen the virtual route of the Internet. On January

31, 2000, the UN launched a new website, www.unglobalcompact.org, which is likely to become the most exhaustive and credible source of information on the regulatory efforts of corporations and the good practices adopted in conformity with such standards. Developed externally, the UN Global Compact website acts as a catalyst for information exchange and discussions on the future of global regulatory initiatives. Among the site's 40 active participants and information providers are the ICC, the WBCSD, the IOE, CEPAA, the Sullivan Principles, Business for Social Responsibility, NGOs such as Amnesty International and Human Rights Watch, and labor unions. The site expounds on the rationale of the Global Compact and provides tools and handbooks on regulation and good practices, including the tools of private sector firms such as KPMG. It also provides access to the databases of NGOs, which supply detailed information and statistics on the human rights and labor rights situations of every country around the world. Finally, the site proposes schemes for granting awards to firms that comply with yet-to-be defined standards.

The dynamic and catalytic nature of the Internet enables all participants to share information and experience in a single place with zero transaction costs. There is no doubt that such an initiative potentially sets the participants on a course toward consolidation and harmonization of standards. Accomplishing the latter, however, will not naturally result from a web-based exchange of data. It will require a political decision on the part of the UN system and political goodwill on the part of private sector actors. The UN must decide whether it is ready to play a leading normative role in the context of globalization, and match its decision with adequate resources. Corporations and private regulatory agencies must decide whether they are willing to give up some measure of autonomy to back a universal effort, and in turn put their capacities and knowledge at the service of a UN-led initiative.

Once such political decisions have been made by each actor, a UN-led standard-setting initiative could take the form of a "global public policy network."[32] Because global public policy networks "can help overcome stalemates in highly conflict-ridden policy arenas,"[33] the UN could invite business associations, UN normative bodies, and regulatory agencies to coalesce in a decentralized yet focused manner in the search for a consensus on norms in the three issue areas of the Compact. Building on their "structured informality," networks facilitate the exchange of data; build trust between the parties by closing the "participatory gap;" increase the chances of successful negotiation by not threatening the autonomy of each party; and help revive the UN by giving its agencies the role of "norm entrepreneurs" and revitalizing "weak or weakening conventions," such as the ILO's.[34]

Indeed, of the three UN organizations directly linked to the Compact—the Office of the UN Commissioner for Human Rights, UNEP, and the

ILO—the latter is the most capable of playing an immediate normative role. In existence since 1919, the ILO has had almost a century to think about and develop policies on labor issues. Its tripartite structure makes it credible to business and labor. Its various declarations on labor have been widely accepted and signed by the majority of states. The signing of the Convention on Child Labor by the United States in November 1999 only strengthened the authority of that document. For the first time since its creation, the ILO's historical hour may finally have arrived.[35] Three questions remain regarding the ILO's future normative power: how to integrate its work within existing regulatory activities at all levels; how to strengthen the authority of its conventions; and how to develop an enforcement mechanism for a future set of universal labor standards.[36] In the post-Seattle context, such work may need to be coordinated with the WTO, as a resumption of trade talks remains a priority irretrievably bound to the provision of solutions to social and domestic concerns.

Translating the Global Compact to UN Partnerships

UN bodies with operational mandates also constitute transmission belts for embedding the Compact's values in UN activities and relationships. These agencies must take the lead in translating the Compact's values to UN-business partnerships, country programs, and field projects. Because they address value concerns, UN guidelines for private sector collaboration are a prime instrument of operationalization of the Compact. But corporations that enter into partnerships with UN bodies represent a minority of businesses. Operationalization must therefore go beyond the niche of UN-business partnerships to affect the UN's operations in and relations with the approximately 175 nations in which the UN operates.

One method for integrating these values in all UN activities and relationships would be to adopt a series of mini-Compacts targeted to the UN's main mandate areas. Under such a concept, the three value areas of the Compact would be adjusted to six broad UN mandates, each regrouping several UN bodies. The six broad UN mandates can be defined as follows: 1) economic and social development (UNDP, UNEP, UNOPS, HABITAT, UNIDO); 2) peacekeeping (DPKO, some aspects of the activities of UNHCR and WFP); 3) humanitarian assistance and post-conflict work (UNICEF, UNHCR, WFP, UNOPS); 4) health, women, and children (UNICEF, UNFPA, UNDP, WHO, UNAIDS); 5) population and family planning (UNFPA, WHO); 6) the technical mandates (ICAO, ITU, IAEA, etc.).[37] Agencies working in each of these six areas could form working groups to adopt a set of values and principles derived from the Compact's three value areas, but more directly related to the work of the respective agencies. These mini-Compacts would then become the conceptual maps informing the UN's activities, partnerships, and relationships in all major UN mandates. At the agency level, operational staff would further adjust these mini-Compacts to their specific business environment, specifying internal rules and guidelines that would ensure the operational translation of the mini-Compacts' and the Global Compact's values. Such rules could apply to an agency's funding mandate, relationships with governments, procurement and outsourcing regime, recruitment procedures, selection criteria for corporate partners, and communication policy—in such a way as to inform all agency-level activities with principles and values derived from the macro vision of the Compact. If all actors that seek the UN's legitimacy and support were submitted to the respect of these values and operational rules, the Global Compact would begin to affect a wide array of relationships and activities around the world.

The following example in the area of post-conflict illustrates the three-level approach outlined above:

Level I : Macro Level of the Global Compact

Three value areas   Human Rights
                      Labor Rights
                      Environmental Standards

Level II: Intermediate Level of the Mini-Compacts

In the example chosen here, the mini-Compact would address the specific mandate of humanitarian assistance and post-conflict work (including but not limited to rehabilitation, resettlement of refugees, mine action, governance programs and election monitoring, institution-building, and reconstruction of infrastructure).

A list of values derived from the Global Compact and applicable to the specific mandate described above could read as follows. (The list is illustrative and far from exhaustive.)

- Respect of fundamental human rights in UN post-conflict work, including in all partnerships and interactions between UN, state, non-state, and non-UN actors on the ground. A list of "fundamental human rights," derived from the Universal Declaration adopted in 1948, would be defined and appended to this mini-Compact;
- Nondiscrimination on the basis of gender, religion, and ethnicity in all UN recruitment procedures on the ground, including the recruitment of partners of the UN—be they governments, NGOs, or businesses;

- Equitable and nondiscriminatory access to decision-making and economic resources (land, water, housing) in post-conflict societies;
- Neutrality toward ethnic groups in reconciliation and reconstruction processes. This principle would have to be respected by UN organs as well as all partners of the UN in country;
- Nondiscrimination in all UN training and education programs on the ground;
- Encouragement of gender equity in institution-building or reform, economic reconstruction, and the overall political process (elections);
- Total exclusion of child labor or hazardous labor conditions (labor rules would be defined in collaboration with the ILO); and
- Sustainable use of water, air, and land resources throughout UN work in the field. UN partners would be submitted to the same requirements. For example, the resettlement of refugees or the establishment of refugee camps would abide by a set of environmental standards to be defined at the operational level (below).

Level III. Operational Rules

Each UN body would refine the principles of the mini-Compacts to its specific operational environment, although some overlap would appear among the operational guidelines of various agencies. Inasmuch as they both implement projects in post-conflict rehabilitation, for example, UNOPS and UNHCR would share some operational rules for these types of projects. Neither organization would procure goods from a corporation associated in any way with the production of landmines, for example. Yet the activities of both agencies are sufficiently different to require two sets of operational rules adjusted to their respective business environments. Furthermore, agencies with multiple mandates would adopt the values of different mini-Compacts and follow different operational rules depending on the mandate area of each project. UNICEF, for example, would borrow from at least two mini-Compacts: health, women, and children; and humanitarian assistance and post-conflict work.

A sample of rules derived from the mini-Compact of humanitarian assistance and post-conflict work could read as follows:

- Refrain from procuring goods or services from, and partnering with companies associated with landmine production, child labor, unsafe labor conditions, and discriminatory practices;
- Apply nondiscrimination and neutrality clauses to agency-level recruitment procedures. Develop a monitoring mechanism at the agency and project level. Extend these rules to business partners of the agency;
- Develop a monitoring mechanism for the respect of fundamental human rights at the agency and project level;

- Design communication and awareness materials to advocate gender equity and nondiscrimination in local post-conflict projects; and
- Develop standards, quantitative measures, and a monitoring mechanism to ensure the sustainable use of natural resources in refugee camps and the construction of new settlements.

The UNOPS Geneva office has already applied many of these principles and operational guidelines to its post-conflict rehabilitation projects in various countries.[38] The so-called RESS Approach developed by that office also informed the proposals presented by UNOPS in the context of the mine action and post-conflict workshops at the Aid & Trade conference in May 2000. In one such proposal, a New York-based small enterprise, Peace-Works, invested in Guatemala with the political support of the government and the United Nations, the advocacy support of local and international NGOs, the financial involvement of the World Bank, and the logistical backing of UNOPS. The firm specializes in post-conflict investment—a new type of economic activity that promotes peace processes and national reconciliation through economic projects co-owned and co-developed by former enemies in a conflict. The local investment was facilitated by Industrias Para La Paz, a consortium of Guatemalan socially responsible entrepreneurs motivated to strengthen national reconciliation through economic activity.[39]

The application of values to UNOPS's project execution and management mandate demonstrates that no UN operational activity is devoid of value considerations. In fact, the credibility and long-term success of post-conflict work is highly dependent on the ability to embed values and principles in all aspects of operations—a reality demonstrated time and again in UN electoral assistance programs as well as the work of the Clarification Commission in Guatemala, to cite only two examples.[40]

The three-level task outlined above has some intrinsic limits, inasmuch as the UN's operational mandates are likely to decrease and the UN's impact on global economic relations is minimal. The imposition of value considerations to UN procurement relationships would bear little impact, as UN contracts do not amount to more than $3 billion a year. If, however, such considerations were imposed on all partners and actors with which the UN entertains relations around the world, these conditions would begin to make their mark. The UN's name retains a great deal of legitimacy, especially in developing countries, and moral influence should not be discounted. This operationalization effort could therefore be seen as reinforcing both the advocacy campaign and the regulatory work outlined earlier. Furthermore, in imposing on its own activities and those of its partners guidelines derived from the Global Compact's values, the UN would mirror the adoption of good corporate practices by industries and individual corporations. By linking its operational and normative activities together in a consistent conceptual approach, the UN would act as it preaches that business should behave.

While the conclusion to this book deals at length with the question of what is at stake in the Compact's dissemination, suffice it to say that its defeat would vindicate the protectionist pressure groups and their governmental supporters by killing the process of openness. By proposing to sustain globalization and taking global societal concerns seriously, the Global Compact is the best offer that business and civil society are likely to entertain in the coming decade. Any other formula would lead to stalemate by either threatening the interests of the private sector or dismissing the anxieties of the global citizenry. Once the compromise on which the Compact is premised is understood by a large number of actors around the world, it is likely to be supported by them too. Surely the business community should pick up the Compact's flag and tout it to governments as the best alternative to domestic protectionist pressure.

Creating a Favorable Environment

The adoption of new guidelines for cooperation, improvements in the UN's management of legal, financial, and country risks, a clearer definition of conflict of interest, and cultural adjustments were suggested above as means of improving the compatibility of UN and business partners. A more sensitive issue is the development of a new UN staff predisposed toward and skilled to implement the new policy, both in its normative and operational aspects. It is only logical that a new policy should demand new recruits, and renewing the UN's ranks would have a positive impact on the sustainability of UN-business relations.

Organizational Change

The first change that can take place at the agency level is organizational in nature. All UN agencies with a significant NGO and private sector outreach should establish a Partnership Division or Unit (depending on the size of their private sector outreach) with a direct reporting line to the agency head. As things now stand in most UN bodies, partnerships are distributed across functional and geographical divisions, which results in multiple lines of reporting and decision-making and creates a great deal of confusion among corporate representatives not accustomed to UN acronyms. While private sector partnerships will continue to overlap across multiple divisions and units within each UN body, UN organizations engaged in this line of work must appoint a focal point responsible for centralizing information and linking directly with the business community. These Partnership Divisions or Units would be charged with conceptualizing the contents of partnerships; seeking new potential partners; ensuring an effective flow of information to and from corporations, as well as linking with civil society; handling media inquiries; producing communication materials; and maintaining a database of best practices and lessons learned. The operational, financial, and legal aspects of partnerships would continue to be managed by the respective geographical and functional divisions, but the business community would benefit from having a single entry point into each UN agency.[41] Establishing such separate divisions or units would also promote the development of a specific culture within them and facilitate the recruitment of new staff members through the creation of new posts. The latter should be filled through open advertising and by reaching out to nontraditional hiring pools.

Human Resources Management

Changes in UN human resources management and recruitment will be essential to maintaining a successful UN-business relationship. This is true both at the policy and at the operational level. The salience of human resources to the UN's private sector outreach lies in the fact that the types of skills and professional profiles needed to manage this new line of work are not widely available in the UN system. Moreover, a portion of the UN bureaucracy remains suspicious of the very policy of rapprochement. As will be reviewed below, training will address some of these shortcomings. But it cannot address them all and it will require more time than the UN can afford. UN agencies therefore must find ways to attract young business professionals, economists, and other policymakers from outside the system.[42]

One quick and politically manageable tactic for attracting new blood consists in increasing the UN recourse to secondment procedures. Under this method, corporations can "lend" members of their staff to UN agencies for a limited period of time under varying financial arrangements. (In some cases, salaries are born entirely by the lending organization; in others they may be shared with the UN body.) Secondment is attractive to both sides: corporations learn the ropes of the UN system, get a political education, and increase their contacts in developing countries. The UN system benefits from the work of talented professionals with desirable skills at low or no cost. While secondment contracts may arouse some internal opposition, their finite duration makes them less contentious than permanent recruiting outside the system. It should be noted that UN member states have consistently stalled the increased use of secondment procedures, which they see as "stealing" job opportunities for their own nationals.

Opening up UN recruitment to the outside world is a long-term project, but it may in fact be aided by the specific requirements of UN-private sector partnerships. Partly responsible for the absence of changes on that front is what I have called elsewhere the "malthusianism" of reform—an attitude imposed on the UN system by a number of member states, the United States first among them.[43] Because UN reform proposals have been dominated by budget and staff cuts, it has become more difficult to create and appoint new recruits to UN posts. As a result, the UN system is engaged in a worldwide recycling exercise whereby UN staff members are shifted among posts and locations, leaving the system with little access to new skills and professional experience. Member states must understand that their obsession with quantitative reform is partly responsible for the failure of qualitative reform, and that ending the freeze on hiring would provide the means for renewing the UN's ranks.

Still, there are ways to decentralize and free recruiting policies, and acquiring the skills necessary to implement UN-business partnerships may provide the justifications for long-awaited changes in UN human resources management. UNOPS is able to hire professional staff members within 10 days, versus an average of 461 days at UN Headquarters. These achievements are due to the establishment by UNOPS of a specific personnel regime, which nonetheless respects UN staff rules and provides UNOPS staff members with equal privileges. This comparative advantage has two positive consequences for human resources reform. Firstly, this personnel regime allows UNOPS to recruit young professionals from all walks of life, although the limited duration of their contracts does not guarantee the longevity of their presence at the UN. Secondly, UN bodies that choose to subcontract their recruitment processes to UNOPS can equally achieve the benefits of fast and open recruiting.[44] Meanwhile, a report on recruitment reform applicable to the UN Secretariat had failed to deliver any concrete change by the end of 1999.[45] The UN is therefore far from sending clear signals on such business values as an open labor market—issues that have a bearing on the UN's compatibility and collaboration with the private sector.

Finally, training programs specifically tailored to UN-business partnering will improve the skills of UN staff members as well as their responsiveness to the concept of UN-private sector collaboration. Under a $500,000 grant from the UN Foundation, the UN Staff College and the PWBLF launched a course in the spring of 2000 aimed at UN staff members around the world. Taught by UN, PWBLF, and business representatives in situ, the course focuses on partnering techniques between private and public entities, best practices in this area, and case studies of UN-business partnerships. Among the objectives of the course is to foster consistency in partnership approaches, encourage creativity in partnering, and increase commitment to collaboration between the UN and the private sector. Distance learning programs are planned for the year 2001 to increase access to the course by UN field staff around the world. Representatives of corporations were invited to make substantive contributions to the course and provide instructors. Their viewpoint as equal partners in UN-business partnerships can only benefit UN staff members. One hopes that in time the course may develop into a mini business- training program with sessions on such topics as accounting, business planning, marketing strategy, and corporate communication. Again, the objective here is not to turn UN professionals into business experts but to contribute to the development of a common language that will improve communication and therefore operational efficiency.

From Partnership to Representation?

Giving nonstate actors a representative status within the United Nations is not a novel idea. Through its Article 71, which allows for the accreditation of civil society groups to the United Nations, the crafters of the UN Charter demonstrated that they understood the need to institutionalize the relationship between states and nonstate actors. As was stated in chapter 1, in the first years of the UN's existence only the ICC, followed by labor and employers' unions, took the UN up on its offer. More recently, NGOs have led the movement toward more meaningful representation—by increasing their participation in UN international conferences and seeking a substantive role in their proceedings, for example. In 1997, the watershed achievement of a ban against landmines by the International Campaign to Ban Landmines confirmed the entrance of civil society in the most securely guarded province of the state: disarmament and arms control. While this success did not give it a seat on the UN General Assembly disarmament committee, the campaign has managed to impose itself as the inescapable partner, mediator, and broker on all issues related to the ban, including its implementation and ratification by additional states. These marginal increases in civil society power cannot therefore be equated with a formal institutionalization of its status and function; yet it is doubtful that NGOs will stop their quest for stepped-up representation. Displaying a behavior that befits the hush-hush of executive boardrooms, the private sector has been more discreet in its representational claims, but two factors make it likely that corporations will catch up.

The Logic of Representation

While UN member states can be expected to fight the trend, forward-thinking scholars and policymakers understand that nonstate actors have become and will increasingly be key participants in the global political process. The question therefore arises as to how to channel their claims, contributions, and potential solutions to the problems of the global era in an international system of nation-states. Failing to institutionalize their participation would result in a number of dysfunctions at the level of global policymaking. These institutional shortcomings would leave the public relations power of non-state groups intact, at the same time as their accountability to the public would be weak since their input would not be mediated by an institutional setting. Alternatively, the continued absence of representation could reduce their participation in the global political process, either because such participation would be difficult to organize outside of institutions, or because nonstate groups would lose interest in a process that does not reward them with formal representation in exchange for their resources. It is doubtful, indeed, that both business and civil society groups will continue to put their multifaceted resources—time, people, money, expertise, technology—at the service of states and multilateral institutions without some form of political payoff. Furthermore, as was argued at length in chapter 1, the global polity cannot expect to address the challenges of the coming century without the resources of metanational actors.

By definition riveted to the national dimension, governments cannot expect to compete with the geographical reach of global corporations and NGOs. As public sector actors, they also cannot keep up with the pace of corporate life. Finally, the Schumpeterian creative capitalism that characterizes the global economy enables corporations to craft more complex responses to the paradoxical contiguity of globalization and localization.[46] There is no circumventing the capacities of nonstate actors, therefore, lest governments fail their responsibility to provide the public good of relevant and peacemaking policies, for which societies give them legitimacy in the first place. The issue of integrating nonstate actors in intergovernmental bodies therefore comes down to when and how.

The UN's Comparative Advantage

The United Nations boasts several advantages in the search for ways to institutionalize the contributions of nonstate actors to the global political process. Firstly, Article 71 of the UN Charter already provides a mechanism for doing so. Secondly, as the sole universal organization of the world community, the United Nations presents a natural setting for integrating the diverse faces and groups of the global polity. Thirdly, UN bodies enjoy fruitful and long-established working relations with these actors. NGOs and UN agencies work together, know each other, and often exchange staff. Finally, as an intergovernmental organization, the United Nations is in the best position to act as mediator and broker in the new relationship between state and nonstate actors. Key to this brokering role in the coming years will be the ability to reassure UN member states as to their ultimate political authority while convincing them of the dangers inherent in failing to institutionalize the participation in and contributions of nonstate actors to the global political process. The international system that began to be crafted in the seventeenth century served the international community through the twentieth because it provided means for institutionalizing the role and tapping the capacities of nation-states. To be equally successful, the global polity that is being constructed in our era must devise appropriate ways for integrating nonstate actors in its norms, institutions, and actions.

Proposals for Giving Business a UN Representative Status

1. Business Advisory Boards

Beyond the ICC's accreditation to the UN in 1946, the only precedent aimed at institutionalizing the contribution of a business group within the United Nations was the creation of the ICC's Consultative Committee in 1969. As was stated in chapter 1, the latter fell into oblivion for lack of UN interest and was never reenergized. Discussions on the creation of business advisory boards at the agency level or in the cabinet of the secretary-general have multiplied in recent years, to the point where hardly any UN organ is not entertaining the idea. Little concrete progress has been made at this stage, however. Establishing such a board in the secretary-general's office is fraught with political problems. Too many senior UN officials still oppose the new role of the private sector in UN affairs to make it palatable to impose such a decision from the top. The project is also mired in interagency squabbles regarding the geographical and sector distribution of businesses on a theoretical business advisory board. How to ensure the representation on the board of all industrial and service sectors relevant to all UN agencies finds no easy answer. Issues of gender and geographical equity are thornier yet.

UNOPS's unique status as the business organization of the UN system may again provide an advantage. In the fall of 1999, UNOPS began discussions with a group of five prestigious business and political leaders on ways to establish a UNOPS Business Advisory Council of 10–15 members that would provide counsel directly to the executive director, meet in plenary once or twice a year, and carry out special projects and studies in the interim. UNOPS's specific needs as a project management organization provide an economic rationale for establishing such a board. This unique status enables UNOPS to escape the political pitfalls of similar discussions in the rest of the UN system. To continue to grow and face its competitors, UNOPS must develop a business strategy and secure its access to the best business skills available in such areas as legal policy, marketing strategy, corporate communication, and financial management. The council UNOPS is attempting to form would therefore act as a provider of business expertise rather than as a political body. Were it to succeed in this enterprise, UNOPS's experiment might have positive ripple effects on the rest of the UN system. The creation of the UNOPS Business Advisory Council may deflate the political overtones of the current debate and unfreeze similar plans lying dormant in the drawers of other organizations daunted by the ideological opposition they have encountered thus far.

2. The Business Contribution to UN Reform

The contribution of the private sector to UN reform was outlined in chapter 1. While some critics point out that UN reform has virtually stopped, the secretary-general's outreach to the private sector constitutes the most substantive and radical addition to the reform debate in UN history. Were a forum to be established to begin translating the Global Compact into a set of norms and rules, the business contribution to that effort would constitute a significant step in a real reform of the UN—one aimed at making the organization relevant to the global polity of the twenty-first century. Although it remains controversial, the role of the private sector in supplying operational reform proposals will hopefully be revitalized as the recovered partnership becomes a fact of life. Once it is created, the UNOPS Business Advisory Council may make itself available to other UN bodies to offer advice on reorganization, human resources and legal management, financial administration, and other business functions. Were a national discussion on UN reform to resume among UN member states, and in the United States in particular, those business groups that have increased their ties with the UN system in recent years ought to be key interlocutors and information providers in this discussion. Business leaders should play a vital role in outlining the benefits of the UN to their private sector counterparts and renewing the national commitment to multilateralism. In the United States, several business associations are in good positions to organize congressional hearings in which business executives could inform national lawmakers on ongoing UN policy changes. From the vantage point of their recent experiences with the United Nations, business representatives could outline a reform agenda and recommend concrete measures needed to secure a fruitful and long-term UN-business relationship. Another proposal for integrating business in a discussion of the UN's future would consist of reviving the Consultative Committee provided by the ICC in the 1970s. The ICC is likely to play a significant role in the formulation of a post-Seattle strategy between UN agencies and the WTO. Based on the regular and highly compatible relationship that now links the ICC and the secretary-general's office, a group of ICC business executives may elicit greater interest from the UN system in 2000 than 30 years ago.

3. An Official Representative Status: Some Possibilities

The participation of business groups in UN international conferences became a regular occurrence in the 1990s. Business representatives, however, have often regretted the absence of concrete outcomes resulting from their attendance. Institutionalizing the representation of business groups at international conferences would require the approval of the General Assembly—a political milestone that probably lies years ahead of us. Specifically, it would imply extending the "features" of international conferences to the General Assembly, thereby giving NGOs and business groups an official participation in General Assembly debates.[48] In practical terms, nonstate actors would derive no clear benefits from obtaining a representative status within the General Assembly. The latter's representatives are not primarily concerned with, nor skilled to discuss and solve the challenges of globalization. As the UN's primary legislative body, however, the General Assembly retains ultimate voting power over UN agendas, reforms, and institutional structures. Because it is mandated to address economic and social matters, a more logical forum to integrate the contributions of nonstate actors would be ECOSOC. Formalizing the representation of private sector and NGO groups in its midst, however, would require the approval of the General Assembly, whose legislative power ECOSOC does not match. The GA cannot be circumvented, which explains the slow pace of changes regarding the participation of nonstate actors in UN deliberations and decision-making.

The weakness and irrelevance of ECOSOC to the challenges of the global era have led to a flurry of reform proposals in recent years, including the suggestion to eliminate ECOSOC altogether. ECOSOC's very shortcomings and threatened future provide an opening for integrating the private sector in its midst. If the member states that constitute the General Assembly hope to justify the existence and functions of ECOSOC in the coming decades, the latter ought to build the internal capacity to think seriously about and devise strategies for addressing the problems of the global economy. Formulating a relevant message and useful solutions in the context of globalization implies a recognition of the business nature of that process and the accompanying power of global corporations. Based on this understanding, ECOSOC could welcome the private sector into its deliberations and policymaking process as a means of revamping its mission and salvaging its very existence as a body dedicated to social and economic issues.

A starting point for the inclusion of the private sector in ECOSOC would be to engage business groups in the follow-up to global conferences by integrating a business component in post-conference implementation taskforces or committees at the agency or interagency level. Business groups could be associated to the drafting of follow-up reports, as well as the definition of timelines and strategies for achieving objectives. UN agencies ought to review the possibility of moving toward such a reform without ECOSOC's or the General Assembly's approval. Without the commitment, resources, and substantive contributions of the private sector, the recommendations of global conferences will only fill the dustbins of history. As was demonstrated in chapter 1, the ICC played a more active role in League of Nations conferences in the 1920s than it does in UN conferences today. Given the central position of business in the process of globalization, this backward movement is fundamentally irrational and fraught with dangers. UN agencies must begin a discussion with member states on allowing large international business groups such as the ICC to co-sign the final declarations of international conferences and other significant UN texts on economic and social issues. Making the private sector the co-signatory of relevant UN documents would bind corporations to the realization of societal goals, thereby dramatically increasing the credibility and power of these texts and the resolutions that emerge from UN international conferences. As things currently stand, the actors most concerned with the subject matter of economic and social conferences and best equipped to translate their injunctions into reality are left out of the negotiation and implementation process. The lack of progress on the recommendations of these international meetings cannot be dissociated from the larger challenge of global governance.

The road toward a reformulation of global governance arrangements is long and pitted with obstacles, but the UN system and its member states must engage in an urgent debate on the matter. Leaving aside the UN's peace and security mandates, the construction of an institutional format linking the main actors of the global polity is the only significant challenge facing the UN system in the economic and social realm. Were the UN to be incapable of reinterpreting its Charter and transforming its structures to allow for the inclusion of nonstate actors in the formulation and implementation of economic and social policy, there is little doubt that a novel institutional mechanism—organization, forum, or else—would arise in due course to fulfill this function.

• • •

The lessons drawn from the recent experience of UN-private sector partnerships and the directions set for the coming years point to the size and sensitivity of the challenge of sustaining the UN relationship with the private sector. While the crafters of the policy of rapprochement correctly stress that the UN's normative functions are its best assets and most important contribution to the process of globalization, business leaders are typically more interested in the operational aspects of policy and their impact on the bottom line. Both sides are correct and must see their respective functions as compatible and mutually reinforcing. As work begins to operationalize the

Global Compact both at the regulatory level and in UN activities and relationships, it will soon become apparent that what is at stake is a larger challenge indeed, one questioning the capacity of the global polity to craft a new arrangement for a new era. Not since the seventeenth century has the community of the world's peoples confronted such a task.

CONCLUSION

What Is at Stake?

I n his biography of Secretary of State Dean Acheson, James Chace points out that when he was not elaborating the plans of the future NATO, Acheson liked to build wooden furniture. Of cabinet-making, the secretary of state once said: "The great thing about this hobby is that when I have finished a table or a chair and I put it down, it either stands or falls. It's not like foreign policy, you don't have to wait for twenty years to see whether it works."[1]

Having first entered my professional life as a draftsman in an architect's office, the parallels between architecture and international relations never cease to amaze me. System-building differs from architecture only in the materials one uses to put one's constructs on the ground. Where the architect uses steel and glass, the political analyst resorts to language and ideas. If the architect meets the test of truth long before the political scientist, it is because the gravity of physical matter is less elusive than that of concepts. The system of governance proposed in this book and the ideas that underpin it will not only require time to demonstrate their validity; they will take years to build. Before considering what is at stake in this vision, I wish to briefly summarize the argument.

The Argument

Because it is premised on pluralism and openness, the process of globalization that began in the early 1990s is, from a liberal viewpoint, fundamentally positive. This statement is consciously ideological. It runs counter to the belief that history and its accompanying ideologies have ended and counter to "Third Way" thinking, itself another incarnation of the end of history argument. Freedom and openness are no more neutral values today than they were in the eighteenth century or during the Cold War. Without delving into the intellectual roots of liberalism, support of the process of globalization assumes an endorsement of political and economic openness that itself makes specific claims about the individual, human society, peace and war, and the pursuit of the good. Criticism of globalization on the basis of the dislocations and imbalances it creates usually conceals an ideological opposition to openness and cosmopolitanism. As the media repeat ad nauseam the cliché of the end of ideologies in the age of the Internet, it is useful to correct what this author, at least, perceives as an erroneous reading of the zeitgeist.

It is precisely because trade and other forms of exchange are seen as peace-promoting that globalization must be sustained. Concerns about the negative externalities of globalization—global warming, child labor, a widening of inequalities, the AIDS pandemic—lead to the search for remedial actions that can ensure rather than stall the continuation of the process. The Global Compact and other statements issued by UN Secretary-General Kofi Annan since 1997 are premised on the need to sustain and indeed increase free trade and the access of the developing countries to export markets. Poverty and glaring inequalities in access to health, education, and information are seen as major threats to international stability. Scenarios for a large-scale disruption of the process of globalization are varied, but all assume a social reaction against openness with potential war-causing effects that could spread globally. In both Asia and Russia in 1998, economic turmoil was accompanied by social unrest. The liberal assumption according to which trade is the best remedy against poverty and social inequalities underpins the Global Compact. As Secretary-General Kofi Annan wrote in a 1999 editorial, "trade is cheaper than aid."[2] Moreover, official aid is unlikely to return to its pre-1990 level. The role of trade in reducing poverty therefore makes resuming multilateral trade talks and controlling domestic protectionist pressures in the developed world two indivisible priorities of UN and world policymakers.

Because the trade system ought to be protected from social and environmental clauses that conceal protectionist interests, other mechanisms must be found to address the societal concerns that threaten the sustainability of globalization. The Global Compact proposes that UN normative and regulatory agencies be strengthened and reformed in order that they might propose universally applicable norms that will guarantee the respect of fundamental values in the areas of human rights, labor, and the environment. These UN organs, as well as UN operational agencies working in partnership with the private sector, must develop ways to embed these norms and values in the global economy. The approach also requires the support and coordinated actions of states and civil society. Of the former, it was said that while they have lost the capacity to regulate global economic and financial exchanges, they retain the authority to approve and support policies—an authority demonstrated by their status as the only voting members of such intergovernmental organizations as the United Nations. Additionally, they retain the primary allegiance of their citizens, even if the buds of a global citizenry are blooming here and there. Civil society, for its part, has sprouted across borders and agendas. Swelling the ranks of UN forums to which they are accredited, NGOs have become key variables in the global policy equation. The three value areas of the Global Compact match the overriding interests of global NGOs, 80 percent of which devote their activism to human rights, labor rights, and the environment. The capacity of the International Campaign to Ban Landmines to literally force its agenda on a majority of world governments in 1997 signaled a radical shift in the distribution of power among global policymakers, the implications of which have not been fully digested by nation-states.

In 1997, Secretary-General Kofi Annan embarked on a consistent and determined policy of rapprochement with the private sector. This decision was premised on the conviction that, without the support of global business, large and small, sustaining globalization in the respect of fundamental values could only fail. The Global Compact hinges on a renewed and productive UN-business relationship for three reasons. Firstly, the end of the Cold War eliminated non-market-based economic theories as credible rivals of free markets and free enterprise. The role of private sector firms, private philanthropies, and private consultants in providing the policy advice and the actual plans followed by the countries of Eastern Europe and the former Soviet Union in their transition to the free market was symptomatic of a shift to the privatization not only of enterprises but also of policymaking. Despite establishing offices throughout the region, the UN was not apt to devise pro-market policies as it emerged from two decades of a Marxist-inclined, structuralist economic discourse. Secondly, most analysts agree that globalization is a business-led process driven initially by the financial industry, followed by manufacturing and other service sectors, and now the entertainment industry as well. The Internet—this archetypal icon of globalization—owes its growth and success to the genius and inventiveness of risk-taking entrepreneurs based mostly in the United States. Because globalization is first and foremost a creation of business, devising a policy and structures suited to its specificity will necessarily require the contribution and support of those actors who generated it and remain its primary movers. Finally, the outreach of the UN system to the business community follows four decades of at best mitigated results in international assistance to the developing world, a half-baked success (or failure) that has entailed so-called "donor fatigue" and the disaffection of developing nations toward the schemes of aid organizations. Why the private sector was left out of both the debate on and the implementation of development policies for the better part of the UN's history owes much to the ideological nature of the Cold War. It took the end of that conflict to put the private sector back where it belonged: at the center of development and economic growth. Yet it would be erroneous to see the UN's courtship of multinationals as motivated by a search for lost ODA.

The Future of Development Assistance

Official Development Assistance (ODA) refers to the transfer by developed countries, on a bilateral or multilateral basis, of grants and low-interest loans to developing countries to assist the latter in their economic and social development efforts. Although the general public lumps the funding of UN and other international organizations together with ODA, the two do not overlap entirely. ODA benefits such bodies as UNDP and the World Bank inasmuch as it supports their lending or granting activities. But ODA should not be confused with government contributions to the regular budgets of multilateral institutions themselves. ODA assumes the transfer of funds by developed nations to the developing countries.

The recent literature on ODA and its 40-year record is prolix. In recent years, however, a consensus seems to have emerged on the conditions required to ensure the effective use of ODA. While unconditional defenders of government funding of international assistance still make their voices heard—the UN and bilateral technical cooperation agencies boast quite a few of these activists—the record of ODA is so mitigated and expectations so diminished as to seriously question the relevance of this approach to the economic challenges of the twenty-first century.

Many factors seem to have limited the good use of ODA in the past decades, and they cannot be fully listed here. Among key disincentives to an efficient use of ODA is the lack of ownership of development policies by recipient countries, and the domination of the aid agenda by the own bureaucratic needs and policy preferences of donors.[3] As a result, recipients have had mixed feelings about ODA, needing the money on the one hand, yet convinced that the objectives of its use have been captured by donors and international organizations that know best. The siphoning off of aid through corruption may be partly imputed to the distancing of developing countries from the development policy process and the irresponsibility that ensues. Corruption has had counterproductive effects on aid not only through the sheer waste of ODA funds, but also by lowering private investment, thereby reducing growth. In low-income countries, the cumulative effect of corruption "could quite easily and relatively quickly (five to six years) reduce the impact of aid to such an extent as to render its development justification untenable."[4]

Corruption also explains in part the shift toward the macroeconomic conditionality of aid that took place 15–20 years ago in the development policy literature. The so-called "conditionality paradigm," according to which aid should be delivered to countries with sound and stable macro-economic policies and performance, dominated World Bank and IMF lending policies in the 1980s and early 1990s. Yet macroeconomic conditionality did not prove more effective in guaranteeing the good use of ODA.[5] In recent years, a new emphasis has emerged, this time favoring the institutional conditions of the use of ODA. Because it links quantitative achievements to the qualitative environment in which aid is disbursed, this paradigm proposes a more complete and realistic picture of what ODA can be expected to produce in developing countries. Also influenced by the corruption debate, proponents of this view have insisted on the quality of institutions, the presence of monitoring and regulatory mechanisms, and the quality of the democratic process as the main determinants of effective aid policies. This line of thinking is politically liberal, as it sees development as directly affected by the degree of freedom in society, the presence of checks and balances, and the accountability of elected officials through democratic elections and vibrant civic groups.[6] As a result of this candid assessment of the political environments of developing countries, World Bank and UN policies have shifted toward governance, institutional, and civil society programs.[7]

The record of ODA and the recent shift toward institutional conditions raise a critical question as to whether ODA and its traditional method of delivery are best suited to the creation of open and stable societies. If, as the World Bank proposes, "the evaluation of development aid should focus . . . on the extent to which financial resources have contributed to sound policy environments . . . [and] the extent to which agencies have used their resources to stimulate the policy reforms and institutional change that lead to better outcomes,"[8] it is not clear that the traditional mechanism of bilateral assistance transferred and managed by international organizations constitutes the best strategy for achieving institutional changes.

The involvement of the private sector in the development process through the concept of partnership is likely to affect positively the search for more open societies in the developing world. For one, the private sector itself operates under a model of openness and freedom—political liberalism preceded economic liberalism and the two are mutually reinforcing. As a member of civil society, the private sector can encourage and provide a model for the development of a richer civic environment in the developing countries. Additionally, as was argued in chapter 4, the profit motivation of corporations may provide a more effective antidote against corruption than international organizations have been able to devise thus far. The microeconomic nature of business activities will also increase the control and ownership of local communities in their development. Because business matches the double incarnation of globalization in that it is both global and local, it can constitute an ideal partner in the development of future growth policies with both cross-border and community-level dimensions. Finally, no international organization or government can compete with the advantages enjoyed by corporations in technology, knowledge, best business practice, and adaptability, thereby placing the onus of economic development on the private sector.

What then will happen to ODA and development assistance? In the short term, I predict a status quo; but the declining trend is sure to be confirmed.[9] For mostly bureaucratic reasons, governments will continue to devote a share of their GNPs to official assistance. Too many departments, offices, and careers both at the national and the international level depend on the continuation of this process for it to dry up rapidly. The return of ODA to its Cold War levels, however, seems ruled out. The end of the Cold War precisely discredited governmental approaches to economic management. The quasi-universal acceptance of the superiority of free markets has submitted governments themselves to the rationale of economic efficiency. Domestic constituents expect the use of their tax money to be accounted for, and except in Europe, most citizens prefer their taxes to go down than up. Each year policymakers find it more difficult to ask their parliaments for ODA funding when the vibrancy of private entrepreneurship and philanthropy stares them in the face. ODA, in its traditional form, is simply not part of the zeitgeist, and a new model is already evolving to replace it.

Among recently formulated innovative ideas are the World Bank's Comprehensive Development Framework (CDF), the direction of international assistance toward the provision of public goods, the common pool approach, and global policy networks.[10] By proposing a comprehensive approach to global and country-level challenges that addresses the entire spectrum of requisite conditions for an effective use of official assistance, the CDF takes stock of the past four decades and argues for a matrix integrating the spatial, economic, institutional, and chronological dimensions of development. While it devotes less attention to the means of delivering its vision, the CDF is not incompatible with other recently argued approaches. The focus on public goods has the merit of addressing the very rationale of assistance inasmuch as aid ought to facilitate the production of those goods that individual and national actors have no incentive to produce. It also matches the spatial dimensions of globalization, as public goods may be local, regional, or global and it is not contradictory with private sector involvement in the provision of those goods. The common pool approach and the global policy networks provide two funding models for future development assistance. The former suffers from a lack of oversight on the use of funds.[11] The latter has qualitative advantages, in that networks facilitate the formation of regional institutional settings focused on building policy and implementation capacity in the developing countries themselves, as opposed to leaving such capacities with the funding organizations. The global policy networks can be seen as institutional formats for the production of public goods at various geographical levels, and their loose, decentralized nature is particularly compatible with the context of globalization.

While none of these approaches has become the dominant paradigm, they share several points in common and might in fact coexist quite effectively. In proposing multilevel geographical formats and addressing the nonquantitative dimensions of development, all depart from the traditional project approach that dominated development policy in the 1960s and 1970s and which seems now buried. The authors of these models also foresee multiple decentralized funding arrangements as likely replacements for traditional bilateral assistance. As Mark Malloch Brown stated at Harvard in September 1999: "Maybe ODA is the wrong word because I am not sure it's going to be very official. . . . I am not sure it's going to be government to government."[12] While governments will continue to provide some form of assistance, the formats and objectives of funding will display increasing diversity. Various consortiums will be formed to fund various initiatives, and large corporations as well as major international philanthropists will wield greater financial and intellectual influence on development. Ted Turner's UN Foundation and Bill Gates's funding of global health initiatives already point the way to a certain privatization of aid, which does not question, however, the policy and implementation functions of multilateral institutions.

The new approaches also rely on multiple stakeholders for the production and delivery of the public goods of development—states, civil society, international organizations, and the private sector. Except in specific cases, they put the onus of responsibility and ownership on the developing countries and argue for a decentralization of multilateral programs rather than the construction of new institutions.[13] Finally, by assigning to multilateral organizations the role of providing advice and ideas, they assume that these organizations will turn away from operational activities and continue to reform themselves into knowledge-based institutions "selling" advisory services.[14] In the context of globalization, the image that emerges from the development literature is one of diversity in funding sources, spatial and chronological orientation of activities, actors and stakeholders, mandates and institutional formats.

Implications for the UN

This brief review of a matter to which economists have devoted millions of pages in the past 50 years was required to dispel misconceptions regarding the outreach of the UN to the private sector. It ought to be clear in light of the current transformation of development policy that the UN's policy of rapprochement with the business community is not motivated by an attempt to replace ODA, but rather to regain policy relevance in the context of a global world. The idea that corporate funds should replace ODA is surprising, if not preposterous. Multinationals have no reason to wish to relay governments in funding a model discredited by its own record and the ideological changes that accompanied the end of the Cold War. What is taking place is not a shift of funding sources but a shift of paradigm.

The implications of this shift will take time to seep through the UN system in its entirety, but they are probably unavoidable if the United Nations is to retain (some would say regain) political influence. The main change likely to affect UN agencies in the coming decade is a move away from direct operational involvement in project implementation and execution to a gradual delegation of this role to the private sector. As has already been stated, the project approach is being replaced by macro frameworks that no single multilateral organization has the competence or capacity to implement in full. The complexity and diversity of the future model of development assistance will require the coordinated actions of multiple actors—an area where UN and other multilateral organizations enjoy a comparative advantage. At the heart of the partnership approach, however, is the realization that only private sector firms can provide the research, technology, and development capacity to address the global health, environmental, and information challenges of the coming decade—to cite only three priorities of international action. What will UNDP do then? In the words of its own administrator, it must "be an advocate of good policy [and provide the advisors to implement it]; promote and facilitate regional cooperation; and strengthen [its] role in the areas of national policy formation, institution-building, and governance support."[15]

Because such a transformation will necessarily deplete the ranks of UN staff members working at the operational level in the field and at agency headquarters, it will require both time and willpower to be carried out. As in the case of ODA, UN jobs provide states with too many opportunities for political patronage for them to agree readily to qualitative reforms that, while making the UN more relevant, would also curtail its traditional activities. Operational tasks, however, will not disappear; they will only move elsewhere. Job opportunities in developing countries may be provided by other organizations, by corporations and consulting firms in particular. Providing UN staff with business training and professional retooling opportunities takes particular salience in this context. UN agencies will also issue a decreasing number of procurement contracts for goods and services themselves. Specialized procurement firms as well as procurement agencies in the developing countries are likely to pick up contracting responsibilities. Emerging markets rather than the UN market offer the largest potential for companies seeking contracts abroad. In addition to trickling out of the UN system, operational activities will be decentralized around the world. This conforms to efforts aimed at increasing the ownership and responsibilities of developing countries in crafting their own future.

Contrary to the argument according to which folding several agencies under the same roof would produce efficiency gains, the UN system is unlikely to consolidate into larger agencies with more diverse mandates. UN agencies with specialized mandates cannot derive economies of scale from being merged with incompatible bodies. The problem does not lie in the wide diversity of UN acronyms—even if their number unnerves those who cannot decipher them. At issue rather are the relevance, expertise, and efficiency of UN bodies in delivering their mandates. The technological nature of many of the challenges of development and current cross-border problems will require the specialized knowledge of focused expert bodies, not the fuzzy wisdom of multisectoral mastodons. The UN system will therefore remain diverse, if constituted of smaller organizations, and it will become more, not less decentralized. Governments, on the other hand, will increasingly assess the level of their contribution mandate by mandate and agency by agency. This has already become common practice in the United States and, like the domestic public sector before them, UN bodies can expect to be submitted to more stringent expectations of economic efficiency and more rigorous cost-benefit analyses.

The main challenge facing UN organizations in the coming decade, therefore, is to provide their private sector partners with the incentives to invest in the poorest countries, connect Africa to the Internet, help staunch the AIDS epidemic, and adopt universal environmental standards for sustainable growth. The public goods literature outlines several interesting opportunities for giving corporations incentives to produce impurely public goods, especially joint products and club goods.[16] Ultimately, the largest interest of the business community in joining hands with multilateral institutions lies in the unrealized markets of Africa, and to a great extent still, of Asia and Latin America. Multilateral organizations will use their comparative advantage to broker and legitimize relations between the private sector, civil society, and governments. Under the partnership approach, they will provide policy guidance where they have the capacity to do so, develop lessons learned on development policies, coordinate the actions of actors and stakeholders, and communicate the rationale for partnerships by demonstrating the business interest in them. They will lend their legitimacy to and participate in various institutional settings—World Bank, development banks, global policy networks, national institutions—but they will increasingly leave the business of implementation to those whose business it is.

The U.S.-UN Relationship

The role played by the United States in the creation of the United Nations and the incomparable advantage enjoyed by American corporations in the global economy make restoring America's active engagement in UN affairs a priority of whichever administration enters the White House in January 2001. As aloof and unproductive as the relationship has been allowed to become in the past decade, the trend can only be seen as an anomaly that, in the context of a more interconnected world, must be reversed.

Parallels between the constitutive beliefs of America and those of the UN Charter were hinted at in the introduction.[17] Early in the twentieth century, President Wilson described the principles of the League of Nations he was trying to build as "American principles."[18] The rule of law, the supreme values of human dignity and freedom that form the basis of equality between human beings, the modern notion of human rights that evolved out of the former, and the principle of nondiscrimination—all constitute the fundamental ideational constructs of the American "imagined community," which the United States has projected time and again on the international order and its institutions.[19] America's inorganic, civic nationalism is therefore highly compatible with international organizations that give equal rights to all nations and creatures irrespective of creed, ethnicity, race, and gender. These principles are inscribed both in the UN Charter and the UN Declaration of Human Rights, in whose adoption by the General Assembly in 1948 yet another American, Eleanor Roosevelt, played a leading role. The multilateral nature of the UN system finds its ideological justification not in the organic communities of the Old World, but in the idea-lism of the new.[20] It is not surprising therefore that "America has produced some of the world's most vigorous enthusiasts for international cooperation and most creative architects of international institutions."[21]

But the exceptionalism of the "city on a hill"—"the well-wisher to the freedom and independence of all . . . the champion and vindicator only of her own"[22]—has been difficult to reconcile with a policy of engagement and cooperation with the Old World of unprincipled power politics. The dilemma of America's "peerless" yet "indispensable" status plagued its stance toward multilateralism and its interactions with multilateral institutions during the entire twentieth century.[23] Overall, it took strong leaders with an outstanding talent at building coalitions to silence the populist, anticosmopolitan isolationists that questioned American engagement in international organizations since the League of Nations debate.[24] While both the League and the UN were created under the leadership of Democratic administrations, it would be erroneous to blame the Republican Party as a whole for the failure to support multilateralism. Populism has its adherents on both sides of the ideological divide, and several Republican presidents stood as great internationalist defenders of engagement. The vociferous opposition of a minority to the principles of multilateralism does not illustrate the isolationism of an entire party as much as it points to a textbook political phenomenon: the collective action problem.

In their excellent survey of American attitudes toward international organizations, Kull and Destler provide endless evidence of wide public support for a policy of sustained American engagement and cooperation.[25] Pointing to a disconnection between the opinion the policy elites have formed about public attitudes and those attitudes themselves, the authors demonstrate that a large majority of Americans support full payment of U.S. dues to the UN, American participation in UN peacekeeping, assistance to developing countries, and humanitarian intervention to stop human suffering. The latter is particularly interesting, as it supports the thesis that multilateral institutions operate in accordance with American values. Asked how the international community should respond to genocide, one survey participant replied: "I think any reason for deciding whether someone lives or dies because of culture or race . . . or religion is wrong . . . If Bosnia was an issue of . . . territory, then maybe you should just let them fight it out. But . . . genocide is wrong and when that is occurring, something needs to be done to stop it."[26]

Because it is easier to organize a minority than a majority of actors, the isolationist and protectionist minorities make their voices heard louder than the majorities of interventionists and free-traders.[27] Grassroots political action is also biased toward the expression of negative values: groups have greater incentives to form in opposition to policies than to support them.[28] According to Kull and Destler, other dysfunctions of the democratic process account for the mismatch between the public and the elites. The latter tend to underestimate the ability of the former to educate itself and form opinions about international affairs.[29] Moreover, foreign policy issues are rarely critical in general elections, coming to the fore only during presidential campaigns. As a result, there is no marketplace for the discussion of foreign policy matters, and the perception that the cost of addressing such issues is greater than any expected benefit reinforces the politics of silence.[30]

Whatever the reasons for the disaffection of the U.S. Congress toward multilateralism, the United States cannot afford to remain at the periphery of the impending debate on the future of global governance. If addressing Congress in 1947 on the U.S. interest in supporting the UN, Truman could state that "no nation has a higher stake in the outcome than our own," the stakes are only greater when American values permeate the globe and American corporations stand to lose the most from a disruption of globalization.[31] Because the multilateral system has been fashioned according to the values of the American republic, this nation has not only material but ideological interests in sustaining and reforming its institutions. The likely evolution of international assistance sketched above also conforms to American preferences regarding the optimal organization of economic activity—one that favors the role of business, relies on philanthropic responsibility, and shies away from government intervention. It would be ironic indeed that after decades of mismatch between UN and American economic policies, the United States would stay away from UN forums at the very moment when the organization strengthens its ties with the private sector.

The quandary of integrating business and civil society groups in an intergovernmental organization is one to which the United States is ideally suited to propose solutions. Because the success of the American democratic model owes much to the vibrancy of civil society, the United States ought to favor raising the profile of civic groups at the United Nations as a means of making the world body more democratic and accountable to a diverse global polity. The increased participation of the private sector in UN debates and the possibility of institutionalizing its contributions should not be seen as supporting primarily American business interests. The identity of multinationals bearing an American name is not domestic but global. The main argument that ought to militate for the raised profile of these corporations in UN forums, and which the next administration should champion, is that the world community cannot hope to address the challenges and negative externalities of globalization without the capacities and support of corporations in the definition and implementation of solutions. While the economic, cultural, and ideational assets of its "soft power" give America incomparable incentives to sustain the process of globalization, so does the rest of the world stand to benefit from American leadership in crafting proactively the governance structure of the twenty-first century.[32] Finally, an increasingly diverse world polity will mirror America's mosaic of ethnic, linguistic, racial, and religious groups—a unique national context that the principle of nondiscrimination embedded in multilateral institutions can help manage.[33]

The United Nations: Pro and Con

Before considering the possibility that the United Nations may not provide the requisite setting for the construction of a tripartite governance structure, one must reiterate the significant comparative advantage enjoyed by the UN system.

In its conceptual, nonfunctionalist acceptation, multilateralism refers to the application of the principles of nondiscrimination, equality, and reciprocity to all the members of a system, institution, or regime.[34] As the only organization linking all states, the United Nations can make a claim of universalism that reinforces the legitimacy and credibility of its positions. Legitimacy can be defined as "the normative belief by an actor that a rule or institution ought to be obeyed. It is a subjective quality, relational between actor and institution, and defined by the actor's *perception* of the institution."[35] Adherence to the rules of a legitimate organization therefore proceeds from "an internal sense of moral obligation" rather than coercion, and a shared definition of what is legitimate is the basis upon which communities are built. Legitimacy so defined is far more powerful than raw power. Because participants in a legitimate community have no incentive to calculate how specific outcomes benefit their self-interests, legitimacy discourages revisionism and guarantees greater stability. The moral power of the United Nations therefore rests on two related principles. Because legitimacy is based on the internalization of values and beliefs, the construction of a legitimate UN community is entirely dependent on the authority of the values of the Charter, and, by extension, of the Global Compact in the context that concerns us here. Secondly, the moral authority of these values is compounded by the principle of multilateralism and the universal nature of an organization of all states. This analysis implies that the UN system enjoys an incomparable advantage in defining the structure of the global polity. Assuming that such construction rests on ideational values, the UN has the moral capacity to define in the coming decades a legitimate and universal community of states and nonstate actors. The question remains as to whether it has the political will and material resources to match.

One other characteristic of legitimate communities is their reliance on symbolism. Be they objects or words, symbols represent the adhesion of those who use them to a set of values and beliefs that are group-constituting. Symbols are "us," and while their use at the UN has been decried time and again, those who question the salience of symbols need only walk down the street of a mid-size American town on the Fourth of July and wonder whether the display of flags reflects only shallow symbolism. In such UN forums as the General Assembly and the Security Council, now obsolete topics remain on the agenda because they reflect the symbol of state sovereignty or Security Council membership inherent in the power to keep issues on the agenda and/or vote on them. Participation in UN peacekeeping has also acquired symbolic value as it has raised the status of nonpermanent members and nonmembers of the Security Council.[36] But symbols may translate the impotence of an organization when they are not backed by material capacity and the joint action of those who subscribe to them. The symbolic value of the American flag—as testified by the violence of the debate over its desecration—lies in the deep allegiance of the American people to the values it represents as well as the material capacities America can bring to bear on the defense of these values.

Among the pathologies of institutional life therefore is a proclivity toward assigning symbolic value to things or ideas for the sake of symbolism. Max Weber has shown that because they rely on technical knowledge to "specialize and compartmentalize," bureaucracies take on the appearance of apolitical creatures, which increases their claims on authority and power. [37] UN officials have relied on the assertion of specialized knowledge to define and control such concepts as development policy or the principle of neutrality in refugee assistance. As a result of bureaucratic control, such definitions "may become so embedded and powerful that they determine ends and the way the organization defines its goals," irrespective of efficiency considerations and the achievement of outcomes.[38] Such policies may take on lives of their own and escape the tests of timely relevance and contextual impact. The construction and functioning of organizations according to values and concepts therefore does not guarantee positive and pertinent results.

The potential pathological behavior of organizations has clear implications for the Global Compact and the policy of rapprochement with the private sector. The validity of the model of the Compact and the relevance of its values to the global context do not ensure an effective transformation of the UN's role and structure in the coming decades. The language of the Global Compact could be captured by bureaucratic interests to restructure the discourse of the United Nations in an attractive manner without necessarily leading to actual policy changes.[39] Too little time has elapsed since it was enounced at Davos in 1999 to point to such dysfunctional diversion of the Compact's objectives by the UN bureaucracy. But its implementation and operationalization will constitute critical tests of how serious the UN is about engaging the private sector and civil society in a substantive and substantial redefinition of UN mandates.

Other factors could derail the visionary policy courageously elaborated since 1997. Displaying increasingly obsolete attitudes, the UN's member states remain wary of inviting nonstate actors to the table. The failure of the November 1999 WTO meeting demonstrated the dangers inherent in such obscurantism, and it will take all the talent of the UN's best diplomats, starting with the secretary-general himself, to steer nation-states toward an acceptance of diversity and its implications. What was needed in Seattle and remains an urgent priority is the formation of a broad coalition between developed and developing countries, based on a deep understanding of their irretrievably interconnected fates. The work of such economists as Jagdish Bhagwati will remain essential in pointing to the misperceptions and mis-representations of trade as a pauperizing phenomenon in the developed world. Beyond economics, however, rich and poor nations must see their partnership as the sine qua non of political stability in a global world. Member countries of the G77 must be convinced that the policy of outreach to the private sector does not conceal a neocolonialist agenda of economic domination, but indeed has the potential of benefiting them most. Indeed, the record of reactions emanating from developing nations toward the UN's policy of rapprochement with the business community points to an encouraging understanding of the prospects of this renewed partnership for developing economies. Possibly because they enjoy larger aggregate power and therefore have more to lose, G-8 nations display comparatively greater resistance to the inclusion of nonstate actors in global policymaking. The necessity of a North-South coalition provides the United States with a unique opportunity to restructure its historically troubled relationship with Latin America—an overdue transformation that the United States would pay a high price for delaying yet again. It also provides the key for finally integrating Africa into the affairs of the world, a policy in which Europe has much at stake even if the new generation emerging on the African continent is keen to develop ties across the Atlantic.

Given the historical record, one is hard-pressed to be forcefully optimistic about the ability of UN member states to allow greater participation and give stepped-up representation to NGOs and corporations in the deliberations and votes of such bodies as ECOSOC and the General Assembly. Attempts to extend to the General Assembly the features of UN international conferences, in which nonstate actors participate, have failed thus far. For all the ink that has been poured on the subject, the reform of ECOSOC has made similar progress, leaving that body dejected on the sidelines of the economic and social policymaking process. Like the Trusteeship Council in a postcolonial world, however, it is legitimate to ask what can justify the existence of ECOSOC if the latter fails to regenerate its ranks and mandate. And doing so without engaging nonstate actors in the context of globalization is unthinkable.

Civil society will constitute a critical ally in the effort to bring nation-states on board. Inasmuch as democratic nations base their longevity and legitimacy on the allegiance of their citizens, the latter will continue to exert significant influence on the behavior and policy choices of states in the global arena. Those metanational civil society groups that have emerged in the past decade will continue to grow, bringing their rising power to bear on the resolution of global issues. To become partners in the UN's search for a tripartite governance formula, civil society organizations must be confident that the future policy role of the business community will not develop at the expense of their representation and agenda. They must be convinced that they are not the weak link of the global policy chain, but rather can derive moral authority from the willingness of states and corporations to accept that NGOs speak for the global community. On the other hand, the ability of NGO activists to disrupt international meetings will not translate into policymaking clout unless civil society makes the necessary compromises to partner with its nemesis and Siamese twin in the private sector.

Finally, the UN must give itself the means of its policy. In addition to political goodwill and courage, the success of the UN's effort at reinventing itself will require material resources and time. While it was argued above that UN operational activities will decline in size and importance, the implementation of the Global Compact implies strengthening UN normative and regulatory functions and bodies. As real reform always requires additional investments rather than across-the-board cuts, these organizations will require funds to expand, hire new staff, and create new programs. Happily, in the context of a policy of rapprochement with the private sector, such funding may not come exclusively from UN member states but may be provided selectively by corporations and private philanthropic institutions. Those UN departments charged with conceptualizing and implementing the outreach to the private sector and the resulting UN-business partnerships will also need to acquire new staff and skills outside the UN system. Other expenses likely to accompany the new policy will be in the areas of information technology, website and database development, teleconferencing, distance learning, and other multimedia technologies that are slowly becoming the staples of business life. But in light of the political and organizational challenges faced by the UN system to effect a conceptual and institutional transformation in the coming decade, the acquisition of material resources is a small concern unlikely to stand in the way.

If Not the United Nations, Then What?

While it boasts significant advantages to constitute the global forum of the twenty-first century, the bureaucratic and political obstacles it faces could prevent the United Nations from remaining the universal institution of the world polity. Trained to plan for bad scenarios rather than good ones, the political analyst must ask what institutional setting could in time replace the UN and whence it would emerge.

Before outlining a few possibilities, it is useful to keep in mind the overwhelming obstacles that stand in the way of institution-building. Intergovernmental institutions of the type discussed in this book are creatures of the twentieth century. In their capacities, legitimacy, size, and universality, no institution resembled the World Bank or the United Nations before 1919. The League of Nations is the only comparable predecessor to the organizations created in 1945, although its membership diminished by American absence and its policy record have irremediably impaired its historical legacy. In addition to being a new occupation in which the human community has had relatively little experience, institution-building also demands colossal political and financial investments. To begin with, both in 1919 and 1945, the creation of international organizations occurred in the wake of a global conflict. While a causal relationship cannot be derived from the correlation of war and institution-building, it is significant that international organizations of similar scope have never emerged under conditions of systemic stability. A third World War ought not to precede the design of the governance mechanism of the global era. Secondly, despite the backdrop of destruction and despair against which the League and the UN emerged, in both cases again, the creation of these organizations required the leadership of a great generation of individuals who spared no personal effort and dedicated their careers to the creation of institutions. The generation of Jean Monnet, Dean Acheson, Robert Schuman, Averell Harriman, and George Kennan—even if he was no fan of multilateralism—displayed a genius and a commitment that will be difficult to replicate. At the UN's creation, the wealth and benevolent hegemony of the United States were key factors in ensuring that the new organization would obtain the resources it needed to get off the ground, and if Europe later was able to contribute, it was to a great extent because the Marshall Plan had restored its productive capacities. The ideological bent of the Keynesian compromise also provided a favorable context for endowing international organizations with government resources—a situation that does not abide today, although private funding could take the relay. Even in 1945, ratification of the UN Charter by the U.S. Senate required the orchestration of a deliberate campaign at all levels of the American polity, from the grassroots to the executive board rooms. Needless to say, there is little evidence that the U.S. Senate requires less lobbying on behalf of global governance in 2000 than in 1945.

These precedents imply that the emergence in the coming years of structures, forums, or institutional networks parallel to the United Nations would necessarily be a more decentralized, less costly, and less ambitious process than the institution-building activity that took place in 1919 and 1945. Such new settings would also arise alongside and collaboratively with the United Nations and the Bretton Woods institutions rather than in competition with them. In fact, such forums could be offshoots of these existing organizations initiated by some of their current or former staff members. They would also be transitional institutions that could serve as a useful bridge toward the creation of a global governance organization. But likely to exhibit a loose format and limited in their scope, they could not pretend to replace quickly the institutions created in 1945.

The global policy networks developed by Wolfgang Reinicke point to one possible new institutional setting.[40] Because they involve multilateral organizations, civil society, corporations, and at times governmental bodies, these networks are a step in the direction of multipartite governance structures suited to the conditions of the global era. Their loose and decentralized structure, their policy expertise backed by information technology, and their concern with global negative externalities demonstrate their applicability to the geography, pace, and complexity of globalization.[41] They display two main weaknesses, however: they are issue-specific, which limits their scope; and they do not involve the private sector sufficiently or consistently. One interesting avenue of growth for the global policy network approach would be to link several of them in a few overarching multipartite bodies tied to larger issue areas. Such overarching networks could coalesce around global standards (as envisioned in chapter 4), security issues, environmental stewardship, and financial governance, among other broad topics. These informal yet highly connected networks would derive their legitimacy from their multilateral membership drawn from the ranks of governments, civil society, corporations, and multilateral organizations. Acting as epistemic communities, their expertise in each issue area, linked to their ability to disseminate information and propose innovative policy solutions, would constitute another source of credibility, and hence of legitimacy. Their rise to political prominence would derive not from their ability to threaten national sovereignty, but rather from their capabilities as policy entrepreneurs and solution providers in the vacuum of global governance. Their multiplication, on the one hand, matched by their consolidation around 5–6 major global policy poles would in time increase their influence, interconnectedness, and operational capacities. While such a network of networks could not be equated with the format of international organization as it emerged from the post–World War II period, it may prove as effective, if not more effective, in the context of globalization and begin to chart a course toward a future global governance structure.

The annual meeting of the World Economic Forum in Davos also provides a setting in which corporate, government, and NGO leaders discuss global governance issues. The urgency of creating multipartite institutional settings giving nonstate actors substantive and legislative responsibilities is particularly well understood by members of the WEF's Global Leaders for Tomorrow. A younger generation of corporate, government, and civil society representatives is coming into leadership positions on every continent, and representatives of the developing countries may well constitute the most active and motivated among them. Some are establishing young leadership and corporate responsibility networks in Africa and Latin America, and their global worldview, uninhibited by ethnic or religious considerations, is particularly encouraging. While these efforts are mostly local and lack the traditional aggregates of power, it is not far-fetched to imagine how, within a few years, such local initiatives could be linked into a global network of multipartite associations, NGOs, and think tanks in which young entrepreneurs would play a leadership role. Indeed, these networks of young entrepreneurs could overlap with and strengthen the global public policy networks mentioned above. Such a global network of associations would have much distance to cover before competing with existing institutions, but the legitimacy it would derive from the diversity and commitment of its members could be brought to bear on any future effort to construct a global governance system.

• • •

The ideas sketched above will appear radical to some, obvious to others already working to fulfill them. The aim of this book, however, is not to engage in political fiction but rather to impart to the world community a sense of urgency regarding the inadequacy of current policies and institutional settings to the conditions of the global era. Devoted to a large extent to the renewed partnership between the private sector and the United Nations, this book has argued that the latter stands in good stead to revitalize its mission and structure by welcoming nonstate actors into its deliberative forums and policymaking bodies. But what is at stake is not the future of an institution as much as the future of the global polity of nations, regions, city-states, corporate networks, and metanational civic groups that again will form the fabric of our world in this century.

Notes

Notes for Introduction

1. The only variation between the two headings is in the Charter's use of the plural ("Peoples") vs. the singular form in the U.S. constitution. See preamble to the *Charter of the United Nations and Statute of the International Court of Justice.* UN Department of Information, New York: United Nations.

2. The "compromise of embedded liberalism" is John Ruggie's expression. See John Gerard Ruggie, "International Regimes, Transactions, and Change: Embedded Liberalism in the Postwar Economic Order," in *International Regimes,* ed. Stephen D. Krasner. Ithaca, NY: Cornell University Press, 1983. The concept is further analyzed in chapter 1.

3. The expression is Francis Fukuyama's. See Francis Fukuyama, *The End of History and the Last Man.* New York: Free Press, 1992.

4. This key distinction between authority and control is at the heart of Stephen D. Krasner's latest reflection on sovereignty. See Stephen D. Krasner, *Sovereignty: Organized Hypocrisy.* Princeton: Princeton University Press, 1999.

5. If this entire paragraph appears as the product of social-democratic thinking, see Francis Fukuyama, *The Great Disruption: Human Nature and the Reconstitution of Social Order.* New York: Free Press, 1999. Of course, Max Weber and his followers must be credited for the theory outlined here.

6. Speech delivered at the World Economic Forum, Davos, Switzerland, February 1, 1997. Available on the UN website at *www.un.org/partners/business.*

7. Speech, "A Compact for the New Century," delivered at the World Economic Forum, Davos, Switzerland, January 31, 1999.

Notes for Chapter 1

1. Francis Fukuyama, *The End of History and the Last Man.* New York: Free Press, 1992.

2. This portrayal of Venice's glory can be found in Braudel/Duby, *La Méditerrannée, Les Hommes et l'Héritage.* Paris: Champs Flammarion, 1986; see chapter on Venice. See also Braudel, *Le Modèle Italien.* Paris: Champs Flammarion, 1994.

3. See Jacques Attali, *1492*. Paris: Fayard, 1991, p. 110.

4. John Gerard Ruggie, *Constructing the World Polity: Essays on International Institutionalization*. London: Routledge, 1998, p. 145

5. Henry Kissinger's *Diplomacy* is a vivid and brilliant historical summary of diplomacy since Richelieu. New York: Simon and Schuster, 1994.

6. François Furet, *La Révolution, 1770–1880*. Paris: Hachette Littératures, 1988.

7. It can be argued that President Wilson had not explained the aims and strategies of the League to the American people and had not expended much energy on lobbying members of Congress to support it. The lesson would not be lost on Franklin Roosevelt thirty years later. See John Gerard Ruggie, *Winning the Peace: America and World Order in the New Era*. New York: Columbia University Press, 1996, for an original treatment of U.S. congressional positions toward multilateralism since 1900.

8. Pressure for including labor unions in the ILO came from the fact that in 1914 labor groups rallied to the war effort rather than support the Socialist International's call for labor solidarity against mobilization.

9. Charles Poor Kindleberger, *The World in Depression: 1929–1939*. Berkeley: University of California Press, 1973.

10. See Robert C. Hilderbrand, *Dumbarton Oaks: The Origins of the United Nations and the Search for Postwar Security*. Chapel Hill, NC: University of North Carolina Press, 1990, p. 47.

11. See John Gerard Ruggie, *Winning the Peace*.

12. This is the principle enshrined in NATO's famous article V, according to which an attack on any member of the alliance calls for a collective response by the entire alliance.

13. See Hilderbrand, p. 89.

14. Jacques Fomerand, *The United States and Development Cooperation in the United Nations: Toward a New Deal?* To be published in 2000 by Editions Diderot, New York.

15. See Hildebrand, pp. 85–86 and 88.

16. See Ralph Townley, "The Economic Organs of the United Nations" in *The Evolution of International Organizations,* ed. Evan Luard. New York: Praeger, 1966. See also Hilderbrand, p. 87.

17. Georg Schild, *Bretton Woods and Dumbarton Oaks: American Economic and Political Postwar Planning in the Summer of 1944*. New York: St. Martin's Press, 1995, p. 183.

18. The State Department was not hostile to the idea. It is simply that U.S. policymakers had developed the concept of a tight division of labor between the UN and the Bretton Woods institutions, which business involvement in the former contradicted.

19. The history of the ICC, entitled *World Peace through World Trade, 1919–1979,* is available on the ICC website at www.iccwbo.org.

20. See George L. Ridgeway, *Merchants of Peace*. Paris: ICC, 1959 ed., p. 104.

21. This remarkable telegram was found and made available by Bill Stibravy at USCIB.

22. All aforementioned statements are quoted by Fomerand, cited above.

23. *Charter of the United Nations,* Article 1.3.

24. *Charter of the United Nations,* Article 55.

25. John Gerard Ruggie, "International Regimes, Transactions, and Change: Embedded Liberalism in the Postwar Economic Order," in *International Regimes,* ed. Stephen D. Krasner. Ithaca, NY: Cornell University Press, 1983. A reworked version of the original article can be found in *Constructing the World Polity,* pp. 62–84.

26. This redefinition of multilateralism can be found in John Gerard Ruggie, *Multilateralim: The Anatomy of an Institution,* in *Multilateralism Matters,* ed. John Gerard Ruggie. New York: Columbia Univeristy Press, 1993.

27. *Charter of the United Nations,* Article 63, para. 2.

28. Ibid., Article 66, para. 3.

29. Ibid., Article 13, para. 1b. Also see Article 60 for the authority of the General Assembly over ECOSOC.

30. Ibid., Article 71. It is important to note that the so-called "nongovernmental sector" was understood to include business associations and labor groups. This general understanding still pertains today in some UN circles.

31. The Economic Commissions for Europe and the Asia-Pacific region were both created in 1947. An Economic Commission for Latin America and the Caribbean followed suit in 1948. The Economic Commissions for Africa and Western Asia were established in 1958 and 1973, respectively.

32. The politicization of the ILO's debates led to U.S. withdrawal in 1977. The U.S. rejoined in 1980.

33. See "International Organizations: Scope, Purpose, and Impact on Business," an ICC paper delivered at an international trade conference in Washington D.C. in June 1983. The author, Peter M. Robinson, states on p. 9: "Our concern is that the ITU, in existence since 1965, has increasingly become a forum for political debate, which can have the effect of diverting discussion from telecommunications issues to, for example, general attacks on corporate activity in this area."

34. The contrast with business support of the WTO in 1995 is enlightening.

35. *Basic Facts About the UN,* UN Department of Public Information, 1998, p. 293.

36. Cited in Fomerand.

37. Ibid.

38. Statement by U.S. Deputy Assistant Secretary of State for International Organizations Richard Gardner to the ILO in 1962, cited in Fomerand.

39. Statement by American Permanent Representative to the UN Adlai Stevenson, in 1963, cited in Fomerand.

40. American insistence of the importance of family planning would lead in 1969 to the creation of the UN Population Fund (UNFPA), an agency from

which the U.S. Congress has withdrawn funding intermittently in the past decade.

41. *Report of Expert Group to the UN General Assembly,* 1961.

42. *Cairo Declaration of Developing Countries,* 1962 Conference on the Problems of Economic Development.

43. The Group of 77 still exists today, although it now has 133 members.

44. The following provide good general discussions of structuralist and dependency theories: Joan E. Spero, *The Politics of International Economic Relations.* New York: St. Martin's Press, 1990; Robert Gilpin, *The Political Economy of International Relations.* Princeton: Princeton University Press, 1987; and Jeffry Frieden and David Lake, *International Political Economy: Perspectives on Global Power and Wealth.* New York: St. Martin's Press, 1991. The classic text on the structuralist agenda of third world countries is Stephen D. Krasner, *Structural Conflict: The Third World Against Global Liberalism.* Berkeley: University of California Press, 1985.

45. Lenin's pamphlet, *Imperialism: The Highest Stage of Capitalism,* appeared in 1916. See Frieden and Lake, *International Political Economy.*

46. Spero, p. 210.

47. The U.S. contributed 25 percent of UNDP's budget at that time.

48. Today, UNDP estimates that it is active in 175 countries and territories.

49. Another agency created in 1966, the UN Capital Development Fund (UNCDF), was placed under the administration of UNDP in 1967. Although its creation marked another achievement of the developing countries in the General Assembly—its establishment was opposed by all developed nations—the fund never worked to the anticipated benefit of its creators. In 1973, ECOSOC redirected the fund toward small-scale projects in poor nations, which prompted developed countries to begin making contributions to UNCDF.

50. American opposition stemmed, no doubt, from the reluctance of placing another UN economic agency under the control of the developing countries in the General Assembly. In addition, the United States did not agree with the rationale of separating industrial development from the overall formulation of development policy, a view that has been reiterated in recent efforts to reform UNIDO and place it under the mandate of a larger UN body.

51. The NIEO rested on a rephrasing of the structuralist analysis of the international economy labeled dependency theory. Although political economists separate the two doctrines, it is difficult to dismiss their common assumptions. Both take for granted structural biases against developed countries. Both call for correcting the dependence of developing nations on exports of raw materials. Both stress the presence of sociological and institutional factors as impediments to development. Both point to the consequences of the technological gap in maintaining the backwardness of the developing world. If dependency theory stresses the pernicious effects of transnationals on developing economies, it is simply because transnationals did not exist in the 1940s and 1950s. According to dependency theory, therefore, the transna-

tionals further pervert the economies of the developing world by controlling local resources, introducing inappropriate technologies, repatriating all profits, distorting the local labor market, destroying local entrepreneurship, and widening social inequalities.

52. Spero, p. 213.
53. Gilpin, p. 298.
54. Ibid.
55. ICC News, *Monthly Bulletin of the International Chamber of Commerce*, Vol. XXXV-3, March-April 1969. The 16-member committee was chaired by Dr. Marcus Wallenberg of Sweden, chairman of the board of Enskilda Bank, and included Nathaniel Samuels, managing partner of Kuhn, Loeb, & Co. and U.S. Deputy Under Secretary of State for economic affairs.
56. Ibid.
57. Ibid.
58. Krasner, p. 49.
59. In Asia the NICs were also referred to as the "four tigers," comprising Korea, Taiwan, Singapore, and Hong Kong.
60. Krasner, p.50.
61. During the 1970–1976 period, Saudi Arabia's GDP grew at an annual rate of 14.4 percent, Iraq's at 9.5 percent, and Iran's at 9 percent. See Krasner, p. 50.
62. Quoted by Frieden and Lake, p. 173.
63. Robert Keohane and Joseph Nye. *Power and Interdependence: World Politics in Transition.* Boston: Little, Brown, 1977.
64. Reinhart Helmke reminded me that the only exception was the creation of the International Fund for Agricultural Development (IFAD) whose directorship has gone to an Arab national since its inception.
65. Spero, p.175.
66. The tale of her ambassadorship is vividly recounted in Allan Gerson's *The Kirkpatrick Mission, Diplomacy Without Apology: America at the United Nations, 1981–85.* New York: Free Press, 1991. The author was Ambassador Kirkpatrick's legal counsel at the U.S. Mission to the UN.
67. In 1999, U.S. arrears to the UN topped $1.6 billion, of which the U.S. Senate decided in November 1999 to repay $926 million with various conditions and restrictions of U.S. funding of family planning—a policy formulated by the U.S. itself in the 1960s.
68. Quoted by Fomerand.
69. See, for example, *UN General Assembly Resolution 45/188 of 1990* mentioning "entrepreneurship" as a universal concept central to economic growth and development.
70. See *ECOSOC Resolution 1088/74 of 1988* for an exposition of these concepts.
71. The idea that the United Nations had a role to play in transition countries was not readily accepted and took some time to shape. One of the factors stalling the adoption of a UN policy originated in UN member states rather than in the organization itself. The national technical cooperation ministries

that had been set up in the early 1960s were reluctant to relinquish their power as funders of development assistance to the foreign ministries. This shift of control had to occur, however, as the complexity of political and economic issues in transition countries meant that most governments designated their foreign ministries as coordinators of assistance to Eastern Europe and the former Soviet Union.

72. Internal transcripts of oral report by the president of the 46th UN General Assembly, July 21–23, 1992.

73. Evidence of this emerging consensus can be found in hearings before the 101st U.S. Congress, Committee on Foreign Relations, Subcommittee on International Economic Policy, Oceans and the Environment, second session, October 11, 1990. At these hearings, Abraham Katz, then president of the U.S. Council for International Business, took the view that the code was then acceptable to business interests, although the United Nations was not the best forum to issue it.

74. Mikhail Gorbachev, *Perestroika: New Thinking for Our Country and the World.* New York: Harper & Row, 1987.

75. Few recent publications in the growing literature of globalization explain clearly this fundamental historical break. Wolfgang Reinicke was the first to characterize this distinction in *Global Public Policy: Governing Without Government?* Washington, D.C.: Brookings Institution Press, 1997. The following section is based on his insight.

76. Reinicke, p.11.

77. Jagdish Bhagwati, *A Stream of Windows: Unsettling Reflections on Trade, Immigration, and Democracy.* Cambridge, MA: MIT Press, 1998, pp. 38–39. Bhagwati also notes that the 1990 level must be compared to a share of trade to GNP of 3.6 percent in 1950.

78. Robert Keohane and Joseph Nye, "Globalization: What's New? What's Not? (And So What?)" in *Foreign Policy* (spring 2000), p. 109.

79. Schmiddheiny's views on the business role in promoting environmental responsibility can be found in *Changing Course.* Cambridge, MA: MIT Press, 1992.

80. The expression is John Ruggie's. See *Constructing the World Polity,* p. 248.

81. The UN's largest mission in Somalia, UNOSOM II, was deployed from March 1993 to March 1995 with 28,000 troops under UN command at top strength. The UN's mission in Bosnia, UNPROFOR, lasted from February 1992 to March 1995 and deployed close to 40,000 troops at top strength. These figures include military observers and civilian police. Figures for Somalia do not include 17,700 troops under direct U.S. command. Comprehensive data on UN peacekeeping can be found in *The Blue Helmets,* 3rd ed., New York: UN Department of Public Information, 1996.

82. See Sandrine Tesner, *How to Do Business with the United Nations: The Complete Guide to UN Procurement.* New York: UNA-USA, 1995, 1996, and 1997 editions.

83. This bridging of the gap took place when business executives actually visited UN operations in the field. It did not evolve from contacts at UN Headquarters in New York or elsewhere, which still suffered then (as they do now) from a lack of common understanding.

84. Personal interview with a member of the U.S. consulting firm, carried out in the spring of 1999.

85. Personal interview with Denis Beissel conducted in the spring of 1999.

86. Comment made by the member of the U.S. consulting firm during the interview conducted in the spring of 1999.

87. Some of these recommendations are contained in *Reports on the Fourth and Fifth Annual Peacekeeping Missions,* Sandrine Tesner, Rapporteur, UNA-USA, 1995 and 1996, respectively. Interestingly, the recommendation that peacekeeping mandates should include economic programs is reminiscent of the U.K. proposal, in the 1944–1945 period, to place the UN's social and economic functions under the authority of the Security Council. Several CEOs who participated in the UNA-USA visits in the mid-1990s called for giving the UN Security Council enforcement power over the economic and social planks of peacekeeping missions.

88. *Report of the Special Adviser and Delegate of the Secretary-General on the Reform of the Economic and Social Sectors,* so-called Dadzie Report, February 1993.

89. Report of the taskforce on the Office for Project Services, issued by the Governing Council of UNDP as *document DP/1993/70, June 1, 1993.*

90. Ibid.

91. *Executive Board document DP/1995/1, January 1995, decision 94/12.* The merger of development implementation had been recommended in *Governing Council decision 93/42 of June 18, 1993.*

92. *General Assembly decision 48/501 of September 19, 1994* endorsing *ECOSOC decision 1994/284 of July 26, 1994.*

93. *DP/1994/62 of August 16, 1994.*

94. *Executive Board document DP/1995/6 of November 1994.*

95. As we take up a discussion of the secretary-general's role in determining the course of UN action, it is interesting to note that the title of "Secretary-General" (which had been the title of the head of the League of Nations) was a U.S. concession to the Soviet Union in 1944 at Dumbarton Oaks. The U.S. delegation preferred the title of "Director-General," which was not retained. See Hilderbrand, p. 106.

96. Speech to the World Economic Forum, February 1, 1997, available on the UN website at www.un.org/partners/business.

97. Ibid.

98. The argument for commercial pacifism is Smith's and Schumpeter's while the argument for justice is Kant's. See Michael Doyle, *Ways of War and Peace.* New York: W.W. Norton, 1997, part 2, titled "Liberalism."

99. Speech to the World Economic Forum, January 31, 1998, available on the UN website.

100. Ibid.

101. Ibid.

102. Ibid.

103. For a theoretical background to this speech, see Ruggie, *Constructing the Word Polity,* p. 67, especially the reference to Karl Polanyi: "Laissez-faire was planned." See Karl Polanyi, *The Great Transformation: The Political and Economic Origins of Our Time.* Boston: Beacon Press, 1944.

104. This section and chapter 2 refer repeatedly to "principles," "norms," and "rules." While official UN speeches and texts do not define these terms, it is useful to refer the reader to the classical definitions provided by Krasner in *International Regimes,* ed. Stephen D. Krasner. Ithaca, NY: Cornell University Press. 1983. In the first essay of this volume, Krasner writes on p. 2: "Principles are beliefs of fact, causation, and rectitude. Norms are standards of behavior defined in terms of rights and obligations. Rules are specific prescriptions or proscriptions for action."

105. The entire text of the reform proposal is available in UN *document A/51/950 of July 14, 1997.*

106. para. 213, p. 68.

107. para. 214, p. 68.

108. Action 17c, p. 69.

109. Strategy 7, p. 79.

110. The website address is www.un.org/partners/business.

111. That recommendation is contained in para. 41, p. 18 of the reform proposal.

112. Action 11, p. 56.

113. A special UN division, the UN Fund for International Partnership (UNFIP), was created to work with the UN Foundation in managing the Turner grants.

114. UNICEF has long been the UN fund-raising champion. UNFPA, UNHCR, and WFP are catching up to its leadership in that area. Some UN fund-raising activities are further developed in chapter 3.

115. The ICC had written Secretary-General Boutros-Ghali to offer similar assistance but received no reply.

116. *Joint Statement on Common Interests,* issued by the UN and the ICC on February 9, 1998. The text can be found on both the ICC website (*www.iccwbo.org*) and the UN website (*www.un.org/partners/business).*

117. Ibid.

118. Ibid.

119. The *Geneva Business Declaration* is available on the ICC website as well as in a conference report published by and available from the ICC.

120. Ibid.

121. The July 1999 joint statement is available on both the UN and the ICC websites, addresses cited above.

122. Ibid.

123. All quotes are taken from an internal UN memorandum.

124. The Prince of Wales Business Leaders Forum has published two manuals on partnering between private and public organizations. Jane Nelson, *Business*

as Partners in Development. London: Prince of Wales Business Leaders Forum, 1996, and Ros Tennyson, *Managing Partnerships.* London: Prince of Wales Business Leaders Forum, 1998.

125. The history of BCUN is interesting from the viewpoint of UN-business relations. BCUN was born in 1958 as UN We Believe, an American NGO launched by two United Airlines pilots with the backing of the UN. The pilots, who had participated in an airlift of food and supplies to Hungary in 1956, lamented the lack of power of the UN in that country's October 1956 crisis—a weakness they attributed to lack of U.S. support for the organization. They thought that a U.S. grassroots organization backed by corporations could enhance U.S. understanding of the UN's role. They eventually managed to have United Airlines place on the tails of its aircraft a logo that integrated the UN logo within it and sets an interesting precedent for UN lending of its logo to a corporation. For this oral history, I thank Paul Underwood, vice president of BCUN.

126. The speech delivered by the secretary-general to the U.S. Chamber of Commerce on June 8, 1999 is available on the UN website.

127. UNCTAD Secretary-General Rubens Ricupero referred to UNCTAD as "a typical 'child of the 1960s'" in a speech delivered at a UNESCO conference in February 1999. The speech can be found on the UNESCO website at *www.unesco.org.*

128. These speeches can be found on the UNCTAD website at *www.unctad.org.* Mr. Ricupero also addressed the 1998 Davos conference.

129. The full program of Partners for Development as well as Mr. Ricupero's follow-up report can be found on the UNCTAD website.

130. On the dangers of reading Russia's past in Russia's present, see Martin Malia, *Russia Under Western Eyes.* Cambridge, MA: Harvard University Press, 1999.

131. The "longue durée" is a key concept in Fernand Braudel's historiography.

Notes for Chapter 2

1. This section borrows its argument and a number of data from "Global Markets and Social Legitimacy: The Case of the 'Global Compact,'" a paper by Georg Kell and John G. Ruggie presented at a conference held at York University, Toronto, Canada, November 4–6, 1999.

2. See Albert O. Hirshmann, *National Power and the Structure of Foreign Trade.* Berkeley: University of California Press, 1945, as well as Charles Kindleberger, *The World in Depression, 1929–1939.* Berkeley: University of California Press, 1973.

3. Keohane and Nye write that "interdependence refers to a condition, a state of affairs . . . Globalization and deglobalization refer to the increase or decrease of globalism." They define "globalism" as "a state of the world involving networks of interdependence at multicontinental distances." See "Globalization: What's New? What's Not? (And So What?)" in *Foreign Policy* (spring 2000), p. 105.

4. Robert Wade, "Globalization and its Limits: Reports of the Death of the National Economy are Greatly Exaggerated," in *National Diversity and Global Capitalism*, eds. S. Berger and R. Dove. Ithaca: Cornell University Press, 1996.

5. UNCTAD, *World Investment Report*, 1999. UNCTAD's transnationality index of the top 100 multinationals has increased from 51 percent to 55 percent since 1990, largely as a result of the internationalization of assets (which grew particularly fast between 1993 and 1996).

6. Kell and Ruggie, p. 3.

7. Keohane and Nye, "Globalization," p. 113.

8. Dani Rodrik, *Has Globalization Gone Too Far?* Washington, D.C.: Institute for International Economics, 1997, p. 2.

9. Rodrik writes that the traditional tax base of governments has become "footloose."

10. Rodrik, p. 5.

11. Kelland Ruggie, p. 3. See Ruggie's concept of "embedded liberalism" for the origin of this rephrasing.

12. Kell and Ruggie, p. 3.

13. Kelland Ruggie, p. 3. I have edited "international" to "inter-national."

14. Secretary-General Kofi Annan demonstrated that he favors such interpretative efforts in his speech to the opening session of the 55th UN General Assembly (September 20, 1999), where he argued for the need to reinterpret the Charter to promote international interventions against ethnic conflicts and gross human rights abuses. The speech is available on the UN website, www.un.org.

15. Kell and Ruggie, p. 4.

16. Kell and Ruggie define an NGO as "any non-profit, voluntary citizens group that is constituted at the local, national, or international level," p. 3.

17. The coalition has over 1,400 NGO members today and keeps adding new recruits.

18. Kell and Ruggie citing D. Henderson, *The MAI Affair: A Story and Its Lessons.* London: The Royal Institute of International Affairs, 1999.

19. Kell and Ruggie, p. 5.

20. According to Kell and Ruggie, "CSR can be understood as the conditions under which society grants private corporations the right to pursue the maximization of profits. This social contract between a corporation and its host society implies legal requirements or can be understood to include implicit assumptions and expectations." See 1999 UNCTAD *World Investment Report* for a good overview of the social responsibility of multinationals.

21. Kell and Ruggie point out that this is especially true in developing countries. For example, sales by leading multinationals exceed the GDPs of such regional giants as Thailand and South Africa, according to the UNDP *Human Development Report.* New York: Oxford University Press, 1999, p. 32.

22. Peter Schwartz and Blair Glibb, *When Good Companies Do Bad Things. Responsibility and Risk in an Age of Globalization.* New York: John Wiley, 1999.

See chapter 1 for an excellent exposition of the salience of corporate responsibility in the context of globalization.

23. Kell and Ruggie citing Wild, "A Review of Corporate Citizenship and Social Initiatives," prepared for the International Labor Organization's Bureau for Employers' Activities, October 1–2, 1998. Geneva: ILO.

24. Kell and Ruggie, p.6. See also Schwartz and Glibb.

25. Kell and Ruggie citing G. Cramb, "Greenpeace Stepping Up Threat to Multinationals," in *Financial Times,* August 18, 1999, and R. Cramb and R. Corzine, "Shell Audit Tells of Action on Global Warming," in *Financial Times,* July 14, 1998.

26. Kell and Ruggie, p. 6.

27. The leading text on the ethical interest of firms is John Dalla Costa, *The Ethical Imperative: Why Moral Leadership is Good Business.* New York: Perseus Books, 1998. See also the principles developed by the Caux Roundtable, at www.cauxroundtable.org.

28. See Dalla Costa, "The Golden Rule Across Cultures," in Dalla Costa, pp. 141–42.

29. This quote, excerpted from the Copenhagen Declaration on Social Development, is used by the Triglav Circle to frame the objectives of its activities. Paper distributed by the Triglav Circle at an informal gathering, November 5–6, 1999.

30. See Daniel Cohen, *The Wealth of the World and the Poverty of Nations.* Cambridge, MA: MIT Press, 1998.

31. Kell and Ruggie, p. 7.

32. Kell and Ruggie, p. 8.

33. "Beyond the Multilateral Trading System," address by Renato Ruggiero, director general of the WTO, Geneva, April 12, 1999.

34. Kell and Ruggie, p. 7.

35. "World Business Priorities for a New Round of Multilateral Trade Negotiations," Policy Statement for Submission to the Third Ministerial Conference Of the World Trade Organization. ICC: April 1999. See the ICC website.

36. Kell and Ruggie, p. 8.

37. Jagdish Bhagwati offers numerous data to back this claim in *A Stream of Windows: Unsettling Reflections on Trade, Immigration, and Democracy.* Cambridge, MA: MIT Press, 1998. See p. 11 for the influence of trade on employment and pp. 43–45 for the implications of trade on wage levels. See p. 304 for the argument that trade has favored development through job creation in the "South."

38. The statement appeared in the *Earth Times,* September 16–30, 1999, a New York newspaper that often reflects the NGO agenda.

39. Ibid.

40. The follow-up process to UNCED exemplifies this trend. Indications are that "Copenhagen +5" will be comparably sobering.

41. Kell and Ruggie, p. 10.

42. See the Global Compact website at www.unglobalcompact.org.

43. Kell and Ruggie, p. 11.

44. There are multiple reasons for this new attitude. Kofi Annan's outreach to the business community and his unquestionable commitment to defending an open multilateral trade and financial system have put the concerns of corporate leaders to rest. The discourse of protectionist NGOs has been uncovered by developing countries, and their majority at the UN would ensure that the protectionist agendas of some developed countries are not allowed to interfere with free trade and export-led growth. The times are different and governments and NGOs, like corporations, are submitted to the hard necessity of economic efficiency. The debate is therefore no longer ideological but rather one of protectionism vs. opportunities for developing countries.

45. Kofi Annan. "Help the Third World Help Itself," in the *Wall Street Journal*, November 29, 1999.

46. Ibid.

47. The following discussion is based on *The United Nations and Global Commerce*, a report by Dr. Mark Zacher, Institute of International Relations, University of British Columbia. Published by the UN Department of Public Information in September 1999. Available from the UN at no charge.

48. *The United Nations and Global Commerce*, p. 17.

49. Ibid., p. 18.

50. John Gerard Ruggie, ed., *Multilateralism Matters*. New York: Columbia University Press, 1993, p. 21.

51. See Inge Kaul, et al., eds., *Global Public Goods*, a publication of the UN Development Program (UNDP). New York: Oxford University Press, 1999. The bibliography provided in this book contains the most important academic texts on the concept of public good.

52. The ability of states to organize numerous actors solves the so-called collective action problem. This political concept states that it is more difficult to generate action on an issue supported by a majority of the public than one supported by a minority. This is so because it is harder to organize a large number rather than a small number of actors. This explains why protectionists in the United States, although a minority, are more vocal than the vast majority of free-traders.

53. Personal interview, December 1999.

54. Personal interview, December 1999.

55. "Toward Greater International Cooperation," ICC Paper by Jean-Jacques Oechslin, 1977.

56. "Business and the Global Economy," ICC Statement on Behalf of World Business to the Heads of State and Governments Attending the Birmingham Summit, May 15–17, 1998. Available on the ICC website.

57. Both quotes from the ICC Statement at the Birmingham Summit, May 15–17, 1998. See also Karl Polanyi's statement, "Laissez-faire was planned," quoted in John Gerard Ruggie, *Constructing the World Polity: Essays on International Institutionalization*. London: Routledge, 1998, p. 67.

58. ICC Statement on Behalf of World Business to the Heads of State and Governments Attending the Cologne Summit, June 18–20, 1999. Available on the ICC website.

59. Ibid.

60. ICC press release, May 20, 1999. "Settle Current Rows and Launch New Trade Round, Business Tells G7."

61. "The World Needs the Millennium Round," statement by ICC President Adnan Kassar to the Third Ministerial Meeting of the WTO issued ahead of the November 1999 Seattle meeting. Available from the ICC.

62. Internal UN survey conducted by the UN Department of Economic and Social Affairs, fall 1998.

63. Personal phone interview carried out in the spring of 1999.

64. Oechslin, p. 8.

65. Oechslin, p. 7.

66. Speech by Mary Robinson, UN high commissioner for human rights, to the Business and Social Responsibility Conference, San Francisco, November 3, 1999.

67. See Kell and Ruggie, p. 7. Also see Schwartz and Glibb, chapter 7.

68. See Kell and Ruggie, p. 7.

69. Examples include the U.K. ethical trading initiative, the development of national ethics codes in Canada and Norway, and the work of the World Bank on best practices in the extracting industry. Many other initiatives are sponsored by business NGOs such as the WBCSD (World Business Council for Sustainable Development) and the PWBLF (Prince of Wales Business Leaders Forum).

70. See Sandrine Tesner, *How to do Business with the United Nations.*

71. The current increase in peacekeeping procurement is due to the deployment of new missions in East Timor and Africa, but it should not overshadow the long-term declining trend.

72. ICC Statement on Behalf of World Business to the Heads of State and Governments Attending the Birmingham Summit, May 15–17, 1998. Available on the ICC website.

73. The interview was carried out at UN Headquarters in New York on October 22, 1999.

74. It was stressed in chapter 1 that UNOPS represents the beginning of an inclusion of business principles in the workings of a UN body.

75. Views expressed in a personal interview, October 22, 1999.

76. Colum Lynch, "Annan Crusades to Rebuild U.S. Support for UN," in *The Boston Globe,* July 10, 1998.

77. All three quotes are excerpted from the letter signed by the presidents of the U.S. Chamber of Commerce, the Business Roundtable, and the National Association of Manufacturers. The text can be found on the website of the Better World Fund, at www.betterworldfund.org.

78. The statistics quoted by the Better World Campaign are available at www.betterworldfund.org.

79. My contention on the minority status of liberal parties in Europe is based on the latter's election results, typically hovering at or below 15 percent of the electorate in France, the U.K., and Germany.

Notes for Chapter 3

1. It is important to remember that the UN secretary-general does not wield authority over the entire UN system and that the only weapon at his disposal is his power of conviction rather than coercion. The forthcoming guidelines will therefore be indicative and not binding.

2. The documents used for Part 1 of this chapter are internal guidelines used by each UN agency to guide collaboration with the private sector. These documents were shared among members of the UN Working Group on Operational Guidelines and do not bear official UN document numbers. Unless stated otherwise, all quotes in Part 1 of this chapter are excerpted from the guidelines of each respective UN agency. It is important to note that the UN Working Group on Operational Guidelines used World Bank documents as a reference only and did not include the World Bank in an internal UN policy-drafting effort.

3. Jane Nelson and Simon Zadek, "The Partnership Alchemy," a brochure of the Copenhagen Center produced with the PWBLF. See www.copenhagencentre.org.

4. While UNDP is most open in stating "illegal financial transactions" as unacceptable behavior on the part of potential corporate partners, it is interesting to note that the UN had not, at press time, adopted an official anti-bribery policy in its collaboration with the private sector. Given the UN's recent emphasis on good governance and the World Bank's own attention to corruption issues, such a policy ought to be considered.

5. Bryan A. Garner, ed. *Black's Law Dictionary,* 7th ed. St. Paul, MN: West Group, 1999.

6. The annual reports and the respective websites of UN agencies provide the best sources of information on the content of their partnerships with corporations. The internal survey of UN-business partnerships carried out by the UN in the fall of 1998 was also used in this section. A good overview of the status of UN-business cooperation, including a description of partnership examples, is provided by the UN Joint Inspection Unit in its report entitled "Private Sector Involvement and Cooperation with the United Nations System," September 1999.

7. While the latter—the link between peace and democracy—is not openly stated in joint UN-ICC declarations, it seems implied in the Global Compact's focus on human rights and the secretary-general's activist reading of the Charter favoring UN intervention against oppressive regimes. The ICC's support of the Global Compact indirectly acknowledges this orientation, as well as past ICC documents such as *Merchants of Peace* (published in 1938).

8. See The Global Compact at *www.unglobalcompact.org.*

9. These items are drawn from an internal PWBLF memorandum dated July 1, 1999. Many of the ideas hereby presented, however, can also be found in the PWBLF literature. See bibliography.

10. Letter by IOE President Ashraf Tabani, dated November 16, 1999.

11. IOE and the Global Compact. Memo by IOE Secretary-General Antonio Peñalosa, dated December 17, 1999.

12. UNCTAD, *World Investment Report,* 1999.

13. See, for example, *New Challenges,* a biannual newsletter jointly produced by UNCTAD and UNDP, first issued in July 1999 and aimed, according to the two sponsoring agencies, at addressing "the negative spin-offs of globalization." The newsletter lists an array of joint policy and governance initiatives in the areas of globalization, trade, and investment.

14. See UNCTAD at *www.unctad.org/en/pub/fdiafrica_frame.htm* The booklet on investing in Africa is also available from the UNCTAD website.

15. See UNDP Media Advisory dated July 14, 1999 in which Malloch Brown stated "UNDP, as a matter of policy, neither advocates nor supports any so-called global tax, nor any other form of international levy, as a means of funding development aid."

16. Annual Report of the U.S. Committee for UNICEF, 1998–99, p. 4.

17. *The Business Response to HIV/AIDS: Innovation and Partnership.* Published by UNAIDS and PWBLF, 1997.

18. Quotes and other data provided in this section can be found on the website of the UN Foundation at *www.unfoundation.org.*

19. See the *New York Times,* May 5, 1999.

20. Internal E-mail sent by UNDP Administrator Mark Malloch-Brown on September 8, 1999.

21. See *www.thehungersite.org.*

22. UNEP reply to the fall 1998 survey conducted by the UN Department of Economic and Social Affairs.

23. At press time, Glaxo and Smithkline Beecham had just announced their merger. It was too early to establish whether the merged organization would maintain its cooperation with UNAIDS.

24. Internal UNDP draft proposal on the GSDF, dated March 22, 1999.

Notes for Chapter 4

1. Convincing evidence of this point is provided by Dani Rodrik. See Dani Rodrik, *Has Globalization Gone Too Far?* Washington, DC: Institute for International Economics, 1997; Daniel Cohen, *The Wealth of Nations and the Poverty of the World.* Cambridge, MA: MIT Press, 1998; and Stephen Krasner, *Sovereignty: Organized Hypocrisy.* Princeton: Princeton University Press, 1999.

2. The comments quoted below are excerpted from an internal survey carried out by the UN Department for Economic and Social Affairs in 1998.

3. Carol Bellamy, "Sharing Responsibilities: Public, Private, and Civil Society," address delivered to the Harvard International Development Conference, Harvard University, April 16, 1999.

4. Speech delivered by Mark Malloch Brown at UN Headquarters in New York on July 1, 1999. Available on the UNDP website, www.undp.org.

5. Speech delivered by Mark Malloch Brown to the third regular session of the UNDP/UNFPA Executive Board, UN Headquarters, September 13, 1999. Available on the UNDP website, *www.undp.org*. In an article published in the spring of 1999, Malloch Brown's predecessor, Gustave Speth, wrote that "the United States has been particularly stingy with its aid budget." He appealed to the West and the United States to "increase their investment in less-developed countries." See James Gustave Speth, "The Plight of the Poor," in *Foreign Affairs,* 78, no. 3, May-June 1999.

6. Quoted from an internal survey carried out by the UN Department for Economic and Social Affairs in 1998.

7. Brazil's Instituto Ethos, Guatemala's Industrias Para La Paz, and Latin America's Empresa network are three excellent examples of the rapid growth of corporate social responsibility in the so-called "South."

8. The cooperative behaviors of several developing nations toward private sector partnerships in the months leading to Aid & Trade 2000 demonstrated the potential support of these countries for the UN policy of outreach to the private sector.

9. See Susan Rose-Ackerman, *Corruption and Government: Causes, Consequences, and Reform.* New York: Cambridge University Press, 1999, and the World Bank Development Report, *The Role of the State in a Changing World,* World Bank, 1997, which devotes quite a few pages to the issue of corruption.

10. See *The Future of Development Assistance: Common Pools and International Public Goods.* Washington, D.C.: Overseas Development Council (ODC), 1999, pp. 25–27.

11. This of course implies a well-functioning market economy, not a virtual one, as can be said to exist in Russia today. History cannot be rewritten, but it is interesting to wonder whether corruption would have prevailed in Russia in the last decade to such an extent if Russia's enterprises had been truly privatized through the development of a middle-class shareholder base, open and transparent ownership, an open and critical media, and the deliberate dismantling of oligopolies, monopolies, and corporatist networks. The prevalence of corruption in the case of Russian economic reform cannot be separated from the incomplete and bungled nature of the reform itself.

12. Carol Bellamy, "Sharing Responsibilities," 1999.

13. An exhaustive list of articles is not possible here. Suffice it to mention "UN Reformer Looks for New Friends in World of Business," in *Financial Times,* March 17, 1998; "UN Boosts its Brand Identity," in *The Guardian,* February 23, 1998; "Annan Fears Backlash Over Global Crisis," in the *New York Times,* February 1, 1999; "Annan Urges Firms to Enforce Values," in *International*

Herald Tribune, February 1,1999; "La ONU Establecerá un Acuerdo de Co-operación Económica y Social," *El Heraldo de México,* 6 de Julio de 1999; "L'ONU Salue le Monde des Affaires," *Le Figaro,* 6 juillet 1999.

14. The transcript of the interview by Kevin Newman can be found on the ABC website at www.abcnews.com, *World News Tonight.*

15. Some representatives of the media have understood the larger picture and the prevalence of mutual benefits in collaboration. An excellent example was provided by Claudia H. Deutsch in "Unlikely Allies at the United Nations," in the *New York Times,* December 10,1999.

16. Quoted from an internal survey carried out by the UN Department for Economic and Social Affairs in 1998.

17. Claudia Deutsch, "Unlikely Allies," 1999.

18. The existence of these groups accounts for the outrage caused by President Clinton's denunciation of the use of child labor by Brazilian shoe manufacturers at the November 1999 WTO meeting. As it turned out, the Brazilian shoe industry does not resort to child workers, although the coal industry does.

19. All statements in this paragraph are excerpted from the internal survey carried out by the UN Department for Economic and Social Affairs in 1998.

20. New "draft general principles on the use of the UN name and emblem and the name and emblem of UN funds and programs in the context of partnership with the private sector," circulated to members of the working group in the first quarter of 2000.

21. "The United Nations and the Business Community: Why, With Whom, On What Terms?" paper prepared by UNDP and UNICEF and circulated to members of the working group in the first quarter of 2000.

22. Ibid.

23. Ibid.

24. Draft UN Guidelines circulated to members of the working group in March 2000.

25. Ibid.

26. Ibid.

27. Ibid.

28. Phone interview carried out in the spring of 1999.

29. This culture is readily observable at UNICEF, where the marketing division occupies two floors. By contrast, no other UN body has a marketing department or division.

30. Kofi Annan, "Help the Third World Help Itself," in the *Wall Street Journal,* November 29, 1999.

31. For the unraveling of the financial system and its consequences for the assumptions of the 1945 compromise, see John Gerard Ruggie, *Constructing the World Polity: Essays on International Institutionalization.* London: Routledge, 1998, pp. 79–81.

32. See Wolfgang Reinicke and Francis Deng, *Critical Choices: The United Nations, Networks, and the Future of Global Governance.* Published on the website of Global Public Policy (*www.globalpublicpolicy.net*) in March 2000 and

forthcoming in 2000 in book format. Examples of global public policy networks include the International Campaign to Ban Landmines and the Global Commission on Dams.

33. Ibid. p. ix.

34. Ibid. pp. ix - xiv. See pp. 79–89 for a further refinement of these proposals.

35. For a good outline of that argument, see Elizabeth Olson, "ILO, Long in Eclipse, Regains Some Prominence," in the *New York Times,* March 23, 2000.

36. The ILO's director-general, Juan Somavía, however, does not believe that lack of enforcement power necessarily condemns the ILO to impotence. In the article by Elizabeth Olson, quoted above, he states: "I would not be in agreement that unless you have [penalties], there is nothing you can do. . . . When countries ratify [labor] conventions, they become national law and are enforceable in national courts." The ability to shame countries was also cited as one source of ILO power.

37. The non-UN reader may wonder why I propose to separate "women and children" and "population and family planning" in two distinct categories. While the model outlined here was not discussed with UN agencies prior to its release, it is likely that UNFPA would argue for the specificity and political complexity of its mandate vs. other issues of women and child care. I would concur that family planning faces a set of unique challenges and political conditions in the realm of UN activities, and that it would therefore require a specific mini-Compact.

38. See *The RESS Approach,* a periodical publication of the UNOPS Geneva office. The UNOPS Geneva Office is finalizing an operational manual that applies these values to all phases and tasks of post-conflict projects and provides staff with a concrete strategy for embedding these values in project definition and management.

39. The corporate involvement in conflict prevention and post-conflict reconciliation is becoming substantive and significant. In May 2000, The Prince of Wales Business Leaders Forum published the most comprehensive review of business activities in support of these two areas to date. See Harriet Fletcher, *The Business of Peace: The Private Sector as a Partner in Conflict Prevention and Resolution.* London: The Prince of Wales Business Leaders Forum, 2000. On April 29, 2000, New York University convened a conference on the same topics with participants drawn from business, management consulting, the United Nations, and academia.

40. In elections monitored or organized by the UN, the credibility of results is dependent on such operational "details" as the number of voting booths, the design of ballots, and the reassuring, yet not intimidating, presence of security. In the case of the Clarification Commission that investigated the human rights abuses perpetrated during Guatemala's 35-year civil war, the credibility of the report hinged on deploying a sufficient amount of UN outposts throughout the country to collect the stories of a representative amount of local inhabitants.

41. The private sector has long complained about the widely decentralized and confusing UN procurement system. The UN should learn from this experience and facilitate the private sector's access to information about private sector partnerships.

42. Reinicke and Deng concur that, as it sets on a trilateral approach to its activities, "the current structure, skill mix, and resources of the organization [read the UN] may pose real limits." See Reinicke and Deng, *Critical Choices,* p. 82.

43. Sandrine Tesner, *How to Do Business with the United Nations: The 1997 Update.* UNA-USA, 1997, p. 226.

44. In 1999, however, UNOPS approached the UNDP Executive Board to acquire the last remnants of its authority in personnel matters, as this so-called "delegated authority" had been foreseen at the creation of UNOPS in 1995. Opposition to finalizing the UNOPS personnel regime arose from both the ranks of member states and the UN bureaucracy, providing further evidence of a widespread ambiguity toward economic efficiency and competition. Finally, a wider delegation of authority in personnel and recruiting procedures was granted in the fall of 1999, but the process was not complete and many operational hurdles remained in the way of implementation.

45. As this book was being finalized in March 2000, a Secretariat report proposed to cut the 461-day recruiting period to 200.

46. For the lack of a governmental comparative advantage across space, time, and complexity, see Wolfgang Reinicke, "The Other World Wide Web: Global Public Policy Networks," in *Foreign Policy* (winter 1999–2000), p 45. See also Reinicke and Deng, *Critical Choices,* released in March 2000 on www.globalpublicpolicy.net.

47. See Action 17 in the secretary-general's reform proposal of July 1997.

Notes for Conclusion

1. James Chace, *Acheson: The Secretary of State that Created the American World.* New York: Simon & Schuster, 1998, p. 142.

2. Kofi Annan, "Help the Third World Help Itself," in the *Wall Street Journal,* November 29, 1999.

3. See *The Future of Development Assistance: Common Pools and International Public Goods.* Washington, D.C.: Overseas Development Council (ODC), 1999, chapter 2. This is also the underlying argument in Roger Riddell, *Aid in the 21st Century.* UNDP/ODS Discussion Series. New York: United Nations, 1996.

4. Riddell, p. 36.

5. See Overseas Development Council, *The Future of Development Assistance,* 1999, p. 23.

6. See Amartya Sen, *Development as Freedom.* New York: Knopf, 1999, for an exposition of the link between democratic institutions and economic development.

7. On the critical value of civil society and civil liberties, see Amartya Sen and World Bank, *Assessing Aid: What Works, What Doesn't, and Why.* New York: Oxford University Press, 1998, p. 136: "While electoral democracy and civil liberties are obviously closely linked, both in practice and in the data, the main channel of influence appears to be the availability of civil liberties rather than the more purely political mechanisms of choosing leaders."

8. World Bank, *Assessing Aid,* 1998, p. 6.

9. According to the OECD, since 1992 overall flows of ODA have fallen from an average .33 percent of the combined national product of donor countries to .22 percent in 1997. See Organization of Economic Cooperation and Development, *1998 Development Cooperation Report.* Paris: February 1999.

10. The CDF was exposed in a speech given by World Bank President James Wolfenshon in January 1999 (see the World Bank website at www.worldbank.org). The public good argument is the topic of *Global Public Goods,* Inge Kaul, et al., eds., a publication of the UN Developmment Program (UNDP).New York: Oxford University Press, 1999, and *The Future of Development Assistance,* ODC, 1999. The common pool approach can be found in the latter report. Finally, global policy networks are presented in Wolfgang Reinicke, "The Other World Wide Web: Global Public Policy Networks," in *Foreign Policy* (winter 1999–2000). See also www.globalpublicpolicy.net.

11. This approach basically argues that funders of development assistance should make their contributions to a common pool established in each country and over which the country would have total allocation and management control. Funders would therefore no longer be in a position to define development priorities and make aid conditional on the achievement of objectives defined by them.

12. Mark Malloch Brown, "Development Assistance in the 21st Century: Challenging the Conventional Wisdom," speech delivered at Harvard University on September 30, 1999.

13. *The Future of Development Assistance,* ODC, 1999, advocates transferring to regional organizations the responsibility of providing regional public goods, and Reinicke argues that the value of global policy networks is precisely that they are not institutions (see Reinicke, "The Other World Wide Web"). In the case of weak-link or best-shot aggregation techniques for the provision of certain public goods, the developed nations are better off providing the goods themselves than transferring funds to the developing countries. (see ODC, 1999, pp. 70–72).

14. For an outline of this necessary reform in the objectives of multilateral organizations, see World Bank, *Assessing Aid,* p. 119.

15. Mark Malloch Brown, "Development in the 21st Century: The Evolving Role of UNDP," speech delivered at Columbia University's School of International and Public Affairs, October 25, 1999. In September 1999, Mark Malloch Brown told a Harvard audience that UNDP must "develop a first-class governance and policy advisory service." See Malloch Brown, "Development Assistance in the 21st Century: Challenging the Conventional Wisdom."

16. See *The Future of Development Assistance,* ODC, 1999, pp. 63–66 and 76.

17. I am referring here to the similar incipits of the U.S. constitution and the UN Charter.

18. See John Gerard Ruggie, *Constructing the World Polity: Essays on International Institutionalization.* London: Routledge, 1998, p. 223.

19. The expression "imagined community" is borrowed from Benedict Anderson, *Imagined Communities.* London: Verso, 1983.

20. See Ruggie, *Constructing the World Polity,* pp. 218–19 for a full development of these ideas.

21. Edward Luck, *Mixed Messages: American Politics and International Organization, 1919–1999.* Washington, D.C.: Brookings Institution Press, 1999, p. 3.

22. John Quincy Adams quoted by Ruggie, in *Constructing the World Polity,* p. 203.

23. "A Special Nation, Peerless and Indispensable," is the title of the second chapter of Luck's book *Mixed Messages.*

24. See John Gerard Ruggie, *Winning the Peace: America and World Order in the New Era* for a discussion of how such coalitions and consensus were built by Roosevelt in particular. See *Mixed Messages,* p. 20, for a quote by U.S. Representative to the UN Adlai Stevenson, seeking to reconcile American exceptionalism with cooperation with the rest of the world.

25. Steven Kull and I. M. Destler, *Misreading the Public: The Myth of a New Isolationism.* Washington, D.C.: Brookings Institution Press, 1999.

26. Kull and Destler, p. 95.

27. As Ruggie demonstrated in *Winning the Peace,* the isolationist camp at times conceals its motivation under the guises of unilateralism.

28. Kull and Destler, p. 217.

29. Ibid. pp. 222–28.

30. See Kull and Destler, chapter 11 for a discussion of these arguments.

31. Kull and Destler, p. 20.

32. The definition of American "soft power" is owed to Joseph Nye. See *Bound to Lead.* New York: Basic Books. 1990.

33. See Ruggie, *Constructing the World Polity,* pp. 219–23 for how multilateralism can help address the complex relationships and potential tensions of a multiethnic nation.

34. John Gerard Ruggie, *Multilateralism Matters: The Theory and Practice of an Institutional Forum.* New York: Columbia University Press, 1993.

35. See Ian Hurd, "Legitimacy and Authority in International Politics," in *International Organization,* 53, no. 2 (spring 1999), p. 381 and subsequent pages for several points made here. The italics are Hurd's.

36. For a full analysis of these examples, see Ian Hurd, "Legitimacy and the Symbolic Life of the Security Council," paper presented to the International Studies Association, Yale University, February 1999.

37. See Michael Barnett and Martha Finnemore, "The Politics, Power, and Pathologies of International Organizations," *International Organization,* 53, no.4 (fall 1999).

38. Ibid., p. 720.

39. The stalled institutional expansion of UNOPS already points to this pathological behavior inasmuch as the UN's intent in 1995 to create a UN body that operates "like a business" has not been backed by the requisite follow-up actions.

40. See Reinicke, "The Other World Wide Web;" See also Reinicke and Francis M. Deng, *Critical Choices: The United Nations, Networks, and the Future of Global Governance.* Report on the UN Vision Project on Global Public Policy Networks, March 2000. Available at www.globalpublicpolicy.net.

41. Reinicke calls the decentralized format of networks "structured informality." See *Critical Choices,* p. xii.

Bibliography

Annan, Kofi. "Global Values: The United Nations and the Rule of Law in the 21st Century." 18th Singapore Lecture. Singapore, February 14, 2000.

———. "Help the Third World Help Itself." *Wall Street Journal.* November 29, 1999.

———. "A Compact for the New Century." Address to the World Economic Forum. Davos, Switzerland, January 31, 1999.

———. "Unite Power of Markets with Authority of Universal Values." Address to the World Economic Forum (WEF), Davos, Switzerland, January 30,1998.

———. Address to the World Economic Forum (WEF), Davos, Switzerland, February 1, 1997.

Attali, Jacques. *1492.* Paris: Fayard, 1991.

Barnett, M. and Finnemore, M. "The Politics, Power, and Pathologies of International Organizations." *International Organization* 53, no. 4 (fall 1999).

Basic Facts About the United Nations. United Nations Department of Public Information. New York: United Nations, 1998.

Bellamy, Carol. "Sharing Responsibilities: Public, Private, and Civil Society." Address delivered at Harvard University, April 16, 1999.

Bhagwati, Jagdish. *A Stream of Windows: Unsettling Reflections on Trade, Immigration, and Democracy.* Cambridge, MA: The MIT Press, 1998.

The Blue Helmets. 3rd ed. United Nations Department of Public Information. New York: United Nations, 1996.

Braudel, Fernand. *Le Model Italien.* Paris: Champs Flammarion, 1994.

Braudel, Fernand, and Georges Duby. *La Méditerranée, Les Hommes et l'Héritage.* Paris: Champs Flammarion, 1986.

Burtless, Gary, R.Z. Lawrence, R.E. Litan, and R.J. Shapiro. *Globaphobia: Confronting Fears About Open Trade.* Washington, D.C.: Brookings Institution Press, 1998.

Business and the Global Economy: ICC Statement on Behalf of World Business to the Heads of State and Government Attending the Cologne Summit, June 18–20, 1999. Paris: International Chamber of Commerce (ICC), 1999.

Business and the Global Economy: ICC Statement on Behalf of World Business to the Heads of State and Government Attending the Birmingham Summit, May 15–17, 1998. Paris: International Chamber of Commerce (ICC), 1998.

The Business Response to HIV/AIDS: Innovation and Partnership. Geneva: UNAIDS and The Prince of Wales Business Leaders Forum, 1997.

Cairo Declaration of Developing Countries. 1962 Conference on the Problems of Economic Development.

Chase, James. *Acheson: The Secretary of State that Created the American World.* New York: Simon & Schuster, 1998.

Cohen, Daniel. *The Wealth of the World and the Poverty of Nations.* Cambridge, MA: The MIT Press, 1998.

Cowell, Alan. "Annan Fears Backlash Over Global Crisis." *New York Times,* February 1, 1999.

Cramb, G. "Greenpeace Stepping up Threat to Multinationals." *Financial Times,* August 18,1999.

Cramb, G. and R. Corzine. "Shell Audit Tells of Action on Global Warming." *Financial Times,* July 14, 1998.

Dalla Costa, John. *The Ethical Imperative: Why Moral Leadership is Good Business.* Reading, MA: Perseus Books, 1998.

Deutsch, C.H. "Unlikely Allies at the United Nations." *New York Times,* December 10, 1999.

Development Cooperation Report, 1998. Paris: Organization for Economic Cooperation & Development (OECD), February, 1999.

Doyle, Michael W. *Ways of War and Peace: Realism, Liberalism, and Socialism.* New York: W.W. Norton, 1997.

Fomerand, Jacques. *The United States and Development Cooperation in the United Nations: Toward a New Deal.* New York: Editions Diderot, 2000.

Frieden, Jeffry A. and David A. Lake. *International Political Economy: Perspectives on Global Power and Wealth.* New York: St. Martin's Press, 1991.

Friedman, Thomas. *The Lexus and the Olive Tree.* New York: Farrar, Straus, & Giroux, 1999.

Fukuyama, Francis. *The Great Disruption: Human Nature and the Reconstitution of Social Order.* New York: Free Press, 1999.

———. *The End of History and the Last Man.* New York: Free Press, 1992.

Furet, François. *La Révolution, 1780–1880.* Paris: Hachette Littératures, 1988.

Garner, Bryan A., ed. *Black's Law Dictionary,* 7th ed. St. Paul, MN: West Group, 1999.

Gerson, Allan. *The Kirkpatrick Mission: Diplomacy without Apology: America at the United Nations, 1981–85.* New York: Free Press, 1991.

Gilpin, Robert. *The Political Economy of International Relations.* Princeton: Princeton University Press, 1987.

Gorbachev, Mikhail. *Perestroika: New Thinking for our Country and the World.* New York: Harper & Row, 1987.

Henderson, D. *The MAI Affair: A Story and its Lessons.* London: The Royal Institute of International Affairs, 1999.

Hilderbrand, Robert C. *Dumbarton Oaks: The Origins of the United Nations and the Search for Postwar Security.* Chapel Hill, NC: University of North Carolina Press, 1990.

Hirschmann, Albert O. *National Power and the Structure of Foreign Trade.* Berkeley: University of California Press, 1945.

Human Development Report, 1999. United Nations Development Program (UNDP). New York: Oxford University Press, 1999.

Hurd, Ian. "Legitimacy and Authority in International Politics." *International Organization* 53, no. 2 (spring 1999).

———. "Legitimacy and the Symbolic Life of the Security Council." Paper Presented to the International Studies Association at Yale University, February, 1999.

International Chamber of Commerce News. Monthly Bulletin of the ICC. Volume XXXV-3, March-April 1969.

Joint Statement on Common Interests. New York and Geneva: United Nations and International Chamber of Commerce (ICC), February 9, 1998.

Kandur, Ravi and Todd Sandler with Kevin M. Morrison. *The Future of Development Assistance: Common Pools and International Public Goods.* Washington, D.C.: Overseas Development Council, 1999.

Kane, A. *Non-Governmental Organizations and The United Nations: A Relationship in Flux.* Conference on Responses to Insecurity, October 23–24, 1998. New Haven: The Academic Council on the United Nations at Yale University.

Kaul, Inge, Isabelle Grunberg, and Marc A. Stern, eds. *Global Public Goods: International Cooperation in the 21st Century.* New York: Oxford University Press for UNDP, 1999.

Keohane, Robert and Joseph Nye. "Globalization: What's New? What's Not? (And So What?)." *Foreign Policy* (spring 2000): 105.

———. *Power and Interdependence.* Boston: Little, Brown, 1977.

Kindleberger, Charles Poor. *The World in Depression, 1929–1939.* Berkeley: University Of California, 1973.

Kissinger, Henry. *Diplomacy.* New York: Simon & Schuster, 1994.

Krasner, Stephen D. *Sovereignty: Organized Hypocrisy.* Princeton: Princeton University Press, 1999.

———. *Structural Conflict: The Third World Against Global Liberalism.* Berkeley: University of California Press, 1985.

———. *International Regimes.* Ithaca, NY: Cornell University Press, 1983.

Kull, Steven and I.M. Destler. *Misreading the Public: The Myth of a New Isolationism.* Washington, D.C.: Brookings Institution Press, 1999.

Luard, Evan, ed. *The Evolution of International Organizations.* New York: Frederick A. Praeger, 1966.

Luck, Edward. *Mixed Messages: American Politics and International Organization, 1919- 1999.* Washington, D.C.: Brookings Institution Press, 1999.

Lynch, Colum. "Annan Crusades to Rebuild U.S. Support for UN." *The Boston Globe,* July 19, 1998.

Malia, Martin. *Russia Under Western Eyes.* Cambridge, MA: Harvard University Press, 1999.

Malloch Brown, Mark. "Development in the 21st Century: The Evolving Role of UNDP." Address to the School of International and Public Affairs. Columbia University, New York, October 25, 1999.

———. "Development Assistance in the 21st Century: Challenging the Conventional Wisdom on Assistance and Development." Address to the Harvard Institute for

International Development. Harvard University, Cambridge, MA, September 30, 1999.

The Millennium Poll on Corporate Social Responsibility: Executive Briefing. Environics International, Ltd. in Cooperation with The Prince of Wales Business Leaders Forum and The Conference Board. Toronto: Environics International Ltd, 1999.

Monks, Robert A.G. *The Emperor's Nightingale: Restoring the Integrity of the Corporation In the Age of Shareholder Activism.* Reading, MA: Addison-Wesley, 1998.

Mossu, Laurent. "L'ONU Salue le Monde des Affaires." *Le Figaro,* July 6, 1999.

Nelson, Jane. *The Business of Peace: The Private Sector as a Partner in Conflict Prevention and Resolution.* London: The Prince of Wales Business Leaders Forum, 2000.

―――. *Building Competitiveness and Communities: How World Class Companies Are Creating Shareholder Value and Societal Value.* London: The Prince of Wales Business Leaders Forum, 1998.

―――. *Business as Partners in Development: Creating Wealth for Countries, Companies and Communities.* London: The Prince of Wales Business Leaders Forum, 1996.

Nelson, Jane and Simon Zadek. "The Partnership Alchemy." Brochure of the Copenhagen Center produced with The Prince of Wales Business Leaders Forum. Available at www.copenhagencentre.org.

Nye, Joseph S. *Bound to Lead: The Changing Nature of American Power.* New York: Basic Books, 1990.

Oechslin, Jean-Jacques. "Toward Greater International Cooperation." International Chamber of Commerce (ICC) Paper, 1977.

Olson, Elizabeth. "ILO, Long in Eclipse, Regains Some Prominence." *New York Times,* March 23, 2000.

"La ONU Establecerá un Acuerdo de Cooperación Económica y Social." *El Heraldo de México.* July 6, 1999.

Polyani, Karl. *The Great Transformation: The Political and Economic Origins of Our Time.* Boston: Beacon Press, 1944.

Private Sector Involvement and Cooperation with the United Nations System. Report of the United Nations Joint Inspection Unit (JIU), Geneva: United Nations, 1999.

Reinicke, Wolfgang H. "The Other World Wide Web: Global Public Policy Networks." *Foreign Policy,* winter 1999–2000.

―――. *Global Public Policy: Governing Without Government?* Washington, D.C.: Brookings Institution Press, 1998.

Reinicke, Wolfgang H. and Francis M. Deng. *Critical Choices: The United Nations, Networks, and the Future of Global Governance.* Report of the UN Vision Project on Global Public Policy Networks, March 2000. Available at *www.globalpublicpolicy.net*

Renewing the United Nations: A Program for Reform. Report of the Secretary-General, July 14, 1997. United Nations General Assembly Document A/51/950.

Report of Expert Group to the United Nations General Assembly. United Nations, 1961.

Report of the Special Adviser and Delegate of the Secretary-General on the Reform of the Economic and Social Sectors, so-called *Dazdie Report.* United Nations, February 1993.

Report of the Taskforce on the Office of Project Services. Issued by the Governing Council of the United Nations Development Program (UNDP) as document DP/1993/70, June 1, 1993.

The RESS Approach. Geneva: United Nations Office of Project Services, Quarterly publication.

Riddell, Roger. *Aid in the 21ˢᵗ Century.* UNDP/ODS Discussion Series. New York: United Nations, 1996.

Ridgeway, George L. *Merchants of Peace.* Paris: International Chamber of Commerce (ICC), 1938.

Rodrik, Dani. *Has Globalization Gone Too Far?* Washington, D.C.: Institute for International Economics. 1997.

Rose-Ackerman, Susan. *Corruption and Government: Causes, Consequences, and Reform.* New York: Cambridge University Press, 1999.

Ruggie, John Gerard. *Constructing the World Polity: Essays on International Institutionalization.* London: Routledge, 1998.

———. *Winning the Peace: America and World Order in the New Era.* New York: Columbia University Press, 1996

———. *Multilateralism Matters: The Theory and Praxis of an Institutional Form.* New York: Columbia University Press. 1993

Ruggie, John G. and Georg Kell. "Global Markets and Social Legitimacy: The Case of the Global Compact." Paper presented at York University, Toronto, Canada, November 1999.

Ruggiero, Renato, Director-General of the WTO. "Beyond the Multilateral Trading System." Address delivered at the 20th Seminar on International Security, Politics, and Economics. Geneva, April 12, 1999.

Sharp, Walter R. *The United Nations Economic and Social Council.* New York: Columbia University Press, 1969.

Schild, Georg. *Bretton Woods and Dumbarton Oaks: American Economic and Political Postwar Planning in the Summer of 1944.* New York: St. Martin's Press, 1995.

Schmiddheiny, Stephan. *Changing Course.* Cambridge, MA: The MIT Press, 1992.

Schwartz, Peter and Blair Glibb. *When Good Companies Do Bad Things: Responsibility and Risk in an Age of Globalization.* New York: John Wiley & Sons, 1999.

Sen, Amartya. *Development as Freedom.* New York: Knopf, 1999

"Settle Current Rows and Launch New Trade Round, Business Tells G7." International Chamber of Commerce (ICC) Press Release dated May 20, 1999.

Silber, Laura. "UN Reformer Looks for New Friends in the World of Business." *Financial Times,* March 17, 1998.

Spero, Joan Edelman. *The Politics of International Economic Relations.* New York: St. Martin's Press, 1990.

Speth, James Gustave. "The Plight of the Poor." *Foreign Affairs* 78, no. 3 (May-June 1999).

Suzman, Mark. "Internal Turmoil Turns the Tables on Aid Agency." *Financial Times,* October 19, 1999.

Swardson, Anne. "Annan Urges Firms to Enforce Values." *International Herald Tribune,* February 1, 1999.

Tennyson, Ros. *Managing Partnerships: Tools for Mobilizing the Public Sector, Business and Civil Society As Partners in Development.* London: The Prince of Wales Business Leaders Forum, 1998.

Tesner, Sandrine. *How to Do Business with the United Nations: The 1997 Update.* UNA- USA, 1997.

———. *How to Do Business with the United Nations: The 1996 Update.* New York: UNA-USA, 1996.

———. *How to Do Business with the United Nations: The Complete Guide to UN Procurement.* New York: UNA-USA, 1995.

———. *Report on the Fifth Annual Peacekeeping Mission: Rwanda and Angola.* New York: UNA-USA, 1996.

———. *Report on the Fourth Annual Peacekeeping Mission: Haiti.* New York: UNA-USA, 1995.

"Third World Intellectuals and NGOs: Statement Against Linkage." *Earth Times,* September 1999, pp. 16–30.

Townley, Ralph. "The Economic Organs of the United Nations." In *The Evolution of International Organizations,* ed. Evan Luard. New York: Praeger, 1966.

Tran, Mark. "UN Boosts its Brand Identity." *The Guardian,* February 23, 1998.

UNDP Executive Board Document DP/1995/6 of November 1994. New York: United Nations, 1994.

UNDP Governing Council Document DP/1994/62 of August 16, 1994. New York: United Nations, 1994.

U.S. Committee for UNICEF. *Annual Report, 1998–99.* New York: UNICEF, 1999.

Wade, Robert. "Globalization and its Limits: Reports of the Death of the National Economy are Greatly Exaggerated." In S. Berger and R. Dove, *National Diversity and Global Capitalism.* Ithaca, NY: Cornell University Press, 1996.

World Bank. *Annual Report 1999.* Available at *http://www.worldbank.org/html/extpb/annrep/index.htm*

———. *Assessing Aid. What Works, What Doesn't, and Why.* New York: Oxford University Press. 1998

———. *World Development Report 1999–2000. Entering the 21st Century: The Changing Development Landscape.* New York: Oxford University Press, 1999.

———. *World Development Report 1997. The State in a Changing World.* New York: Oxford University Press. 1997.

"World Business Priorities for a New Round of Multilateral Trade Negotiations." Policy Statement for Submission to the Third Ministerial Conference of the World Trade Organization. November 30-December 3, 1999, Seattle. Released by the International Chamber of Commerce (ICC) in May 1999.

World Investment Report 1999: Foreign Direct Investment and the Challenge of Development. United Nations Conference on Trade and Development. New York and Geneva: United Nations, 1999.

World Investment Report 1998: Trends and Determinants. United Nations Conference on Trade and Development. New York and Geneva: United Nations, 1998.

Zacher, Mark. *The United Nations and Global Commerce.* New York: United Nations Department of Public Information, 1999.

Index